The Political Invention of Fragile States

This book investigates the emergence, the dissemination and the reception of the notion of 'state fragility'. It analyses the process of conceptualisation, examining how the 'fragile states' concept was framed by policy makers to describe reality in accordance with their priorities in the fields of development and security. Contributors investigate the instrumental use of the 'state fragility' label in the legitimisation of Western policy interventions in countries facing violence and profound poverty. They also emphasise the agency of actors 'on the receiving end', describing how the elites and governments in so-called 'fragile states' have incorporated and reinterpreted the concept to fit their own political agendas. A first set of articles examines the role played by the World Bank, the OECD, the European Union and the G7+ in the transnational diffusion of the concept, which is understood as a critical element in the new discourse on international aid and security. A second set of papers employs three case studies (Sudan, Indonesia and Uganda) to explore the processes of appropriation, reinterpretation and the strategic use of the 'fragile state' concept.

This book was originally published as a special issue of *Third World Quarterly*.

Sonja Grimm is a Senior Lecturer in the Department of Politics and Public Administration, University of Konstanz, Germany. She publishes on democratization in post-conflict societies and democracy promotion and has co-edited special issues of *Democratization* on "War and Democratization" (2008) and "Do All Good Things Go Together? Conflicting Objectives in Democracy Promotion" (2012). More about her can be found at [www.sonja-grimm.eu].

Nicolas Lemay-Hébert is a Senior Lecturer in the International Development Department, University of Birmingham, UK. He is the co-editor of the *Journal of Intervention and Statebuilding* (with Florian Kuhn). His most recent book is 'Semantics of Statebuilding: Language, Meanings and Sovereignty' (2014; co-edited with N. Onuf, V. Rakic, and P. Bojanic).

Olivier Nay is a Professor of Political Science at the University of Paris 1 – Panthéon Sorbonne, France. He is the Vice-president of the French Association of Political Science and the Chair of the Political Science section at the National Academic Council. He specialises on the reform of international organizations, bureaucratic change and the transnational diffusion of policy ideas. Please see [univ-paris1.academia.edu/OlivierNay].

Thirdworlds

Edited by Shahid Qadir, University of London

THIRDWORLDS will focus on the political economy, development and cultures of those parts of the world that have experienced the most political, social, and economic upheaval, and which have faced the greatest challenges of the postcolonial world under globalisation: poverty, displacement and diaspora, environmental degradation, human and civil rights abuses, war, hunger, and disease.

THIRDWORLDS serves as a signifier of oppositional emerging economies and cultures ranging from Africa, Asia, Latin America, Middle East, and even those 'Souths' within a larger perceived North, such as the U.S. South and Mediterranean Europe. The study of these otherwise disparate and discontinuous areas, known collectively as the Global South, demonstrates that as globalisation pervades the planet, the south, as a synonym for subalterity, also transcends geographical and ideological frontiers.

Terrorism and the Politics of Naming
Edited by Michael Bhatia

Reconstructing Post-Saddam Iraq
Edited by Sultan Barakat

From Nation-Building to State-Building
Edited by Mark T. Berger

Connecting Cultures
Edited by Emma Bainbridge

The Politics of Rights
Dilemmas for feminist praxis
Edited by Andrea Cornwall and Maxine Molyneux

The Long War – Insurgency, Counterinsurgency and Collapsing States
Edited by Mark T. Berger and Douglas A. Borer

Market-led Agrarian Reform
Edited by Saturnino M. Borras, Jr.

After the Third World?
Edited by Mark T. Berger

Developmental and Cultural Nationalisms
Edited by Radhika Desai

Globalisation and Migration
New issues, new politics
Edited by Ronaldo Munck

Domestic and International Perspectives on Kyrgyzstan's 'Tulip Revolution'
Motives, mobilizations and meanings
Edited by Sarah Cummings

War and Revolution in the Caucasus
Georgia Ablaze
Edited by Stephen F. Jones

War, Peace and Progress in the 21st Century
Development, Violence and Insecurities
Edited by Mark T. Berger and Heloise Weber

Renewing International Labour Studies
Edited by Marcus Taylor

Youth in the Former Soviet South
Everyday Lives between Experimentation and Regulation
Edited by Stefan B. Kirmse

Political Civility in the Middle East
Edited by Frédéric Volpi

The Transformation of Tajikistan
Sources of Statehood
Edited by John Heathershaw

Movement, Power and Place in Central Asia and Beyond
Contested Trajectories
Edited by Madeleine Reeves

People Power in an Era of Global Crisis
Rebellion, Resistance and Liberation
Edited by Barry K. Gills and Kevin Gray

EU Strategies on Governance Reform
Between Development and State-building
Edited by Wil Hout

Identity, Inequity and Inequality in India and China
Governing Difference
Edited by Ravinder Kaur and Ayo Wahlberg

The Personal and the Professional in Aid Work
Edited by Anne-Meike Fechter

Rising Powers and the Future of Global Governance
Edited by Kevin Gray and Craig N. Murphy

The Millennium Development Goals: Challenges, Prospects and Opportunities
Edited by Nana Poku

Development Perspectives from the Antipodes
Edited by Susanne Schech

Health, Drugs and Healing in Central Asia
Edited by Alisher Latypov

The Global Politics of Impairment and Disability
Processes and Embodiments
Edited by Karen Soldatic and Helen Meekosha

Negotiating Well-being in Central Asia
Edited by David W. Montgomery

New Actors and Alliances in Development
Edited by Lisa Ann Richey and Stefano Ponte

The Political Invention of Fragile States
The Power of Ideas
Edited by Sonja Grimm, Nicolas Lemay-Hébert and Olivier Nay

Global Land Grabs
History, Theory and Method
Edited by Marc Edelman, Carlos Oya and Saturnino M. Borras Jr.

The Afghan Conundrum: intervention, statebuilding and resistance
Edited by Jonathan Goodhand and Mark Desra

The Political Invention of Fragile States

The Power of Ideas

Edited by

Sonja Grimm, Nicolas Lemay-Hébert and Olivier Nay

Routledge
Taylor & Francis Group
LONDON AND NEW YORK

First published 2015
by Routledge
2 Park Square, Milton Park, Abingdon, Oxfordshire OX14 4RN

and by Routledge
711 Third Avenue, New York, NY 10017, USA

First issued in paperback 2016

Routledge is an imprint of the Taylor & Francis Group, an informa business

British Library Cataloguing in Publication Data
A catalogue record for this book is available from the British Library

ISBN 13: 978-1-138-20972-5 (pbk)
ISBN 13: 978-1-138-80153-0 (hbk)

Typeset in Times New Roman
by RefineCatch Limited, Bungay, Suffolk

Publisher's Note
The publisher accepts responsibility for any inconsistencies that may have arisen during the conversion of this book from journal articles to book chapters, namely the possible inclusion of journal terminology.

Contents

Contents

Citation Information

The chapters in this book were originally published in *Third World Quarterly*, volume 35, issue 2 (2014). When citing this material, please use the original page numbering for each article, as follows:

Chapter 1
'Fragile States': introducing a political concept
Sonja Grimm, Nicolas Lemay-Hébert and Olivier Nay
Third World Quarterly, volume 35, issue 2 (2014) pp. 197–209

Chapter 2
International Organisations and the Production of Hegemonic Knowledge: how the World Bank and the OECD helped invent the Fragile State Concept
Olivier Nay
Third World Quarterly, volume 35, issue 2 (2014) pp. 210–231

Chapter 3
The OECD's discourse on fragile states: expertise and the normalisation of knowledge production
Nicolas Lemay-Hébert and Xavier Mathieu
Third World Quarterly, volume 35, issue 2 (2014) pp. 232–251

Chapter 4
The European Union's ambiguous concept of 'state fragility'
Sonja Grimm
Third World Quarterly, volume 35, issue 2 (2014) pp. 252–267

Chapter 5
Measuring and managing 'state fragility': the production of statistics by the World Bank, Timor-Leste and the g7+
Isabel Rocha De Siqueira
Third World Quarterly, volume 35, issue 2 (2014) pp. 268–283

Chapter 6
How Sudan's 'rogue' state label shaped US responses to the Darfur conflict: what's the problem and who's in charge?
Maria Gabrielsen Jumbert
Third World Quarterly, volume 35, issue 2 (2014) pp. 284–299

Chapter 7

State disintegration and power politics in Post-Suharto Indonesia
Felix Heiduk
Third World Quarterly, volume 35, issue 2 (2014) pp. 300–315

Chapter 8

When it pays to be a 'fragile state': Uganda's use and abuse of a dubious concept
Jonathan Fisher
Third World Quarterly, volume 35, issue 2 (2014) pp. 316–332

Chapter 9

State fragility and failure as wicked problems: beyond naming and taming
Derick W. Brinkerhoff
Third World Quarterly, volume 35, issue 2 (2014) pp. 333–344

Please direct any queries you may have about the citations to
clsuk.permissions@cengage.com

‘Fragile States’: introducing a political concept

Sonja Grimm[a], Nicolas Lemay-Hébert[b] and Olivier Nay[c]

[a]*Department of Politics and Public Administration, University of Konstanz, Konstanz, Germany;* [b]*Department of International Development, University of Birmingham, UK;* [c]*Department of Political Science, Paris 1 – Panthéon Sorbonne, Paris, France*

The special issue ‘Fragile States: A Political Concept’ investigates the emergence, dissemination and reception of the notion of ‘state fragility’. It analyses the process of conceptualisation, examining how the ‘fragile states’ concept was framed by policy makers to describe reality in accordance with their priorities in the fields of development and security. The contributors to the issue investigate the instrumental use of the ‘state fragility’ label in the legitimisation of Western policy interventions in countries facing violence and profound poverty. They also emphasise the agency of actors ‘on the receiving end’, describing how the elites and governments in so-called ‘fragile states’ have incorporated and reinterpreted the concept to fit their own political agendas. A first set of articles examines the role played by the World Bank, the OECD, the European Union and the g7+ coalition of ‘fragile states’ in the transnational diffusion of the concept, which is understood as a critical element in the new discourse on international aid and security. A second set of papers employs three case studies (Sudan, Indonesia and Uganda) to explore the processes of appropriation, reinterpretation and the strategic use of the ‘fragile state’ concept.

Introduction

> The terminology ‘fragile states’ should only be used with caution [...] I strongly feel that it is not a neutral terminology. Apart from the emotional implications, it has financial and political implications. Moreover, it gives us a bad image in the eyes of the investors we so badly need. (Address by Pierre Nkurunziza, President of Burundi, to the United Nations General Assembly, March 2009)

The capacity to shape the representation of reality is now commonly viewed as an attribute of power, along with military and diplomatic capacities. In this context the concept of 'fragile states' can be seen as an attempt by state powers to describe reality in accordance with their foreign policy priorities. The contributors to this special issue seek to disentangle this reality by exploring the notion of 'state fragility', the conditions under which the label 'state fragility' emerged in certain policy circles and how it has been received by actors in fragile states. Hence the contributions to this issue are twofold in nature: they examine both the transnational emergence and diffusion of the notion of 'state fragility' and its reception in the so-called 'fragile countries'. In the first part of the issue the contributors focus on major Western donors and their understanding and use of 'state fragility', opening the 'black box' and exploring the strategies at work behind the process of conceptualisation. In the second, they investigate how countries that have been labelled 'fragile' have internalised and reinterpreted the 'fragile state' classification, and how they have exploited the concept for their own strategic purposes. Scholars included in the issue argue that, on the donor side, the concept is primarily used to classify states facing major political crises or extreme poverty as 'fragile', 'failing' or 'failed' in order to legitimise aid spending and interventionist strategies. On the recipient side, although such labelling is generally contested, it is also frequently accepted and reinterpreted when there is the potential for political gains. The contributors find that aid-dependent states frequently exploit the notion for their own purposes, in order to delay political reforms or to convince donors to invest more aid money in 'situations of fragility' (especially in periods of economic crisis, when Western countries might otherwise opt for cutbacks in foreign aid spending). The ambiguous definitions of the concept open room for different processes of appropriation at the international and local levels.

The rise of the 'fragile state' agenda

Expressions such as 'weak state', 'failing state', 'collapsed state' and other variations have become pervasive, not only in practitioners' discourses but also in scholarly works. New perspectives – such as 'whole-of-government', '3D' ('defence, diplomacy, development') and '3C' ('coherent, coordinated, complementary') approaches – have been developed in order to promote Western humanitarian, reconstruction and security policies with regard to these so-called 'fragile states'. 'Principles of good international engagement in fragile states' have been drawn up by many international and regional organisations, among them the World Bank, the Organisation for Economic Co-operation and Development (OECD) and the European Union.[1] In the US context the National Security Guidelines of September 2002 declared failed states to be a greater threat than states with ambitions of conquest.[2] The EU followed suit in 2003, announcing that failed states constituted a major threat to European security as well.[3] This represented a policy shift, a recognition that modern wars are 'less a problem of the relations between states than a problem within states'.[4] This analysis has been substantiated by quantitative studies showing that 'state weakness' is now one of the most critical factors underlying armed violence (along with outside intervention).[5]

This policy development echoes a similar shift in academic work (especially in peace and conflict studies), as reflected in the conceptual proliferation of new terms to describe the same basic phenomenon: 'collapsed state', 'failed state', 'fragile state', 'imaginary state', 'absent state', 'lame Leviathan', and 'soft state', to list just a few.[6] Every concept has a specific motivation – for example, 'lame Leviathan' or 'quasi-state' focus on sovereignty and international recognition issues, while terms like 'fragile states' and 'weak states' target service delivery and 'renegade regimes' and 'rogue states' concern state behaviour.[7] Nonetheless, many of these conceptual nuances boil down to insufficient state capacity or the unwillingness of a state to meet its obligations, generally understood as delivering 'core functions to the majority of its people'.[8] This intersection between policy and research priorities was the crucial element behind the rise of the 'fragile state' agenda in the 1990s.

Although there is nothing fundamentally new in the contemporary fragile state agenda – many anthropologists and political scientists discussed similar issues following the decolonisation movement, for instance – the agenda truly started to pick up steam in mainstream international relations in the mid-1990s. Helman and Ratner's 1993 article played a crucial role in attracting policy and academic attention to 'failed states', understood here as 'a situation where governmental structures are overwhelmed by circumstances'.[9] Although the authors make a loose distinction between degrees of collapse,[10] and advocate new conservatorships to deal with *bona fide* failed states, they do not delve much deeper into the analysis of the failed state phenomenon. Their contribution is nevertheless considered 'authoritative',[11] in the sense that it succeeded in setting a new research agenda. A similar research agenda was at the same time pursued by Rotberg and Fukuyama, while being nuanced and given more complexity by the likes of Zartmann from the start.[12]

Helman and Ratner's initial article was clearly informed by the collapse of Somalia and the Socialist Federal Republic of Yugoslavia (SFRY) in the early 1990s. Significantly this period also featured rising interest from major donors and international organisations in state fragility issues. For instance, the United Nations Research Institute for Social Development (UNRISD) convened its first research-preparatory workshop on this topic in April 1993, and the United Nations Development Programme (UNDP) organised a programme on 'Linking Rehabilitation to Development: Management Revitalization of War-torn Societies' at around the same time.[13] The 1990s also saw a gradual *rapprochement* between the development and security fields – what has been termed the 'security–development nexus' – under the overarching umbrella of the fragile state agenda, primarily through a merger of security and development policy and the re-problematisation of security as both the result of and the precondition for development in a broader sense.[14] The concept of 'fragile states', the term generally preferred by development experts, intersected with the concept of 'failed states', which was favoured by security experts and diplomats (as exemplified in speeches by former UN Secretary-General Boutros Boutros-Ghali and former US Secretary of State Madeleine Albright).[15]

The idea that 'state fragility' could be a threat to the national security of Western countries gained additional traction after 9/11, when the al-Qaeda terrorist network attacked the World Trade Center in New York and the Pentagon in Washington, DC. Because the government of Afghanistan was hosting members of this terrorist network, countries with no legitimate or institutionalised government were suddenly perceived as potential sanctuaries for criminal activities and global terrorism. Whether they were considered 'failed' or 'failing' in the US discourse on security, or 'fragile' from a development aid perspective, most analysts agreed that new policies for international security would require a focus on the capacity of national governments in the South to control security within their territories and to provide essential services to their citizens. The emerging discourse on fragile states played a role in the diffusion of this new conception of foreign policy based on the security and development 'nexus'. The implications of the 'securitisation' of the fragile state discourse are spelled out in Kofi Annan's re-conceptualisation of security threats after 9/11. For the UN Secretary-General it was clear that these threats were increasingly coming from governments that were being 'allowed to violate the rights of their individual citizens'. These countries had thus 'become a menace not only to their own people, but also to their own neighbours, and indeed the world'.[16] An estimated 105 countries with oppressive or semi-oppressive governments fall under Annan's sprawling definition of potential terrorist threats,[17] justifying all forms of intervention by the 'core' democratic countries.[18]

In the field of development the focus on addressing the capacity of state institutions in countries facing turbulence stems from the shift towards a new aid allocation system in international assistance. In the late 1990s, while the World Bank was expressing renewed interest in the impact of adequate governance institutions on results in the implementation of aid programmes at the country level, the major traditional donors opened a debate on 'aid effectiveness' that resulted in the 'Monterey Consensus on Financing Development' in 2002.[19] The idea that donors should better target recipient countries according to their policy and institutional performance prepared the development community for the establishment of new resource allocation mechanisms. These mechanisms were based on the evaluation of the 'performance' of national institutions, ie their effective capacity to maintain governance mechanisms ensuring the effectiveness of disbursements in official development assistance (ODA). Aid allocation began to be channelled through a 'selectivity' principle, dedicating the most resources to countries with 'efficient' institutions and policies.

The Western donors' interest in fragile states emerged as an indirect consequence of the donors' shift towards aid selectivity. Despite the focus of aid flows on poverty reduction (rather than economic growth), several countries with weak capacities or in political crisis were unable to meet the new benchmarks. The observation that the concentration of aid flows on 'good performers' was resulting in the marginalisation of countries with 'ineffective' institutions and policies inspired growing criticism of the international financial institutions from the US Congress. The outcry led the World Bank to establish, in 2001, an initiative targeting 'low-income countries under stress' to address the specific challenges of recipient countries suffering from the effects of war, violence and political disruption.[20] Two separate World Bank internal units (the Fragile State Unit and the Conflict Prevention and Reconstruction Unit) contributed to the reframing of the discussion, moving from a focus on aid efficiency to a greater emphasis on state- and peace building.

Between 2001 and 2003 the OECD Development Aid Committee (OECD-DAC) also held a series of meetings on 'poor performers' and 'difficult partnerships', which resulted in the creation of a Fragile State Group in 2003. This group paved the way for the organisation of a 'Senior Level Forum on Development Effectiveness in Fragile States' (held in London in 2005) tasked with the formulation of the 'Principles for Good International Engagement in Fragile States and Situations'.[21] The Forum was presented as a milestone on the way to a consensual and shared recognition of the problem of 'fragile states' as a new major challenge for development. In the same year, in its *Human Development Report*, the UNDP published a list of 59 'top priority' and 'high priority' countries most in need of support; these states were characterised by a combination of low human development and poor performance.[22]

Two major public donors, the USA and the UK, played a leading role in the construction of the policy agenda on fragility within these multilateral organisations. The new UK bilateral cooperation (following the creation of the Department for International Development (DFID) in 1997) placed special emphasis on poverty reduction, human security and the recognition of the role of the state within developing countries, supporting economic arrangements and providing laws and regulations to protect human rights.[23] US development assistance programmes also played a critical role in the emergence of the 'fragile state' concept in the new doctrine of aid selectivity, despite a systematic focus on foreign policy and national security concerns after 9/11. In 2004, for example, the US Congress refocused the mandate of the US Agency for International Development (USAID) to emphasise support for poor countries; it also established the Millennium Challenge Corporation, an independent agency, to assist countries selected on the basis of their policy-performance and institutional capacities. This internalisation of the principle of selectivity within the organisational design of the US bilateral assistance scheme created conditions that allowed the initiation of a policy discussion on state fragility and development. In 2005 USAID drew up specific policy objectives for intervention in fragile states (described either as 'vulnerable states' or 'states in crisis'), depending on the degree of weakness of the political authority over the territory, the capacity of the state to deliver basic services to the population and the legitimacy of the government.[24] In line with the '3D' doctrine, the aid agency incorporated defence and diplomatic objectives into its strategy for development.

In the same year developed and developing countries under the aegis of the OECD endorsed the *Paris Declaration on Aid Effectiveness*, committing to make aid effectiveness a high priority (along with other principles, such as 'harmonisation', 'alignment' and the 'ownership' of aid delivery').[25] These aid effectiveness principles were equally applied to fragile states and 'to environments of weak ownership and capacity and to immediate needs for basic service delivery'.[26] Thus, promoted by a vast array of organisations including the World Bank, the OECD and major aid donors (including the USA, the UK and the EU), the 'fragile state' agenda progressively gained traction in the 2000s.

Critical studies vs policy analysis

Scholarly research on fragile states has undergone a similar expansion since Helman and Ratner's seminal contribution. At the centre of this contemporary literature lies a complex dichotomy between 'problem solvers' and 'critical scholars'.[27] Problem solvers focus on performance issues, seeking ways to provide recommendations for governments, international institutions and technical agencies, whereas critical scholars are inclined to question the values and assumptions underpinning the fragile state concept. From a problem-solving perspective some have explored the issue of the classification of 'fragile states' and the possibility of forecasting state collapse.[28] Others have examined the importance of traditional and non-traditional actors in state-building processes, as well as the current production of normative standards and good practices ('soft laws') in international state building.[29] In this context certain scholars have adopted a quantitative approach to measuring state fragility, while others have opted for a qualitative approach, investigating the specific mechanisms of state fragility in specific case studies.[30]

Another strand of the literature has approached the recent conceptualisation of 'fragile states' from a more critical perspective, and has done so from two angles. On the one hand, scholars have examined the manipulation of the norm by powerful state actors, a process that has deprived local actors of their agency and legitimised interventions by Western governmental agencies. These researchers have also questioned the linkages between failed or fragile states and terrorism, which underlie the rationale behind the security–development nexus.[31] On the other hand, scholars have criticised the analytical validity of the 'fragile state' concept itself. Ziaja and Fabra Mata show that, while most indices agree on the classification of certain countries (such as Afghanistan, the Democratic Republic of Congo (DRC) and Iraq) as fragile, the same indices significantly diverge regarding the status of other countries (including Cuba, North Korea, Israel and China). Hagman and Hoehne critically emphasise the 'teleological belief in the convergence of all nation-states' inherent in the Western concept of 'state failure', demonstrating the negative implications of the use of the concept by means of empirical evidence from the Somali territories. Having analysed the US intervention policies in Iraq and Afghanistan, Nuruzzaman similarly highlights the negative effects of the unreflective use of the concepts of 'state failure' and 'state failing' in international relations. Call criticises the concept of 'state failure' as deficient because it conflates states as diverse as Colombia, Malawi, Somalia, Iraq, Haiti and Tajikistan and prescribes that aid donors 'react in a formulaic manner' to enhance state capacity – even though these countries drastically differ in terms of security, capacity and legitimacy. Nay disputes the analytical underpinning of the research agenda on fragile and failed states, interpreting the framework as the reactivation of 'developmentalist' theories. Both Call and Nay argue for the abandonment of the concept, as its use in such widely divergent and problematic ways proves that it has lost all analytical utility.[32]

The contribution of this special issue

The concepts of 'fragile' or 'failed' states (and other derivatives) are still in widespread use, and are arguably more central to the academic literature and to policy making than ever before. Thanks to an increasing awareness among scholars and policy makers of the shortcomings and limitations of the concept, more diplomatically formulated versions of the label have emerged, such as 'situations of fragility' (proposed in 2007 by the OECD) and 'countries and regions in crisis, post-crisis and fragile situation' (a recent reframing by the EU).[33] In this context the purpose of this special issue is to underline certain political dynamics at play behind the logics of labelling. Building on the existing literature (especially the critical strand), the papers assembled here explore the development of the research agenda from two different angles.

A first set of contributors investigates the development of the policy agenda on fragile states from the donor perspective, questioning the structural conditions under which international agencies have promoted (or have avoided promoting) the discourse on fragile states. The contributors take a peek behind the scenes, analysing the discourse of specific actors and examining the conditions of knowledge production. Nay investigates the role played by the World Bank and the OECD in the development and transnational dissemination of the fragile state discourse in relation to the major traditional donors' conception of international aid. He focuses particular attention on three distinct cognitive and normative processes affecting the policy-oriented concepts used on the international stage: 'normalisation', 'fragmentation' and 'assimilation'. Based on an analysis of the emergence of the concept through these processes, he shows that the World Bank and the OECD have played an instrumental part in the development of transnational knowledge that promotes key Western-driven political standards, conceptions and beliefs. In Nay's interpretation the processes of making and shaping knowledge function as contemporary forms of international hegemony.

Lemay-Hébert and Mathieu shed light on the current orthodoxy of state building in 'fragile' states through the investigation of concept formation within the OECD-DAC. By combining an analysis of the discourse of the OECD with insights into how this discourse is produced, their paper reveals the underlying concept of 'legitimacy' that informs OECD reports and policies. Depending on how 'legitimacy' is conceived, the actions and practices of state builders can differ substantially. Lemay-Hébert and Mathieu identify two approaches to legitimacy under which most scholars and international organisations can be classified: the 'institutionalist' (or 'neo-Weberian') approach, focusing on institutional reconstruction, and the social legitimacy approach, emphasising the importance of social cohesion for successful state building. Through an analysis of the normative production of the OECD, the contribution shows that both conceptions are present in most of the institution's reports, but also that the neo-Weberian approach tends to prevail. The authors attribute this finding to the specific dynamics of knowledge production within the OECD: the norms of the organisation have become a way of being and working for insiders, and the practice of these norms by insiders helps to reproduce the organisation and its culture.

In her article Grimm criticises the fact that the EU has not (yet) agreed on a clear-cut definition of 'state fragility'. She highlights three factors that explain this situation: first, the Union's complex institutional framework, which impedes policy coherence; second, developments at the international level that require the Union's compliance; and third, the EU's diplomatic efforts to preserve cooperative relationships with aid-recipient countries that have been labelled 'fragile'. This last aspect reveals a central dilemma facing many aid donors: although they may seek to avoid classification via a label that is perceived as highly political, the lack of a clear-cut strategy to deal with the consequences of state 'fragility' can deprive donors of the capacity to develop meaningful and sustainable country-sensitive policies to overcome deficits in governance, socioeconomic development and security.

Siqueira critically assesses the role of indicators and statistics in the labelling and management of 'fragile states'. After emphasising the difficulties of attributing ownership of numerical claims in fragile contexts, she subsequently questions the validity and reliability of these quantitative classifications. Focusing on the education sector in Timor-Leste and on the World Bank's Country Policy and Institutional Assessment approach, the article shows how accountability and ownership are negotiated within the context of the g7+ group of self-labelled 'fragile states', encouraging an examination of the power relations involved. She concludes that statistical schemes have become increasingly entrenched in international bureaucracy by means of a self-perpetuating process of 'improvement in use'. As a consequence, such schemes become ever more difficult to change. In accepting this reality, the g7+ does not resist the increasingly popular practice of 'fragility' quantification; instead, the group seeks to establish influence over 'numerical claims' by joining the 'multitude of allies' that contributes to the definition and characterisation of 'state fragility'.

The second set of contributors analyses the political use of the 'fragile state' label from a local perspective. These scholars focus on the reception, internalisation and reinterpretation of the 'fragile state' classification from a local perspective, highlighting local agency in the process. Gabrielsen-Jumbert analyses US responses to the conflict in Darfur, examining the ways in which the Sudanese state has been conceptualised by 'outsiders' and how this has affected international intervention. Her analysis reveals that, despite frequent descriptions of Sudan as a 'fragile' or 'failed' state, it is the label 'rogue state' that has truly taken hold in the Darfur context. This distinction has led to the prioritisation of strategies based on 'protection' and 'punishment' over attempts to resolve the underlying causes of the conflict, which a more sophisticated understanding of the Sudanese state's internal weaknesses and instability might have allowed.

In his contribution Heiduk illustrates how discourses on 'state fragility' have been instrumentalised by the Indonesian military in order to consolidate its political and economic powers since the fall of Suharto. In the wake of an impending process of state dissolution in post-Suharto Indonesia the military has managed to re-establish itself as the 'guardian of the nation' by exploiting fears of state disintegration and 'balkanisation'. In this way it has found a way to remove the issue of military reform from the political agenda while reclaiming its former privileges.

Fisher suggests that the aid-dependent government of Uganda has widened its room for manoeuvre with donors by emphasising the degree of instability in the north of the country. By referring to the notion of 'state fragility', the Ugandan regime has successfully persuaded donors to continue their support, despite its domestic transgressions. In parallel the regime has succeeded, according to Fisher, in taking advantage of a contradictory but equally persuasive international discourse that presents Uganda as stable, strong and secure. In exploring how Kampala has successfully employed both narratives to carve out greater agency with donors, the paper emphasises the significance of the donors' physical detachment from the Ugandan 'periphery' in this dynamic. Both Heiduk and Fisher highlight the way local actors have managed to re-appropriate the concept of 'state fragility' and translate it for their own purposes; the end result of such transformations may be far from the original intentions informing the use of the 'fragile state' categorisation.

In his concluding contribution to the issue Brinkerhoff identifies state fragility and failure as 'wicked problems' that affect both international policy discourses and international peace- and state-building interventions. The author explores the various dimensions of 'wicked problems', arguing that these features are easily observable in the fragile state arena. He also suggests that we view the use of the fragile state concept as 'an effort to tame the wickedness of the state fragility/failure problem set'. Complementing the analyses offered in this issue, he recommends not only an examination of the 'naming' and 'taming' of state fragility, but also the development of practices that could help both labellers and the labelled to overcome situations of fragility.

Conclusions

The contributions to this special issue suggest three main conclusions. First, diverging purposes are merged in the 'fragile states' label: the latter seeks to contribute to a conceptual approach addressing states' weaknesses, but at the same time it constitutes a normative tool and a policy label used extensively by international organisations and Western donor countries to legitimise their strategic objectives in foreign policy. Second, the definition of 'fragile states' is far from stable, despite the attempts by many international institutions to create a more rigorous definition. The term is used by various actors with different agendas to describe dissimilar national contexts of political disruption, institutional weakness and economic collapse. As a result, the concept is subject to a variety of interpretations, and its use as an analytical method of understanding the political, social and economic factors that may increase the vulnerability and instability of developing countries is highly problematic. The term 'fragile state' can be better understood as a 'policy narrative', as its meanings reflect the strategic visions and political goals of its main advocates. Finally, actors in so-called 'fragile states' have not remained passive in the process of the transnational dissemination of the concept. Their resources have allowed them 'to resist, ignore, engage with, disengage from, and exploit' international involvement.[34] It is our hope that this special issue will help to increase awareness of these wide-ranging dynamics and provide additional evidence of the limits of the simplistic categorisation of states through the use of the 'fragile states' label.

Acknowledgements

We are very grateful to the contributing authors, who endured numerous meetings (International Studies Association annual meeting in Montreal, International Political Studies Association annual meeting in Madrid) in order to produce a coherent set of articles for this special issue. We also thank our colleagues who served as anonymous reviewers at various stages in the production process. We are grateful to Claire Bacher for her careful proofreading, as well as to Katarina Lavric and Nicki Jeschke for editorial support. The financial support of the Center of Excellence 'Cultural Foundations of Integration' at the University of Konstanz and of the Research Assistant Scheme at the School of Government and Society, University of Birmingham, is gratefully acknowledged.

Notes on Contributors

Sonja Grimm is Senior Lecturer in the Department of Politics and Public Administration, University of Konstanz. She has published various studies on the transition to democracy in post-conflict societies and on international democracy promotion and has previously co-edited special issues of *Democratization* on "War and Democratization: Legality, Legitimacy, and Effectiveness" (15, no. 3 (2008) with Wolfgang Merkel) and "Do all Good Things go Together? Conflicting Objectives in Democracy Promotion" (19, no. 3 (2012) with Julia Leininger and Tina Freyburg). More about her can be found at www.sonja-grimm.eu.

Nicolas Lemay-Hébert is Senior Lecturer in the International Development Department, University of Birmingham. His research interests include peace building and state building, humanitarian interventions in post-conflict or post-disaster contexts, the political economy of international interventions, and local narratives of resistance to international intervention. He has published various articles in *International Studies Perspectives*, *International Peacekeeping*, *Third World Quarterly*, *Democratization*, and the *Journal of Intervention and Statebuilding*, among others. His most recent book is *Semantics of Statebuilding: Language, Meanings and Sovereignty* (2014; co-edited with N. Onuf, V. Rakic and P. Bojanic).

Olivier Nay is Professor of Political Science, University of Paris 1 – Panthéon Sorbonne. He is Vice-president of the French Association of Political Science and Chair of the Political Science section at the National Academic Council. Since 2006 he has been working on the reform of international organisations, bureaucratic change and the transnational diffusion of policy ideas. His most recent articles have been published in the *International Political Science Review* ("Fragile and Failed States"), *Journal of Public Policy* ("How Do Policy Ideas Spread among International Administrations?") and *Governance* ("What Drives Reforms in International Organizations?"). Further information can be found at his personal webpage univ-paris1.academia.edu/OlivierNay.

Notes

1. World Bank, *World Development Report 2011*; OECD, *Principles for Good International Engagement*; Council of the European Union, "An EU Response to Situations of Fragility"; and European Commission, "Towards an EU Response to Situations of Fragility."
2. National Security Council, *The National Security Strategy*. Interestingly this strategy document was drafted amid a period of heightened tension between the People's Republic of China (Mainland China) and the Republic of China (Taiwan) over the policies of the Taiwanese president, Chen Shui-bian.
3. Toje, "The 2003 European Union Security Strategy," 124–127.
4. Holsti, *The State, War and the State of War*, xi.
5. Stepanova, "Trends in Armed Conflicts," 71.
6. Odhiambo, "The Economics of Conflict," 292–296.
7. There is also an element of gradation in the typology of certain authors. For Robert Rotberg, 'it is according to their performances – according to the levels of their effective delivery of the most crucial political goods – that strong states may be distinguished from weak ones, and weak states from failed or collapsed'. Rotberg, "The Failure and Collapse of Nation-states," 2.
8. DFID, *Why We Need to Work More Effectively*.
9. Helman and Ratner, "Saving Failed States," 5.
10. Ibid. Helman and Ratner identify three groups of states whose survival is threatened: failed states, in which the governmental structures have been overwhelmed by circumstances; failing states, where collapse is not imminent but could occur within several years; and, finally, certain newly independent states whose viability is difficult to assess.

11. Wilde, "The Skewed Responsibility Narrative," 425; and Paris, "Ordering the World."
12. Rotberg, "The Failure and Collapse of Nation-states"; Fukuyama, *State-building*; and Zartman, *Collapsed States*.
13. Doornbos, "State Formation and Collapse," 281.
14. Duffield, *Development, Security and Unending War*.
15. Yannis, "State Collapse and its Implications," 64.
16. Annan, "We can Love What We Are."
17. Including 47 'not free countries' and 58 'partly free countries', according to Freedom House's *Freedom in the World 2013* report. Reasoning taken from Dempsey, "Nation Building's Newest Disguise," 416–417.
18. This analogy was developed by Thomas P. M. Barnett, whose book *The Pentagon's New Map* proved influential during the 'neo-conservative moment' in the USA in 2001–2005.
19. United Nations, *Monterrey Consensus*.
20. World Bank, *World Bank Group Work in Low-income Countries under Stress*.
21. The 'Principles for Good International Engagement' were published in 2007 by the OECD; for an overview of the process, see OECD, *International Engagement in Fragile States*.
22. UNDP, *Human Development Report 2003*.
23. DFID, *The Politics of Poverty*.
24. USAID, "Fragile States Strategy."
25. OECD, *Paris Declaration on Aid Effectiveness*, para. 3.
26. Ibid., para. 37.
27. Bellamy, "The 'Next Stage' in Peace Operations Theory?"; and Lemay-Hébert, "Review Essay."
28. Ziaja and Fabra Mata, *State Fragility Indices*; Stewart and Grown, *Fragile States*; and Grimm and Schneider, *Predicting Social Tipping Points*.
29. Brinkerhoff, *Governance in Post-conflict Societies*; Robert Schumann Centre for Advanced Studies, *Overcoming Fragility in Africa*; and Wesley, "The State of the Art."
30. For the former, see Carment, "Assessing State Failure"; and Ikpe, "Challenging the Discourse on Fragile States." For the latter, see Brinkerhoff, "State Fragility and Governance."
31. For the former, see Boas and Jennings, "Failed States and State Failure," 475–485. For the latter, see Hehir, "The Myth of the Failed State"; and Newman, "Weak States."
32. Ziaja and Fabra Mata, *State Fragility Indices*, 3; Hagmann and Hoehne, "Failures of the State Failure Debate," 42; Nuruzzaman, "Revisiting the Category of Fragile and Failed States"; Call, "Beyond the 'Failed State'," 322; Call, "The Fallacy of the 'Failed State'," 1491; and Nay, "Fragile and Failed States."
33. See Lemay-Hébert and Mathieu, as well as Grimm, in this issue. See also Mcloughlin, *Topic Guide*, 9–14.
34. Mac Ginty, *International Peacebuilding and Local Resistance*, 10–11.

Bibliography

Annan, Kofi. "We can Love What We Are, without Hating What – and Who We Are Not." Nobel Lecture, Oslo, 10 December 2001.

Barnett, Thomas P. M. *The Pentagon's New Map*. New York: G. B. Putnam, 2004.

Bellamy, Alex. "The 'Next Stage' in Peace Operations Theory?" In *Peace Operations and Global Order*, edited by Alex Bellamy, and Paul Williams, 17–38. London: Routledge, 2005.

Boas, Morten, and Kathleen M. Jennings. "Failed States and State Failure: Threats or Opportunities?" *Globalizations* 4, no. 4 (2007): 475–485.

Brinkerhoff, Derick, ed. *Governance in Post-conflict Societies: Rebuilding Fragile States*. London: Routledge, 2007.

Brinkerhoff, Derick. "State Fragility and Governance: Conflict Mitigation and Subnational Perspectives." *Development Policy Review* 29, no. 2 (2011): 131–153.

Call, Charles T. "Beyond the 'Failed State': Toward Conceptual Alternatives." *European Journal of International Relations* 17, no. 2 (2011): 303–326.

Call, Charles T. "The Fallacy of the 'Failed State'." *Third World Quarterly* 29, no. 8 (2008): 1491–1507.

Carment, David. "Assessing State Failure: Implications for Theory and Policy." *Third World Quarterly* 24, no. 3 (2003): 407–427.

Council of the European Union. "An EU Response to Situations of Fragility: Conclusions of the Council and the Representatives of the Governments of the Member States Meeting within the Council, 15118/07, 20 November 2007." Brussels, 2007.

Dempsey, Gary. "Nation Building's Newest Disguise." *Orbis* 46, no. 3 (2002): 415–434.

DFID. *The Politics of Poverty: Elites, Citizens and States – Findings from Ten Years of dfid-Funded Research on Governance and Fragile States 2001–2010. A Synthesis Paper*. London: ukaid/Department for International Development, 2010.

DFID. *Why We Need to Work More Effectively in Fragile States*. London: ukaid/Department for International Development, 2005.

Doornbos, Martin. "State Formation and Collapse: Reflections on Identity and Power." In *Pivot Politics: Changing Cultural Identities in Early State Formation Processes*, edited by Martin van Bakel, Renée Hagesteijn, and Pieter van de Velde, 281–285. Amsterdam: Het Spinhuis, 1994.

Duffield, Mark. *Development, Security and Unending War: Governing the World of Peoples*. London: Polity, 2007.

European Commission. "Towards an EU Response to Situations of Fragility: Engaging in Difficult Environments for Sustainable Development, Stability and Peace." Communication from the Commission to the Council, the European Parliament, the European Economic and Social Committee and the Committee of the Regions. Com(2007) 643 Final, 25 October 2007.

Fukuyama, Francis. State-Building: Governance and World Order in the 21st Century. New York, NY: Cornell University Press, 2004.

Grimm, Sonja, and Gerald Schneider. *Predicting Social Tipping Points*. Discussion Paper 8/2011. Bonn: German Development Institute, 2011.

Hagmann, Tobias, and Markus V. Hoehne. "Failures of the State Failure Debate: Evidence from the Somali Territories." *Journal of International Development* 21, no. 1 (2009): 42–57.

Hehir, Aidan. "The Myth of the Failed State and the War on Terror: A Challenge to the Conventional Wisdom." *Journal of Intervention and Statebuilding* 1, no. 3 (2007): 307–332.

Helman, Gerald B., and Steven R. Ratner. "Saving Failed States." *Foreign Policy* 89, no. 4 (1993): 3–20.

Holsti, Kalevi. The State, War and the State of War. Cambridge: Cambridge University Press, 1996.

Ikpe, Eka. "Challenging the Discourse on Fragile States." *Conflict, Security & Development* 7, no. 1 (2007): 85–124.

Lemay-Hébert, Nicolas. "Review Essay: Critical Debates on Liberal Peacebuilding." *Civil Wars* 15, no. 2 (2013): 242–252.

Mac Ginty, Roger. *International Peacebuilding and Local Resistance: Hybrid Forms of Peace*. London: Palgrave Macmillan, 2011.

Mcloughlin, Claire. *Topic Guide on Fragile States*. Brimingham: Governance and Social Development Resource Centre, University of Birmingham, 2012.

National Security Council. *The National Security Strategy, September 2002*. Washington, DC: National Security Council/Administration of President George W. Bush, 2002.

Nay, Olivier. "Fragile and Failed States: Critical Perspectives on Conceptual Hybrids." *International Political Science Review* 34, no. 3 (2013): 326–341.

Newman, Edward. "Weak States, State Failure, and Terrorism." *Terrorism and Political Violence* 19, no. 4 (2007): 463–488.

Nuruzzaman, Mohammed. "Revisiting the Category of Fragile and Failed States in International Relations." *International Studies* 46, no. 3 (2009): 271–294.

Odhiambo, Atieno. "The Economics of Conflict among Marginalized Peoples of Eastern Africa." In *Conflict Resolution in Africa*, edited by Francis Deng, and William Zartman, 292–296. Washington, DC: Brookings, 1991.

OECD. *International Engagement in Fragile States: Can't We Do Better?* Paris: Organisation for Economic Cooperation and Development, 2011.

OECD. *Paris Declaration on Aid Effectiveness*. Final Declaration of the High-Level Forum on Aid Effectiveness. Paris: Organisation for Economic Cooperation and Development, 2005.

OECD. *Principles for Good International Engagement in Fragile States & Situations*. Paris: Organisation for Economic Cooperation and Development, 2007.

Paris, Roland. "Ordering the World: Academic Research and Policymaking on Fragile States." *International Studies Review* 13, no. 1 (2011): 58–74.

Robert Schumann Centre for Advanced Studies. *Overcoming Fragility in Africa: Forging a New European Approach*. European Report on Development 2009. San Domenico di Fiesole: Robert Schuman Centre for Advanced Studies, European University Institute, 2009.

Rotberg, Robert I. "The Failure and Collapse of Nation-states: Breakdown, Prevention, and Repair." In *When States Fail: Causes and Consequences*, edited by Robert I. Rotberg, 1–49. Princeton, NJ: Princeton University Press, 2004.

Stepanova, Ekaterina. "Trends in Armed Conflicts." In *sipri Yearbook 2008: Armaments, Disarmament and International Security*, edited by SIPRI, 43–71. Oxford: Oxford University Press, 2008.

Stewart, Frances, and Graham Grown. *Fragile States*. Overview no. 3. Oxford: Centre for Research on Inequality, Human Security and Ethnicity, June 2010.

Toje, Asle. "The 2003 European Union Security Strategy: A Critical Appraisal." *European Foreign Affairs Review* 10 (2005): 117–133.

UNDP. *Human Development Report 2003: Millennium Development Goals – A Compact among Nations to End Human Poverty*. New York/Oxford: United Nations Development Programme/Oxford University Press, 2003.

United Nations. *Monterrey Consensus on Financing for Development*. Final Text of Agreements and Commitments Adopted at the International Conference on Financing for Development, Monterrey, 18–22 March

2002. New York: United Nations Department of Economic and Social Affairs/Financing for Development Office, 2002.

USAID. "Fragile States Strategy, Pd-Aca-999, January 2005." US Agency for International Development, Washington, DC, 2005.

Wesley, Michael. "The State of the Art on the Art of State Building." *Global Governance* 14, no. 3 (2008): 369–385.

Wilde, Ralph. "The Skewed Responsibility Narrative of the 'Failed States' Concept." *ILSA Journal of International and Comparative Law* 9, no. 2 (2003): 425–429.

World Bank. *World Bank Group Work in Low-income Countries under Stress. A Task Force Report.* Washington, DC: World Bank/Task Force on the Work of the World Bank Group in Low-income Countries Under Stress, 2002.

World Bank. *World Development Report 2011: Conflict, Security and Development.* Washington, DC: World Bank, 2011.

Yannis, Alexandros. "*State Collapse and its Implications for Peace-building and Reconstruction*." In *State Failure, Collapse and Reconstruction*, edited by Jennifer Milliken, 63–80. Oxford: Blackwell, 2003.

Zartman, I. William. *Collapsed States: The Disintegration and Restoration of Legitimate Authority*. Boulder, CO: Lynne Rienner, 1995.

Ziaja, Sebastian, and Javier Fabra Mata. *State Fragility Indices: Potentials, Messages and Limitations.* DIE Briefing Paper 10/2010. Bonn: German Development Institute, 2010.

International Organisations and the Production of Hegemonic Knowledge: how the World Bank and the OECD helped invent the Fragile State Concept

Olivier Nay

Department of Political Science, University of Paris 1 – Panthéon Sorbonne, Paris, France

This article examines the role of the World Bank and the OECD in the emergence and circulation of the 'fragile state' concept. These organisations were critical to the early development of the concept and in the consolidation of a knowledge-based agenda set out by Western aid donors to justify international assistance to poor and conflict-ridden countries. Attention is focused on three normative processes affecting the production of transnational knowledge: normalisation, fragmentation and assimilation. 'Normalisation' is the process by which influential knowledge producers help to transform a rough concept into a widely accepted transnational norm based on expert knowledge, detailed definitions and statistical exercises. Once the concept has been appropriated by several international actors, it undergoes normative 'fragmentation' as it is subjected to various interpretations across time and space. 'Assimilation' is the process by which the overarching concept is renewed, enriched and gradually adapted through the incorporation of additional insights. The article argues that the World Bank and OECD have functioned as central knowledge hubs, facilitating the circulation of new and controversial ideas on fragile states and their integration into the prevailing policies of the most powerful aid donors. The two organisations have thus taken an active role in the consolidation and perpetuation of the aid donors' policy doctrine, ultimately protecting it from major normative dissent.

Introduction

The 'fragile state' concept is one of the few internationally accepted policy categories to have been fully integrated into most policy doctrines on security and development in the post-cold war era. It has gained such prominence in the international political lexicon that many multilateral and bilateral actors now consider fragile states to be a specific priority agenda. Over the past 10 years it has become a core category, used by Western governments to bolster legitimacy for their new foreign assistance strategies towards developing countries. The concept has been promoted by the most influential international organisations, including the World Bank and the OECD. It has been abundantly discussed by diplomats, bureaucrats, decision makers, experts and practitioners in foreign policy circles and development forums. In addition, it has been modelled by databases and matrices using highly sophisticated statistical methods; it has even been conceptualised as a research object in academic discussions.[1]

Global concepts often emerge within a particular epistemic community or in advocacy movements before being appropriated and publicised by governments and administrations. The idea of labelling countries experiencing conflict and severe poverty as 'fragile' – or with other similar qualifications, such as 'failed', 'failing', 'collapsed' or 'in crisis' – was transmitted in the opposite direction: it was initially adopted and actively promoted by a small group of government agencies representing powerful states, before being disseminated among international organisations and gradually extended to wider audiences, including developing countries and non-state actors. The category was developed and promoted by certain Western donor countries as a conceptual tool enabling the creation of a new global agenda in the fields of foreign policy, international cooperation and peacekeeping operations, while supporting the new national security strategies in domestic politics after the attacks of 11 September 2001. Finally, the concept was intended to guide the interactions and relationships between donor countries and recipient countries facing conflict and poverty.

This article views the 'fragile state' concept as a prescriptive category, which has contributed to a definition of the problems experienced in countries from the Southern hemisphere that is highly congruent with Western preoccupations and interests.[2] It argues that the label was coined by leading aid donors in order to promote a new perspective on international assistance. The concept has subsequently been used as a policy category to reshape policy agendas in a manner that has enhanced the legitimacy of major donor-led reforms in the financing of development aid, and has promoted Western policy 'remedies' for war and poverty, such as state-building and peace-building interventions (see the introduction to this special issue).

The article draws on two main underlying assumptions. First, concepts are not politically or ideologically neutral. Although their supporters may claim they are based on rigorous expertise and independent knowledge, concepts are always accompanied by political perceptions and reflect government intentions. They help to frame the comprehension of problems in accordance with the worldviews of the most powerful actors; thus, they form part of the 'structures of knowledge' that are an essential element of the legitimacy of asymmetrical power relationship within the existing world-system.[3] Second, concepts are far from stable in time and space. Once created, they become partially autonomous;

they are then subjected to a multitude of social interpretations as a result of successive reframing processes in a variety of forums. They are the object of diverse ideological appropriations and various forms of resistance. To paraphrase the title of a famous book edited by Appadurai on the cultural biography of objects, concepts have a 'social life'.[4] They may even have multiple lives as they are exposed to various instrumental uses and cultural acclimatisation.

This article focuses on the role of the World Bank and the OECD in the emergence and circulation of the 'fragile state' concept over the past 10 years. It shows how these two organisations participated in the early development of the concept and, once it was widely disseminated, contributed to the perpetuation of the essential premises set out by Western experts. The first section discusses analytical perspectives on the role of the World Bank and the OECD in the transnational circulation of ideas and knowledge on development aid. Using the case of the 'fragile state' concept, the following sections examine how these organisations have been involved in three distinct cognitive and normative processes. The second section draws attention to the role of the World Bank and OECD as knowledge producers participating in the 'normalisation' of the concept, a process in which the 'fragile state' idea was transformed into a transnational norm through successive definition exercises and the use of expert knowledge. The third section focuses on the process of 'fragmentation', whereby the concept was increasingly exposed to a variety of uses and interpretations as it spread among a growing number of international actors. The final section discusses 'assimilation', described as the normative process in which the concept – enriched and adapted through the incorporation of new elements – becomes protected from significant normative dissent over time.

The World Bank, the OECD and the transnational circulation of knowledge on development

International organisations do not operate in isolation as transnational producers and promoters of doctrinal concepts. They participate in knowledge networks and policy forums in which ideas for development aid are actively debated and disputed.[5] In the field of international assistance these transnational networks and forums interconnect a wide range of actors: diplomats and experts from state agencies and international organisations, individual consultants, scholars, journalists and policy analysts working for think-tanks, NGOs, foundations, consulting firms and advocacy groups. They sometimes reflect certain 'ideological constellations', understood as systems of actors that promote convergent ideological views in policy analysis; they may also be linked to 'epistemic communities', professional networks with authoritative and policy-relevant expertise.[6] Despite the claims of most actors that they produce policy-oriented knowledge based on evidence, they usually have their own specific interests, selective policy objectives and individual social beliefs and perceptions. Most often they seek to shape ideas and concepts so that these better reflect their own preferences, objectives and ideological views. The circulation of concepts and knowledge is a selective and competitive process in which actors holding conflicting views, driven by diverging interests and with unequal resource capacities, strive to ensure the success of their personal perspectives in policy analysis.

International organisations play various roles in multi-actor and multi-level dynamics that can affect the circulation and framing of policy ideas. They provide institutional settings where government actors can promote their foreign policy agendas. Some international organisations, through their internal technical resources and their central position in transnational knowledge networks, may acquire even greater capacity to influence prevailing general perceptions and representations in international relations. Three levels of knowledge activity can be identified within international organisations.

First, international organisations operate as policy forums. Their programmes reflect intergovernmental debates; in addition, these organisations are increasingly involved in policy discussions with non-state actors, such as NGOs, advocacy groups and the private sector. They serve as a 'sounding board' for ideas advocated by other actors and also function as 'conveyor belts', contributing to the transnational flow of policy standards and norms. For instance, the OECD played an active role in the dissemination of the market-oriented economic ideas, administration reform models and values associated with New Public Management.[7]

Second, through their administrations, internal units and departments, international organisations play an active role as 'norm entrepreneurs'. Their secretariats frequently include policy specialists involved in expert knowledge production that may shape subsequent public programmes. These experts select, internalise and reframe the ideas advanced by member states or promoted by actors in their direct environment. They are connected to transnational intellectual networks and work in close contact with epistemic communities comprising policy analysts, private consultants, scholars, activists, practitioners and journalists. As such, they can identify emerging and controversial issues that may be integrated into the organisation's agenda, thereby lending these ideas greater legitimacy and political momentum by categorising and codifying them into a perspective that might obtain the support of a majority of member states. At times policy experts working for international organisations are themselves the providers of innovative concepts and norms, as seen with the UN Development Programme (UNDP) and the notion of 'human security' and 'human development indicators'.

Third, international organisations can be enforcers of ideas. They are frequently engaged in the surveillance and monitoring of the ideas implemented by national and local authorities, through the development of benchmarking, reviews and evaluation programmes. Some organisations take part in the concrete application of ideas at country or regional levels. This occurs directly when the organisation is responsible for the operational implementation of the policy programme; alternatively the organisation may act indirectly by participating in the definition and dissemination of the policy instruments and standards to be implemented by national authorities, especially when conditionality links official development aid to the national application of these instruments and standards.

At these three levels international organisations enhance their own legitimacy on the international stage by reinforcing their capacity to disseminate ideas that transcend individual state interests and are expected to help achieve universal goods and values.[8] In particular, the administration of such organisations may gain some autonomy and influence through the development of ideas and knowledge.[9]

The World Bank and the OECD play an instrumental role in the definition and dissemination of legitimate concepts and theories fuelling the international aid agenda. The two institutions have distinct missions and objectives with regard to development policies. The World Bank is a financial institution focused on development that uses the transfer of capital to help reduce poverty, whereas the OECD is a club of wealthy states that serves as a public think-tank for policy development in a large number of fields. The World Bank is legally and operationally in a position to exercise restraint or supervision over the governments of developing countries that receive its financial assistance; in contrast, the OECD lacks the power to enforce compliance with its decisions. The former uses financial instruments and holds sanctioning powers, while the latter functions on a consensus basis and exerts influence through the promotion of policy standards.[10]

Despite these differences, the two organisations have strong institutional linkages, which encourage their bureaucracies to promote similar views on development aid.[11] They have become important hubs of knowledge on development assistance worldwide, thanks to the exceptional enhancement of their research, publication and communication capacities.[12] As Jacobsson describes it,[13] they have gradually become involved in 'inquisitive' activities (based on increased surveillance and monitoring of the actions of national governments through the auditing, evaluation and ranking of state performance) and in 'meditative' activities (based on policy discussions that examine national practices, draw comparisons and disseminate relevant ideas across many countries). To this end, they publish a number of procedural books and technical guides that are central to the dissemination of concepts and ideas through 'good practices'. They also seek to become more involved in transnational knowledge networks, with the aim of participating in and stimulating policy reflection on issues of interest concerning development aid.[14] They therefore operate through 'soft regulations', encouraging the development of standards, informal norms, qualitative approaches, statistical indicators and benchmarks for use by the decision makers, experts and practitioners involved in national policy networks, including both government agencies and non-state actors. Through this knowledge activity they increase their 'cognitive influence', described as the capacity to gather, shape, publicise and circulate the policy standards, information and knowledge used in policy making and the implementation of development programmes.[15]

At the same time these organisations should not be considered 'voluntaristic' in nature. They have no constant or persistent 'will', nor any idiosyncratic capacity to act as independent actors. Their political and bureaucratic structures often suffer from significant internal tensions and may lack consistency.[16] They represent institutional arenas in which individual members, clubs of countries, groups of agents and bureaucratic units lobby and fight to influence internal decision-making processes according to their own views and interests. They are plagued by internal conflicts, misunderstandings and fragmented conceptions.[17] To some extent these tensions reflect the conflicting views and interests of the actors in the environment of the organisations, such as national bureaucracies, other international organisations, market-oriented actors, knowledge producers and advocacy groups, all of whom promote their individual financial, technical and ideological preferences. Therefore, the contribution of international organisations to globalised knowledge should be viewed as the end result of interactional dynamics including both inner struggles for control over concept development and the influence of 'external' actors with the resources to access policy discussions and decision-making processes. The following sections examine the role of the World Bank and the OECD's Development Assistance Committee (OECD-DAC) in the development of the 'fragile state' doctrine through three interconnected processes of knowledge development: normalisation, fragmentation, and assimilation.

Table 1. International organisations and the development of knowledge: three normative processes.

Normalisation	Fragmentation	Assimilation
Process by which international organisations help to transform a rough concept, initially developed in restricted circles of knowledge, into a widely accepted transnational norm based on expert knowledge • Production of detailed definitions, statistical exercises and policy analysis • Increasing use of the concept in public statements and policy programmes • Insertion into regulatory rules and procedures • Inclusion in measurement tools, assessment methods and policy instruments • Dissemination among various audiences	Process by which the concept, once it has gained transnational prominence, is subjected to a variety of local interpretations, as it undergoes multiple uses and acclimatises in diverse ways across time and space • Accumulation of definitions, criteria and indicators that broaden and overload the concept with multiple meanings and understandings • Uncontrolled appropriations, distortions and deviations by new actors in ways that dissociate the concept from its initially agreed-upon interpretation • Resistance from actors who dispute the validity of the concept and its analytical or operational application	Process by which international organisations gradually revise, enrich and perpetuate hegemonic concepts through the steady incorporation of additional insights and critical perspectives into the prevailing paradigm • Incorporation of emerging ideas into the dominant conceptual framework • Integration of critical views in the framework, carefully selected following non-competitive procedures • Rejection of radically diverging interpretations

Normalisation: how international organisations contribute to the standardisation of knowledge

Although no policy entrepreneur or advocate can exercise complete control over the dynamics of policy transfer, some knowledge producers with significant resources can successfully contribute to the shaping and dissemination of a widely agreed-upon definition of a concept. In the following section I argue that the World Bank and the OECD-DAC played a central role in the 'normalisation' of the 'fragile state' concept. Here, I define normalisation as the process by which a concept, initially developed in restricted circles of knowledge, gains acceptance among a wider audience as it begins to be extensively used by decision makers, experts and analysts, practitioners, beneficiaries and stakeholders. Over the course of this process, it becomes both an accepted category for policy development and a transnational 'norm' conveying a set of principles, values and beliefs that are held to be valid and influence how actors perceive reality and evaluate potential actions. Normalisation involves: (1) the increasing use of the concept in the public statements, programmes and reference documents that define the standards of 'good policy', such that the concept becomes part of public agendas; (2) its gradual inclusion as a central category in policy analysis (especially in measurement tools and assessment methods), which allows the concept to become technically associated with the instruments used in policy development, monitoring, implementation and evaluation; (3) its insertion into regulatory rules and procedures; and (4) its dissemination among various audiences in multiple forums and networks.

The World Bank, the inception of expert knowledge and measurement tools for fragile states

Through its initiative on 'low income countries under stress' (LICUS), launched in 2002, the World Bank was the first international agency to develop specific qualitative standards to define countries with limited governmental capacity resulting from severe internal conflicts and deteriorating socioeconomic conditions.[18] Its programme for Liberia, in coordination with UN peacekeeping forces, provided an opportunity to outline specific criteria for policy intervention, focusing on reconstruction. The World Bank also served as an important laboratory in the development of measurement instruments and data production techniques focusing on state fragility associated with poverty and underdevelopment; it also helped promote a highly technical definition of country fragility based on its statistical instrument, the Country Policy and Institutional Assessment (CPIA). The CPIA is an index that was established in the mid-1970s, originally developed as a diagnostic tool to rate the quality of developing countries' policies and institutional arrangements with the aim of guiding the Bank's interventions and assessing financial risks for concessional loans and grants. With the development of country performance ratings for the allocation of resources in the late 1990s, the CPIA became the key instrument used to select countries eligible for financial assistance from the International Development Association, the Bank's fund targeting the poorest countries. In the context of the new LICUS programme the World Bank began to use the index as a rating system to identify countries 'under stress' (called 'fragile' from 2005 onwards), a category that included both conflict-affected countries and countries with weak governance.[19] Initially conceived as an internal instrument that would be restricted to the Bank's experts, the CPIA's numerical scores were disclosed in 2006 and swiftly became reference indicators for other institutions engaged in international support for poor and conflict-ridden countries, including some donor countries, key financial partners (such as the IMF and regional development banks), and certain international organisations (such as the OECD-DAC).

As the Bank's classification tool for the identification and categorisation of poor countries, the CPIA index established definitions and a framework for the discussion of 'fragile state' issues that were then integrated into the donors' agenda on aid effectiveness between 2003 and 2007. Its main criteria provided the basis for a restrictive definition of 'situations of fragility', focusing on the performance of public institutions and governance mechanisms, in a policy framework that prioritised institutional and financial challenges. In this perspective fragility was articulated in terms of the objectives of economic growth and poverty reduction. It was assessed through indicators measuring 'good policies' and criteria of 'effectiveness' with regard to the functioning of the public sector (eg risk management, oversight and supervision of the financial sector, control of budget imbalances, tracking of aid flows and reduction of debt levels). Through its use of universal indicators, the index provided a uniform, non-contextual, ahistorical, state-centred definition of fragility, with attention devoted to 'internal' factors that could exacerbate weak governance, instability and poverty. However, it ignored the major role played by external shocks fuelling the economic and institutional vulnerabilities of so-called fragile countries (eg market fluctuations in the North, the role of global economic actors, transnational crime and trafficking, regional conflicts). The supporters of the index also assumed that the same set of policy reform prescriptions – primarily associated with New Public Management recommendations – would be able to advance economic growth and poverty reduction in all countries, whatever their specific situation. Finally, the diffusion and extensive use of the CPIA laid the foundations for a dominant paradigm establishing a correlation between fragile situations and the lack of capacity of national state institutions, rather than addressing the societal and transnational challenges that may increase vulnerabilities in developing countries.

The dissemination of the CPIA index contributed to the transnational diffusion of a functional approach to fragility dominated by donor-driven interests in policy governance and institutional performance. Along with other indexes on fragility CPIA indicators helped transform the 'fragile state' label into technical knowledge, using sophisticated scoring methods that were compatible with current evaluation and monitoring systems. It depoliticised the debate on fragility at a time when the US administration was advocating a national security strategy based on ideological arguments that referred to 'state failure' as a factor driving immediate threats to the democratic and liberal world. The CPIA indicators transformed the political need of Western donors to differentiate between developing countries according to their institutional and policy efficiency into an indisputable classification objectified through data, indicators and rating systems that used mathematical and scientific language. This turned a policy label into a 'cognitive reality' based on indexation and statistical reasoning. The creation of indicators resulted in the development of ready-to-use knowledge, paving the way for new recommendations, policy standards and financial instruments to be appropriated by development actors, including recipient countries, in the context of a performance-based allocation system for international assistance. The new indicators enabled these actors to converge towards a common understanding of policy priorities in line with the donors' strategic choices.

The OECD as a 'sounding board' for disseminating Western donors' ideas

Over the years the OECD-DAC has established itself as an intergovernmental forum where the world's wealthiest states can engage in policy discussions on development aid and find political consensus. The DAC helps donor countries agree on multilateral strategies and develop joint policy guidance targeting their partners, including governments in the South and non-state actors. Since the creation of the OECD in 1961 the DAC has gained influence through the provision of policy norms and standards on development issues. In particular, it has developed one of the most reliable banks of statistics on development finance. To this end, agents from the OECD's Secretariat (the Development Cooperation Directorate) and from state delegations intensified their exchanges with experts representing recipient countries, policy communities, NGOs, think-tanks and universities; they also hired a considerable number of consultants who were charged with developing official publications. The DAC has significantly contributed to the dissemination of donor-driven policy knowledge addressing critical challenges for development and poverty reduction. It has also provided a setting in which the performance of its members' bilateral cooperation programmes can be critically examined and evaluated through systematic 'peer-reviews', with the support of the Secretariat's agents. In addition, it has become a crucial intergovernmental platform through which its most influential aid donors seek to build coalitions with other OECD members in order to promote specific foreign policy options in the international arena. Although formal agreements on aid policies are usually reached during the preparations for annual high-level meetings, this policy convergence relies on preliminary discussions in 'networks' and 'working parties' that bring together policy makers and analysts from cooperation ministries and technical agencies. Here new ideas can be tested and mutually acceptable compromises reached on issues of relevance for the donor community, such as poverty reduction, governance, gender equality, conflict and trade.

In the early 2000s both the UK Department for International Development (DFID) and the World Bank – the two most active actors in the discussion on development and fragility – used the OECD as the privileged setting for the design of a new policy agenda on fragile states. Because the Bretton Woods institutions were under fire for the inefficiency of the structural adjustment policies they had implemented in developing countries facing economic and financial crises, the OECD-DAC seemed to be the most auspicious forum for donors to engage in a policy discussion on new ideas concerning the reform of official development assistance (ODA). Moreover, as a 'club' insulated from the political pressures of representatives from the developing world, the DAC has long been appreciated by donors as a confidential setting in which 'peers' can build consensus-based agreements on the content of policy guidance.

In 2003 the 'Learning and Advisory Process on Difficult Partnership' (LAP) was established at the OECD under the leadership of the UK delegation, bringing together experts on governance and post-conflict reconstruction from DFID, the World Bank, the IMF, UNDP and the European Commission (EC). This later became the Fragile States Group (FSG), which was given the task of compiling data and knowledge on countries that lacked the capacity to implement development aid strategies and of establishing sound arguments for the inclusion of the new issue of 'fragility' in the OECD-DAC policy agenda. Under the UK's leadership the FSG played a key role in the framing of the discussion on fragility. First, in line with the DFID focus on poverty reduction, no reference was made to the security aspects in fragile contexts, despite the growing influence of new theories concentrating on security and development in US foreign policy circles at the time. Second, the FSG broadened the spectrum of fragility by establishing conflict prevention and peace building as major subjects, as a complement to the World Bank's LICUS programme, which centred on institutional and policy capacities. In focusing equally on state capacity and state reconstruction in post-conflict situations, the framing decisions of the FSG were indicative of the influence wielded by DFID and new groups of British scholars in policy debates.

Through the FSG the governments of the UK and the USA led OECD member states in a first definition exercise that served as the basis for the establishment of a new multilateral agenda on fragile states. In 2005, following the publication of two policy papers by DFID and the US Agency for International Development (USAID), a high-level meeting on development effectiveness in fragile states was jointly held by the DAC, the World Bank, UNDP and the EC. These actors agreed on a vague definition of fragile states as countries confronted with particularly severe development challenges, such as weak governance, limited administrative capacity, chronic humanitarian crisis, persistent social tensions, violence or the legacy of civil war. Despite being hastily organised without prior intergovernmental coordination, this seminal meeting represented a first diplomatic step towards the establishment of a coalition of supporters among OECD donors. It also served as the basis for elaborating a donor-wide policy commitment based on 'guiding principles for good engagement', which were officially endorsed in a later DAC high-level meeting.[20]

The doctrinal foundations of the 'fragile state' label

Through their leading role in the production of widely accessible elements of knowledge related to the new idea of fragile states, the World Bank and the OECD-DAC were instrumental in the invention of a new global concept; they also significantly contributed to its normalisation in the multilateral system in accordance with the strategic views of the most powerful donors. They helped establish seven basic premises that have become the normative foundations of the donors' doctrine of state fragility.

First, the doctrinal approach specifically targets policy and institutional challenges in developing countries affected by conflict and poverty. This does not include the fragilities that may affect countries with advanced economies, highly institutionalised states and democratic systems (states that are generally located in the North). Second, the approach tends to focus on the 'domestic' dimensions of challenges that affect the state order. Consequently little attention is devoted to fragilities stemming from global interdependencies, transnational dynamics or the quest for hegemony in the international space. The approach does not examine externally driven factors that may fuel countries' vulnerability. Third, the donors' approach concentrates primarily on the formal state as the institutional order through which new political arrangements are to be established in response to war and poverty. Even when the causal factors of state fragility are multi-dimensional, policy solutions should focus on the development of state capacities to better regulate the economy and society.

Fourth, this approach prioritises 'functional' criteria to describe stable and robust societies, based on the Weberian assumption that political stability, social integration and economic growth generally stem from institutional arrangements that strengthen the central state's capacity to carry out specific functions. The donors' approach attributes specific traits to countries affected by conflict and poverty; they are considered 'fragile' when their state structures lack the capacity or political will to provide the services necessary for security, justice, economic management and the delivery of social services.[21] This perspective is clearly focused on the tasks traditionally accomplished by the Western modern state, although the need to address state–society relations is also usually mentioned. Fifth, the doctrine of fragile states claims that there is a need for international engagement in fragile states, as effective aid in countries facing problems of weak governance, poverty and conflict will require stabilisation and reconstruction programmes. Hence, the approach justifies externally led interventions that technically and politically assist national governments in rebuilding their own institutions so that they can become more effective, enjoy greater legitimacy and increase the nation's capacity to promote long-term development. Sixth, the fragile state perspective asserts that aid given to these countries should be conditional on their failure to qualify for the financial aid mechanisms created by the donor community in the early 2000s – in particular, the performance-based allocation system for financial assistance – and their inability to follow certain guiding principles set out in the 2005 *Paris Declaration on Aid Effectiveness*, such as ownership and accountability. Therefore, fragile states should be targeted with alternative programmes and instruments. Seventh, international engagement should be based on the premise that security and development are closely interconnected challenges.[22] The two issues should thus be considered through joint strategies in so-called fragile situations (an approach dubbed the 'security–development nexus').

These fundamental premises laid the foundations upon which donor states have justified international interventions in accordance with their pre-existing expertise. They have enabled bilateral aid agencies as well as international financial institutions, the OECD and most UN organisations to promote the restoration of peace and stability as a first step in creating more equitable, resilient and mature societies. In most strategic programmes addressing fragile countries, this basic premise has led to the legitimisation of international engagement in state-building programmes,[23] an intervention promoted as a universal kit of policy solutions and instruments. State building in fragile countries is viewed as a profoundly political process closely associated with the restoration of the authority and legitimacy of the central government, which is expected to result from the enhancement of the state's capacity to effectively fulfil certain 'core functions'. This follows the conventional approach associated with the historical development of the state in Western countries: as a political structure distinct from society, the state is conceived of as a permanent, unified, autonomous institution that is presumed to exert its monopoly of the legitimate use of physical force over a given population and a consolidated territory. It is also seen as a bureaucratic entity whose legitimacy depends on its ability to manage social interventions. Prescriptions provided by the OECD, the World Bank, the EU and most Western governments usually link state-building policies to public administration reforms promoting a 'whole-of-government' approach that involves most public service agencies and international aid actors across traditional portfolio boundaries (conflict resolution, security, finance, development and humanitarian assistance).

Fragmentation: how knowledge producers blur global concepts

As dominant policy concepts gain ground in transnational policy networks and multilateral forums, they are also immersed in a process of increasing fluctuation as various knowledge entrepreneurs expose them to specific uses and individual interpretations. The more they circulate among policy analysts, decision makers and practitioners, the more they come under discussion, fuel policy debate, and arouse controversy. This sets off the process of 'fragmentation', whereby a concept that has gained prominence in the international sphere is subjected to a variety of interpretations as it undergoes multiple uses and acclimatises in diverse ways across time and space. The fragmentation process entails distortions and deviations in meaning that dissociate the concept from its initially agreed-upon interpretation; the process also involves the accumulation of definitions, criteria and indicators that broaden and overload the concept with new understandings. Fragmentation results from three intertwined dynamics affecting circulating concepts: (1) the growing sophistication of analysis, which enriches and stimulates the analytical discussion but at the same time blurs the concept with multiple meanings and approaches; (2) divergent appropriations by actors who take ownership of the concept and use it in ways that differ from those originally conceptualised; and, (3) resistance from actors who dispute the validity of the concept and contest its analytical or operational application. The more a concept circulates among large audiences, the more it is subjected to such processes of fragmentation, resulting in greater conceptual ambiguity and elusiveness. Ironically fragmentation also extends the diffusion of the concept, as it allows multiple actors to use it in different ways for different purposes.

After the OECD and the World Bank served as knowledge incubators between 2003 and 2005, the following years saw three distinct types of 'knowledge entrepreneurs' strenuously engaging in the policy debate on fragile states – specifically, in the reassessment of aid policies towards conflict-affected and poor countries: the government agencies of OECD member states, transnational knowledge networks and the governments of countries classified as 'fragile'. To begin with the initial agreement among OECD members in 2005 created the conditions for selective appropriations and adaptations of the label among aid bureaucracies. Between 2005 and 2007 administrations taking part in early discussions on fragile states maintained distinct positions on fragility, with USAID focusing on security, DFID on poverty reduction and the World Bank on state efficiency and performance. Most other Western governments and their aid agencies, as well as some regional development banks and UN bureaucracies, repositioned themselves by interpreting the OECD-led initial policy discussions on state fragility in accordance with their own agenda priorities. After engaging in the discourse on failed states at an early stage, the Australian government aid agency (AUSAID) built on its regional experiences in 'micro-states' in the Pacific to promote a 'whole-of-government' approach based on capacity development. The Swedish aid agency placed emphasis on the security of citizens in weak states. The Dutch Ministry of Foreign Affairs focused its discussion on conflict prevention and support of reconstruction programmes. The three major EU institutions (the Commission, the Council and the Parliament) also held public debates on 'situations of fragility' in 2007, addressing both the weaknesses of state structures and the political, social, economic and historical factors contributing to the destabilisation of a country's power structure (see Grimm in this special issue). These institutions devoted significant attention to the capacity of states to carry out key functions, with particular emphasis on democratic governance. Some UN entities also used the concept in a very flexible way in order to reinvigorate their own agendas. They included the UN General Assembly's Peacebuilding Commission (on post-crisis intervention), the UNDP Bureau for Crisis Prevention and Recovery (on governance and capacity development), and UNICEF (on capacity- and institution building as a complement to humanitarian assistance and short-term service delivery in post-crisis situations).

Other influential governments warned against the overuse of the label, even while developing their own analytical assessments of state fragility. The German Ministry for Economic Cooperation and Development (BMZ) encouraged contextualised and pragmatic perspectives combining governance, conflict prevention, peace building, service delivery in the social sector, and human rights protection. The Norwegian government concentrated on mediation and reconciliation processes rather than state-building solutions. The Agence française pour le développement (AFD) argued for a greater emphasis on the 'social contract', state legitimacy and the participation of citizens as the foundation for reconstructing political order in post-conflict countries. Within the OECD-DAC, coalitions of interests were assembled, uniting agencies and governments in accordance with their priorities in fragile situations. For example, France, Germany and Norway built an alliance to promote an alternative approach focusing on state–society interactions in the understanding of fragility; agencies from the UK and Japan lent 'outsider' support to this initiative, as the commitment of the three governments represented a good opportunity to strengthen the nascent fragile state concept.

Although the initial appropriation of the OECD framework on fragile states was made by government agencies, the label was also extensively diffused in transnational knowledge networks. These networks unite scholars, independent consultants, policy analysts, journalists and practitioners, all of whom are actors in the production of academic and private research, essays and analytical instruments concerning the policy challenges associated with state fragility, including global and national security, conflicts and wars, humanitarian interventions, peace building and reconstruction, and economic and human development, among others. Although most experts and analysts assert their independence, a great number of them work for or with government-supported research institutions, or are temporarily engaged as subcontracted individual experts for public agencies. Some of them even hold temporary positions within these agencies. Consequently their work influences the decision makers and policy circles within national and international administrations, blurring the boundaries between the bureaucratic sphere and research networks connecting academic teams, independent think-tanks, political foundations, NGOs, consulting firms and the media.

Beginning in 2003 an increasing number of experts and analysts participated in policy discussions on state failures and fragilities, providing government agencies with theoretical foundations, arguments, facts and measurements that fuelled the agenda on 'failed' or 'fragile' states. Most of these scholars were based in the USA, the UK and to a lesser extent in Northern Europe, where public grants were made available for private research (eg, in the USA, the Fund for Peace, the Brookings Institution, the RAND Corporation, the Center for Global Development, the Council on Foreign Relations, the Hoover Institution and the Center for Strategic and International Studies; in the UK and Europe, the Overseas Development Institute, Saferworld, International Alert and the Danish Institute for International Studies). University-based teams and research centres also gained influence by developing new analytical models and statistical instruments for the use of the government agencies in charge of foreign policy, security and development (eg the State Failure Task Force at George Mason University, the Centre for the Study of African Economies at Oxford, and the 'Country Indicators for Foreign Policy' project at the University of Carleton[24]). These various research teams certainly had a significant interest in promoting the new Western agenda on failed and fragile states, but they also developed a corpus of indicators and data that considerably broadened the understanding of the factors fuelling state fragility. These researchers also played a part in the development of approaches promoting conflict and security as issues with a critical impact on the conventional challenges of sustainable development, such as good governance, delivery of social services, economic investment, health and environmental protection. Moreover, some academic institutions actively promoted critical ideas that exerted pressure on international organisations, such as criticism of the focus on central state institutions to the detriment of the complexities of power structures, as well as the international and transnational dynamics fuelling fragile contexts.

The governments of the so-called 'fragile states' themselves emerged as a third group of actors working to shape policy discussion on fragility. These governments represent the countries most affected by Western-led state-building and peace-building interventions. Ironically these countries were not included in the initial reflections of donors at the World Bank and the OECD-DAC. For instance, the two OECD networks of experts that engaged in discussions on issues of peace, security, governance and state building in fragile environments (the DAC Network on Conflict, Peace and Development Cooperation and the DAC FSG) developed their agendas without holding any consultations with the governments of developing countries, until these two groups were merged into a single network in 2008 (the International Network on Conflict and Fragility – INCAF). Most of the countries identified as 'fragile' in studies published by Western aid agencies (including the first list of 38 states released by the OECD in 2006), and some regional organisations (such as the African Union), have strongly criticised the debate on fragile states for its stigmatising effect on countries facing difficulties, particularly those approaches that focus on the domestic factors driving political conflicts and economic hardship.

Despite the establishment of the International Dialogue on Peacebuilding and Statebuilding (a new forum bringing together international donors and the so-called fragile countries) in 2008 under the auspices of the OECD, certain political leaders from the South took the initiative to re-appropriate the label by establishing their own multilateral coalition in 2010, known as the 'g7+'.[25] This initiative set the stage for a fundamental shift: for the first time the competitive process of reframing the fragile state concept included an increasingly influential coalition of the governments of the South. This coalition was designed to collectively promote the views, values and interests of these countries, with the firm intention of giving them adequate representation in the agenda-setting process for the post-2015 development agenda. The advocacy efforts of the g7+ coalition have played a crucial role in the identification of new policy areas viewed as critical and worthy of specific attention in financial flows (eg justice, security, private sector investment, job creation), significantly diverging from the donors' preferences (eg governance, capacity building, anti-corruption, democratisation). The g7+ has also begun to lobby OECD donors to ensure the inclusion of state building and peace building as specific items in the post-2015 agenda for development.

Assimilation: how international organisations reinvigorate orthodox views on fragile states

In the following section, I discuss the adaptive process by which the governments and agencies promoting the fragile state concept within the OECD-DAC and the World Bank have limited the risk of normative fragmentation by engaging in policy convergence through a process involving the 'assimilation' of ideas. This assimilation is accomplished through social activities in which international organisations work to maintain the policy agenda promoted by their most influential member states; this requires the organisations to capture and integrate the inputs and dissenting views that are circulating in their immediate environment. In this perspective international organisations function as incubators of knowledge: They constantly revise, adjust and complement their policy thinking through mechanisms of policy discussion, which allows them to integrate heterodox perspectives into the dominant paradigm.

How do international organisations assimilate knowledge? First, they develop internal resources to capture the policy ideas emerging in their immediate environment and work to enhance their capacity to frame policy debates. The organisations establish permanent 'working groups', 'task forces' and 'networks' consisting of diplomats, bureaucrats and policy experts; they also dedicate significant resources to the production of policy reports, with the support of contracted consultants who are selected according to non-competitive procedures. Additionally they encourage the consultation activities of external scholars, analysts and practitioners who sustain non-conventional and critical perspectives. Although these activities are expected to reinvigorate policy discussion, they are coordinated and brokered by the organisation's policy specialists, who are tasked with adapting controversial ideas into acceptable policy recommendations that comply with the agenda of the organisation and are compatible with its established terminology. External contributions are examined and reviewed in order to determine whether they are congruent with the pre-existing policy framework (see Lemay-Hébert and Mathieu in this issue). Second, international organisations seek to engage in transnational policy forums and knowledge networks. They develop intellectual partnerships with other multilateral organisations, development aid agencies and independent knowledge producers who conduct empirical research and can provide additional insights into the development of the agenda.

These internal and external activities considerably strengthen the ability of the organisations to capture emerging ideas and incorporate them into their own knowledge framework. The insertion of security and conflict-related issues into the donors' approach to fragile states provides a critical example of the capacity of the World Bank and the OECD-DAC to assimilate circulating ideas. In the early stages of the concept the US security-centred approach to 'state failure' did not provoke much interest from the experts at the OECD-DAC and the World Bank, especially since security issues were considered outside the jurisdiction of the two organisations. The 'club culture' prevailing among the members of the OECD and the World Bank, which usually favours consensus-based decisions, justified the rejection of the US security-based approach, as it was likely to draw all OECD members into the new 'war on terror' being launched by the US administration in the context of military interventions in Afghanistan and Iraq. The aid specialists involved in the design of the concept carefully avoided any doctrinal position that seemed too controversial to be fully endorsed by all donors. They primarily articulated the concept along the lines of governance, policy efficiency and institutional performance in a perspective that chiefly focused on poverty reduction and economic development. Nevertheless, after 2005, the World Bank and the OECD-DAC could not remain insulated from the growing belief that security and development should be regarded as interdependent components and should be fully integrated into operational programmes implemented in fragile contexts.

The OECD-DAC experts integrated the security dimension as a complement to their primary focus on issues of state governance capacities and institutional performance. They internalised US arguments advocating assistance policies in 'failed' states.[26] The diversification of the criteria used by the DAC to identify and classify fragile states clearly indicated this new orientation. Whereas earlier reports (from 2005 to 2007) were based on the World Bank's CPIA index, the 2009 list included the security dimension by reference to two additional matrices managed by the Brookings Institution (the Index of State Weakness in the Developing World) and Carleton University (Country Indicators for Foreign Policy). The World Bank also incrementally repositioned its programmes, shifting from a primary focus on weak state capacity and institutions to a more comprehensive programme integrating conflict and political instability. This move sparked tensions between internal units (the FSG and the Conflict Prevention and Reconstruction Unit), resulting in the establishment of a new Fragile and Conflict-Affected Countries Group entrusted with a broader mandate (coordination of sectors, policy analysis, staff training). The focus on 'fragile and conflict-affected situations' as the overarching theme of the 2011 *World Development Report* confirmed the Bank's stated interest in intensifying its focus on development challenges in conflicts and post-conflict situations.[27] Similarly, in 2012, the Bank's sponsorship of a research programme (the Global Center for Conflict, Security and Development) demonstrated its renewed interest in establishing a knowledge network that would be able to develop innovative policy thinking concerning fragile states. Surprisingly the revision of the CPIA index in 2011 did not integrate criteria on security and conflict into its assessment of the policy and institutional framework of poor countries applying for World Bank resources, although many experts use these ratings to rank so-called fragile states.

Moreover, the experts from the OECD-DAC and the World Bank exhibited a capacity to digest critical claims from advocacy groups and independent scholars and incorporate them into their existing agenda on fragile states. In this way the two organisations have co-opted a significant number of the criticisms that contest the donors' state-centred approach. The OECD's method of dealing with the issue of 'legitimacy' provides a concrete example of this mechanism of assimilation. Legitimacy has become an increasingly important focus of the OECD's approach to fragile states, especially because state-building interventions have come under fire for their inability to devote adequate attention to the factors underlying social identity, cohesion and solidarity within society (see Lemay-Hebert and Mathieu in this issue). Many reports published by the DAC were originally grounded in a conceptual framework that viewed political legitimacy in terms of state functions and capacity. This framework promoted an institutional approach to legitimacy concentrating on the capacity of the state to provide basic services to its population (functionalist perspective), protect its citizens within its national boundaries (security perspective) and function through efficient institutions and governance mechanisms (management perspective) grounded in the rule of law and respect for human rights (liberal perspective). This framework was clearly based on the Weberian conception of statehood, which focuses on the bureaucratic foundations of the state and the capacity of the central government to operate within society through the delivery of efficient services.

Reflecting donors' concerns about aid efficiency, this state-centred conception of legitimacy was widely disseminated by the three most influential actors supporting the OECD-DAC's fragile state agenda: DFID, USAID and the World Bank.[28] It held a position of prominence in most of the reports released by the OECD from 2005 to 2010. However, some scholars, NGOs and practitioners began to question this narrow vision of 'political order', and certain influential OECD members (mainly from the French, German and Norwegian delegations) expressed dissenting views within the DAC. These representatives argued for the reconsideration of national political systems through contextualised and historically grounded perspectives, taking into account local powers and the transnational dynamics stemming from globalisation. The OECD-DAC Secretariat and the International Network on Conflict and Fragility (coordinated by the DAC) commissioned reports integrating critical scholars' calls for the development of sociological and anthropological approaches to political legitimacy. One report in 2010 specifically examined the various dimensions of political legitimacy in the social sciences, offering a broader definition of legitimacy and initiating a discussion of the social foundations of political orders, including the various factors that strengthen the 'social contract'.[29] Several OECD reports took up some of these claims, emphasising the need to include local sources of legitimacy in the design of international engagement in fragile states.[30]

In this assimilation process dissenting views are selected, reviewed and incorporated into the policy framework in a way that ensures compliance with the basic premises of the leading donors' doctrine on fragile states. Despite the call for a shift from a 'thin' approach to fragility (centred on the state's capabilities) to a 'thick' understanding that would devote adequate attention to the importance of the 'social contract' and 'state–society relations',[31] the state is still regarded as the overarching authority that unites society, ensures security and enables development. The increase in attention granted to socially grounded forms of authority is understood as a means of consolidating relationships between the state and society, ultimately strengthening state legitimacy as an institution embedded in society. This interpretation reconceptualises traditional legitimacy in a manner compatible with the institutionalist conception of an autonomous state, distinct from society (whereas critical approaches have argued that in many fragile situations, the two should be perceived as part of the same overall social structure). Its perspective on local systems concentrates primarily on their capacity to carry out functions and to achieve results similar to those of the state (through criteria focusing on policy performance and institutional efficiency).

This assimilation process ultimately presented the OECD and World Bank experts with a tough challenge: they had to incorporate the call for sociological approaches to 'situations of fragility' while simultaneously upholding the essential premises of the donors' orthodoxy. On the one hand, they had to acknowledge the multidimensional factors that can undermine security and human development in so-called fragile states; on the other hand, they had to safeguard their donors' doctrines and find a way to keep the agenda centred on state-building and peace-building solutions, maintaining the focus on Weberian state structures. The outcome helped to promote the preferences of Western donors, whose international domination over developing societies is connected to their capacity to maintain direct, stable, predictable transactions with government elites in the South.

Assimilation is a process of normative adaptation in which international organisations actively engage in the consolidation and perpetuation of policy doctrines. This process has two essential characteristics. First, it is a social process: assimilation does not stem from a fixed position representing the political intentions of a coalition of aid donors that control the multilateral system. Even though the OECD and the World Bank are monitored by a club of rich countries, they experience internal conflicts and generate competing normative conceptions with regard to the propriety of interventions in poor and conflict-affected countries. They have no unique rationality or capacity to follow stable preferences. Assimilation consequently results from inner struggles and coalitions of interests between the various actors involved in the definition process inside the organisations – mainly government agencies, but also internal units and departments and contracted experts. Assimilation is also connected to diffuse or direct external pressures from transnational knowledge producers and various national actors with the resources to provide new insights, objections and alternative views, including governments that are aid beneficiaries (such as those represented in the g7+). Nevertheless, the OECD and the World Bank as organisations do not play a neutral role in this social process. Most of their interactions are channelled through the internal procedures and bureaucratic routines of the organisations. Their constant discussions with global knowledge networks allow them to become central hubs where new and controversial ideas can circulate and be integrated to some degree into the main donor agenda. In addition, their experts may have the resources necessary to generate new policy knowledge, shape normative views and influence policy debates, particularly in the World Bank, where internal units have intellectual autonomy and compete to influence ideas on development. At the least, in the OECD-DAC, individual experts play a mediating and filtering role in the policy discussions leading to 'consensus-based' positions adopted by government agencies.

Second, the process of assimilation does not result in the promotion of a stable definition of fragile states that would reflect an initial 'consensus' shared among the main advocates of the fragile state doctrine. Rather, it produces slight alterations, amendments and additions that contribute to the constant adjustment of the agenda of the OECD and the World Bank to the various approaches to fragility. By integrating additional understanding from national government agencies, research institutions, NGOs and advocacy groups, assimilation is instrumental in the incremental adaptation of the policy framework of the two international organisations. Their agenda becomes less dogmatic, more specific and more insightful as it is developed through policy discussion. Assimilation is a dynamic process that ultimately facilitates the incorporation of heterodox views into the dominant paradigm, without revision of the doctrinal foundations set out by the most powerful member states. It helps states to channel their individual claims and to converge upon a consistent policy message; in addition, it allows them to reinvigorate and legitimise the basic premises of the fragile state agenda by capturing and internalising ideas circulated by other knowledge producers. Moreover, it serves to prevent the expansion of normative dissent and therefore reduces the risk of conceptual fragmentation.

Conclusion: policy concepts as a perpetuation of international hegemony

The analysis of the World Bank and OECD contributions to the donor-driven agenda on fragile states offers insights into the cognitive and normative processes associated with the political use of ideologically oriented concepts on the international stage. On the one hand, the analysis suggests that the diffusion of the fragile state concept reflects asymmetrical power relationships in international politics. By reproducing and disseminating a policy framework that advocates state-building solutions to the problems of conflict and extreme poverty in the countries of the South, the concept reflects the interests of Western donor governments, whose international hegemony is tied to their capacity to maintain a Westphalian order based on stable and predictable transactions among central governments. The capacity of the most powerful governments to support policy research networks, develop expertise and fund scholarly activities, as well as their direct access to the main public forums where legitimate knowledge on development is produced – including the central hubs of the World Bank and the OECD – gives them a comparative advantage in disseminating their normative conceptions. On the other hand, the analysis shows that the social trajectory of the fragile state concept does not precisely reflect the intentions of the governments that initially placed them on the international agenda for development, despite the intense definition exercises that have been carried out. As it is disseminated, the concept has encountered distortion, resistance and subversive appropriation from the various actors engaged in transnational governance.

Finally, the study shows that the contributions of the World Bank and OECD to the preservation of the doctrinal views of their most influential member states has heavily depended on the capacity of the two organisations to absorb, filter and reconceptualise conflicting ideas as they emerge in their environment. Their normative influence does not stem solely from their internal capacity to produce and disseminate ideas; it is also not merely the product of an import–export dynamic, consisting of collecting ideas in various knowledge networks and then circulating them in multilateral decision-making processes. To a great extent it results from the ability of these organisations to operate as 'transfer platforms': the World Bank and the OECD shape international norms on development and security through their capacity to generate consensual transnational knowledge, combining the essential doctrinal views of their most powerful members with the diverse approaches undertaken by national bureaucracies, governments from developing countries and the various non-state actors engaged in the production of knowledge worldwide.

Acknowledgements

I am very grateful to my co-editors Sonja and Nicolas, as well as to the two anonymous reviewers who provided insightful comments on an earlier version of this article. I would also like to thank Claire Bacher for her high-quality proofreading, and all the experts and public officials who kindly agreed to be interviewed during the empirical phase of the research.

Notes on Contributor

Olivier Nay is Professor of Political Science, University of Paris 1 – Panthéon Sorbonne. He is Vice-president of the French Association of Political Science and Chair of the Political Science section at the National Academic Council. Since 2006 he has been working on the reform of international organisations, bureaucratic change and the transnational diffusion of policy ideas. His most recent articles have been published in the *International Political Science Review* ("Fragile and Failed States"), *Journal of Public Policy* ("How Do Policy Ideas Spread among International Administrations?") and *Governance* ("What Drives Reforms in International Organizations?"). Further information can be found at his personal webpage univ-paris1.academia.edu/OlivierNay.

Notes

1. Scholars and independent analysts have played an instrumental role in the circulation and legitimisation of the concept in academic fields and intellectual circles, and thus the 'fragile state' concept is now fully integrated into research agendas on development and security. In its own way, this special issue also contributes to the process.
2. Nay, "Fragile and Failed States."
3. Wallerstein, *The End of the World.*
4. Appadurai, *The Social Life of Things.*
5. Djelic and Sahlin-Andersson, "A World of Governance."
6. Adler and Haas, "Conclusion."
7. Sahlin-Andersson, "National, International and Transnational Constructions of New Public Management."
8. Jolly et al., *UN Ideas that Changed the World.*
9. Barnett and Finnemore, *Rules for the World.*
10. Salzman and Terracino, "Labor Rights, Globalization and Institutions."
11. They often share the same technical teams and international boards in the development field. For instance, the World Bank is officially represented at any meeting of the OECD-DAC.
12. Mehta, "The World Bank"; and Mahon and McBride, "Standardizing and Disseminating Knowledge."
13. Jacobsson, "Regulated Regulators."
14. Maxwell and Stone, *Global Knowledge Networks.*
15. Nay, "How do Policy Ideas Spread?"
16. Ness and Brechin, "Bridging the Gap"; and Brechin, *Planting Trees in the Developing World.*
17. Martens, "Why do Aid Agencies Exist?"; and Weaver, *Hypocrisy Trap.*

18. This reorientation resulted in a marked increase in the number of loans granted by the World Bank to LICUS countries during the period 2003–2006.
19. World Bank, *Fragile States*.
20. OECD, *Principles for Good International Engagement*.
21. Initially promoted by DFID, this interpretation was the leading official definition of state fragility for several years.
22. Duffield, *Development, Security and Unending War*; and Chandler, "The Security–Development Nexus."
23. OECD, *Do No Harm*; and OECD, *Supporting Statebuilding*.
24. The Canadian government, in particular the Canadian International Development Agency and the Canadian Department of Foreign Affairs and International Trade followed in the footsteps of the OECD discussion, providing public funding to Carleton University for the development of a new index on state fragility – the Country Indicators for Foreign Policy – which seeks to provide measures of the multidimensional factors leading to fragile situations.
25. In 2013, the g7+ consisted of 19 countries under the chair of the Timor-Leste Ministry of Finance, an institution that was instrumental in the creation of the coalition. The g7+ organisation has received grants from UNDP and the OECD.
26. OECD, *Principles for Good International Engagement*.
27. World Bank, *World Development Report*.
28. DFID, *Why We Need to Work More Effectively*; USAID, *Fragile States Strategy*; and World Bank, *Fragile States*.
29. OECD, *The State's Legitimacy*.
30. OECD, *Do No Harm*; and OECD, *Supporting Statebuilding*.
31. OECD, *Fragile States 2013*.

Bibiliography

Adler, Emmanuel, and Peter Haas. "Conclusion: Epistemic Communities, World Order, and the Creation of a Reflective Research Program." *International Organization* 46, no. 1 (1992): 367–390.

Appadurai, Arjun, ed. *The Social Life of Things: Commodities in Cultural Perspective*. London: Cambridge University Press, 1986.

Barnett, Michael, and Martha Finnemore. *Rules for the World: International Organizations in Global Politics*. Ithaca, NY: Cornell University Press, 2004.

Brechin, Steven. *Planting Trees in the Developing World: A Sociology of International Organizations*. Baltimore, MD: Johns Hopkins University Press, 1997.

Chandler, David. "The Security-Development Nexus and the Rise of 'Anti-Foreign Policy'." *Journal of International Relations and Development* 10 (2007): 362–386.

DFID. *Why We Need to Work More Effectively in Fragile States*. London: DFID, 2005.

Djelic, Marie-Laure, and Kerstin Sahlin-Andersson. "A World of Governance: The Rise of Transnational Regulation." In *Transnational Governance: Institutional Dynamics of Regulation*, edited by Marie-Laure Djelic, and Kerstin Sahlin-Andersson, 1–28. New York: Cambridge University Press, 2006.

Duffield, Mark. *Development, Security and Unending War: Governing the World of Peoples*. Cambridge: Polity, 2007.

Jacobsson, Bengt. "Regulated Regulators: Global Trends of State Transformation." In *Transnational Governance: Institutional Dynamics of Regulation*, edited by Marie-Laure Djelic, and Kerstin Sahlin-Andersson, 205–224. New York: Cambridge University Press, 2006.

Jolly, Richard, Louis Emmerij, and Thomas G. Weiss. *UN Ideas that Changed the World*. Bloomington, IN: Indiana University Press, 2009.

Mahon, Rianne, and Stephen McBride. "Standardizing and Disseminating Knowledge: The Role of the OECD in Global Governance." *European Political Science Review* 1, no. 1 (2009): 83–101.

Martens, Bertin. "Why Do Aid Agencies Exist?" *Development Policy Review* 23, no. 6 (2005): 643–663.

Maxwell, Simon, and Diane Stone, eds. *Global Knowledge Networks and International Development*. Abingdon: Routledge, 2005.

Mehta, Lyla. "The World Bank and its Emerging Knowledge Empire." *Human Organization* 60, no. 2 (2001): 189–196.

Nay, Olivier. "How do Policy Ideas Spread among International Administrations? Policy Entrepreneurs and Bureaucratic Influence in the UN Response to AIDS." *Journal of Public Policy* 31, no. 1 (2012): 53–76.

Nay, Olivier. "Fragile and Failed States: Critical Perspectives on Conceptual Hybrids." *International Political Science Review* 33, no. 1 (2013): 326–341.

Ness, Gayl D., and Steven Brechin. "Bridging the Gap: IOs as Organizations." *International Organization* 42, no. 2 (1988): 245–288.

OECD. *Principles for Good International Engagement in Fragile States and Situations*. Paris: OECD, 2007.

OECD. *Do No Harm: International Support for Statebuilding*. Paris: OECD, 2010.

OECD. *The State's Legitimacy in Fragile Situations: Unpacking Complexity*. Paris: OECD, 2010.

OECD. *Supporting Statebuilding in Situations of Conflict and Fragility: Policy Guidance*. Paris: OECD, 2011.

OECD. *Fragile States 2013: Resource Flows and Trends in a Shifting World*. Paris: OECD, 2013.
Sahlin-Andersson, Kerstin. "National, International and Transnational Constructions of New Public Management." *Score Rapportserie* 2000:4, Stockholm University, 2000.
Salzman, James, and Julio Bacio Terracino. "Labor Rights, Globalization and Institutions: The Role and Influence of the Organisation for Economic Cooperation and Development." In *Social Issues, Globalisation and International Institutions: Labour Rights and the EU, ILO, OECD and WTO*, edited by A. Virginia Learyand Daniel Warner, 318–409. Boston MA: Martinus Nijhoff, 2006.
USAID. *Fragile States Strategy*. Washington, DC: USAID, 2005.
Wallerstein, Immanuel. *The End of the World as We Know It*. MinneapolisMN: University of Minnesota, 1999.
Weaver, Catherine. *Hypocrisy Trap: The World Bank and the Poverty of Reform*. Princeton, NJ: Princeton University Press, 2008.
World Bank. *Fragile States: Good Practices in Country Assistance Strategies*. Washington, DC: World Bank, 2005.
World Bank. *World Development Report: Conflict, Security and Development*. Washington, DC: World Bank, 2011.

The OECD's discourse on fragile states: expertise and the normalisation of knowledge production

Nicolas Lemay-Hébert[a] and Xavier Mathieu[b]

[a]*International Development Department, University of Birmingham, UK;* [b]*Department of Politics, University of Sheffield, UK*

The concept of legitimacy has been highly influential in policy recommendations concerning state building in 'fragile states'. Indeed, depending on how 'legitimacy' is conceived, the actions and practices of state builders can differ substantially. This article discusses what is at stake in the conceptualisation of 'legitimacy' by comparing the academic literature with the normative production of the OECD. Looking at two approaches to legitimacy – the institutionalist or neo-Weberian approach focusing on institutional reconstruction, and the social legitimacy approach emphasising the importance of social cohesion for successful state building – the article shows that both these conceptions are present in most reports, but also that the neo-Weberian approach tends to prevail over the social legitimacy perspective. Through a series of interviews with OECD officials and scholar-practitioners who have participated in the writing process of OECD reports, we hint, finally, at future research avenues on the social conditions of knowledge production and its normalisation.

Introduction

The Iraqi, Kosovar and Timorese experiments have revealed, each in their own way, the limitations of top-down interventions and external imposition of state structures. However, there is no consensus on what should replace international administrations and protectorates as the next paradigm for interventions in fragile states. Although the option of non-intervention or *laissez-faire*, briefly considered by some authors,[1] has found a certain resonance in the 'fresh start' concept based on social evolutionary theory,[2] it has not achieved widespread acceptance among academics or policy makers. Instead, practitioners and scholars dealing with fragile states are increasingly studying and prescribing 'bottom-up' strategies of peace building and local ownership, as well as policies aimed at winning 'hearts and minds'. In these discussions the concept of 'legitimacy' has returned to the fore; far from being secondary or incidental, 'legitimacy' plays a crucial role in determining the type of state that should be (re-)built and how this process should take place.

Based on previous work,[3] this article analyses two different schools of thought on state building in fragile states and their respective views on 'legitimacy': (1) an 'institutional' approach based on a Weberian (or, to be precise, a neo-Weberian) sociological perspective, focusing on the monopolisation of legitimate violence and the importance of institutional reconstruction; and (2) a 'social legitimacy' approach, which is arguably closer to Durkheimian sociology and political anthropology, emphasising the importance of socio-political cohesion in the process of state building. To use the categories developed by Barry Buzan and Kalevi Holsti, the institutional approach focuses on the 'institutional' and 'physical' bases of the state, while the social legitimacy approach is preoccupied with the 'idea of the state', or the social contract binding citizens together.[4] Depending on the approach selected, the concept of legitimacy can be understood in radically different ways. These divergent conceptualisations of legitimacy lead to different visions of the 'reality' of state fragility and to different recommendations for state building. At present the Weberian approach to statehood has arguably attained the status of orthodoxy in the state-building literature.[5] Although it is implicitly portrayed as consensual and apolitical, this institutional approach entails specific consequences for scholarly and policy debates.

To illustrate and inform our discussion, we focus on the case of the Organisation for Economic Co-operation and Development (OECD). The reason for this focus is threefold: First, the OECD – in particular, its Development Assistance Committee (DAC) and the International Network on Conflict and Fragility (INCAF) – has emerged as one of the most influential knowledge producers on state fragility, thanks to 'its reputation, good arguments, and persuasion'.[6] In this context the OECD is a strong normative actor conveying its ideas through the establishment of standards of 'good international engagement'.[7] Second, the OECD subcontracts scholars and practitioners ('experts') alike to produce its reports, consequently blurring the lines between policy and academic circles.[8] This provides us with a unique opportunity to reflect on a specific epistemic community: knowledge producers on state fragility within the OECD. Our use of the idea of 'epistemic community' differs from that of Adler and Haas:[9] we are not interested in the *external* influence that such a group can have, but rather in the *internal* processes leading to the creation of knowledge. As such, we do not view epistemic communities as consensual groups of individuals somehow pre-existing the analysis; instead, we understand them as the sites of a constant struggle over how to define what qualifies as *valid* knowledge. A second difference from Adler and Haas's use of 'epistemic community' is that we do not conceive of such a group as *purely* scientific and opposed to policy makers. These two domains – to the extent that they can be strictly separated at all – are directly connected and work together to produce knowledge within the epistemic community.

The final reason we choose to focus on the OECD is that some of its reports have adopted innovative stances on state fragility, moving beyond the orthodoxy towards anthropological and ethno-political approaches to legitimacy and state building. However, there is an inherent ambiguity in most of the organisation's reports (even in those adopting a social legitimacy approach to state fragility), and the institutionalist perspective tends to predominate in most cases. This article examines the specific epistemic community associated with the OECD discourse on state fragility and suggests that more work should be done to determine how knowledge is produced within the organisation. By focusing on the language and meanings associated with state fragility, legitimacy and state building,[10] and by combining textual analysis with interviews conducted with OECD officials and scholar-practitioners who have participated in writing reports for the OECD,[11] the article seeks to contribute to the discussion on the different meanings of and approaches to state building and state fragility.

The first section describes the institutional approach and the social legitimacy approach, examining their specific understandings of state fragility. The article then moves on to discuss the conceptions of state fragility expressed in various OECD reports. Some reports can be seen as resolutely institutionalist, while others add an interesting complexity to the debate by considering the sociological processes of state formation. The third section elaborates on the difficulty of operationalising social legitimacy approaches and the tensions this creates in certain OECD reports. The final section, based on preliminary data collected through the interview process, attempts to shed light on the predominance of the institutionalist perspective through a study of the social conditions underlying the production of OECD reports. In a context in which the gap between academic research and policy making has been described as 'much lamented but poorly understood',[12] the article questions the very idea of a gap by showing how knowledge is produced in an international organisation and how a dominant discourse is maintained over time by scholars and policy makers alike.

Conceptual approaches to state fragility

The societal logics underpinning what has been dubbed 'state fragility' are rarely specifically defined in the literature; when they are, these definitions tend to rely on a set of undisclosed premises. In this section we will suggest a method of conceptualising such premises by distinguishing between two approaches to state fragility: the institutional approach and the social legitimacy approach. These two perspectives each adopt specific definitions of the state, state fragility and state building based on a specific and (to a certain extent) quite distinct corpus of sociology. These approaches are 'ideal-types' that the scholar can identify as distinctive paradigmatic ways of thinking about the state; however, as subsequent sections will show, the approaches can be combined in policy discourses.

The first approach, institutionalism, relies on a Weberian perspective on statehood. Weber famously defined the state 'as a human community that successfully claims the monopoly of the legitimate use of physical force within a given territory'.[13] For Weber the formation of modern Western states relied on the constant progression of their bureaucratic foundations over time. In addition to security, which is certainly the central criterion of state strength for institutionalists, various authors have also taken other criteria into account, all of which relate to the capability of the state to secure its hold *on* society.

From this perspective a weak or fragile state is a political entity that lacks the institutional capacity to implement and enforce policies. Accordingly state building is conceptualised as the creation of new government institutions and the strengthening of existing ones. Scholars adopting this institutional approach tend to focus on the administrative capabilities of the state and the ability of the state apparatus to affirm its authority over society, thus echoing the 'state autonomy' theory.[14] This conception of the 'autonomous state' has long been equated with Weber's work, although some argue that it represents an inaccurate interpretation of it.[15] Other authors have convincingly asserted that we should understand Weber's political theory in conjunction with his other sociological works.[16] In any case this division between state structures and societal forces conveniently leads to a distinction between state building and nation building, on the premise that one can conduct state-building operations from the outside without entering into the contested (political) sphere of nation building.[17] In other words, it is possible to target the institutions of a given state and to strengthen state capabilities without engaging in the realm of socio-political cohesion of the targeted society.

Despite the diversity of approaches connected to this neo-Weberian understanding of the state, two main branches of institutionalism can be identified: the functionalists and the sovereigntists. Certain scholars are known for their functionalist interpretation of state formation and state building.[18] Helman and Ratner, for example, assert that 'nation-states exist to provide a decentralised method of delivering political (public) goods to persons living within designated parameters'.[19] For the influential US policy scholar Robert Rotberg 'it is according to their performances – according to the levels of their effective delivery of the most crucial political goods – that strong states may be distinguished from weak ones, and weak states from failed or collapsed'.[20] More generally, as stated by Claire Mcloughlin, 'most development agencies define [state fragility] principally as a fundamental failure of the state to perform functions necessary to meet citizens' basic needs and expectations'.[21] Here the term 'public goods' encompasses a variety of state institutions and functions, including security, a transparent and equitable political process, medical and health care, schools and education, railways, harbours and even a beneficent fiscal and institutional context, within which citizens can pursue personal entrepreneurial goals.

The sovereigntists concentrate on state sovereignty, emphasising the presence of capable institutions as evidence of a 'real' sovereignty.[22] Their common starting point is that, historically speaking, 'fragile' states simply disappeared, became divided up into smaller units or were conquered by powerful neighbours; in contrast, collapsed states are now expected to be rebuilt within the same international borders.[23] The Kaplanian 'coming anarchy,' in which the 'classificatory grid of nation-states is going to be replaced by a jagged-glass pattern of city-states, shanty-states, nebulous and anarchic regionalisms' simply has not materialised,[24] as the new states that emerged after the Second World War could not fail: 'they could be weak, even nonexistent on the domestic and international scene, but they could no longer disappear'.[25] In this context, Ashraf Ghani and Claire Lockhart identify a gap between *de jure* and *de facto* sovereignty, a gap that they posit is growing rather than receding.[26] This gap is linked to the critical functions that the modern state is expected to perform: among others, the maintenance of a monopoly on the legitimate means of violence, the nurturing of human capital and the creation and regulation of the market.[27] States are understood to be 'instruments at the service of their people',[28] and the observation that this capacity to provide services is the basis for legitimate and sovereign states has gained support in recent years.[29] Thus, both the functionalists and the sovereigntists are deeply influenced by the Weberian approach to statehood, and both view institution building as the central dynamic behind contemporary state building.

While accepting the institutional approach's focus on the security apparatus and state institutions, especially as a critical first step in state-building processes, the social legitimacy approach adds a layer of complexity by drawing attention to the state's underlying legitimacy. In sociological terms this approach could be described as influenced more by a Durkheimian conception of the state than by a strictly Weberian one. For Durkheim the state 'is the very organ of social thought'; it comprises 'the sentiments, ideals, beliefs that the society has worked out collectively and with time'.[30] Although the state is diffuse in every society, it has specific characteristics that make it a distinct reality: 'it is, in effect, independent of the particular conditions in which individuals are placed: they pass on and it remains'.[31] For the scholars who consciously or unconsciously adopt this approach, the strengths of the state (and, conversely, its weaknesses) must be defined in terms of 'the capacity of state to command loyalty', that is 'the right to rule'.[32] If a state cannot exist without a physical foundation, as the institutionalists emphasise, the reverse is also true: 'without a widespread and quite deeply rooted idea of the state among the population, the state institutions themselves have difficulty functioning and surviving'.[33]

One of the main differences between these two schools of thought – the institutional and social legitimacy approaches – stems from the understanding of the concept of the state. As Anthony Giddens observes, 'the "state" sometimes means an apparatus of government or power, sometimes the overall social system subject to that government or power'.[34] Adopting the former definition of the state as the state apparatus (the Weberian approach) leads scholars to understand state fragility or state weakness as fragility in the apparatus of government, and state building as a scientific, technical and administrative process of strengthening state institutions. In this regard the social legitimacy approach provides a different perspective on state fragility. It emphasises not only institutional collapse but also the collapse of the legitimacy of the central authority. The collapse of legitimate governance – a process sometimes occurring in parallel with but not simply as a by-product of institutional collapse – opens the door to 'political entrepreneurs', allowing them to mobilise the population on the basis of allegiances that displace national ties. Consequently the strength of the state is defined as the capacity to command loyalty in a political marketplace defined by political bargaining.[35] In general the legitimacy approach is more sociologically or anthropologically oriented, rejecting generalising assumptions and emphasising the characteristics of each state and its societal context. 'Building' or 'consolidating' state institutions is not sufficient here – above all these institutions must define, create and solidify a viable collective identity in order to provide the social bond necessary for them to be recognised as legitimate by their citizens. By extension external actors must find efficient and unobtrusive ways of supporting this process. As Alexander Gourevitch suggests, 'the danger of a technical or managerial view of the state, focusing only on its capacity to regulate society, is that it overlooks the fact that policies and institutions need a real political basis'.[36] Disregarding this aspect can result in the creation of disconnected institutions lacking legitimacy and hence efficiency. Re-joining the Durkheimian sociological tradition, this approach thus places emphasis on the logics of social integration and solidarity as well as the logics of *anomie*,[37] not only on the Weberian logics of state capacity.[38]

Different conceptions of state fragility

Institutionalist ideas have become popular in policy-making circles, and numerous national and international organisations have adopted an institutionalist framework in one way or another. Boutros Boutros-Ghali, for one, defines state collapse as 'the collapse of state institutions'.[39] The UK Department for International Development (DFID) has provided one of the most widely accepted definitions of state fragility, associating the term with 'governments that cannot or will not deliver core functions to the majority of [their] people'.[40] In this context the OECD represents an exception, as it combines aspects of a purely institutional approach in certain reports with more nuanced social legitimacy analyses. It is to this example that we now turn, beginning with an analysis of the conceptual framework used in the organisation's reports.

Legitimacy in the context of fragile states became a major issue among OECD members when governance problems were identified as the main cause of development failures, underscoring the need for a better understanding of political processes and legitimacy in fragile states.[41] Even before this process was formally started, the 'Principles for Good International Engagement in Fragile States and Situations', published in 2007, included key ideas on the state and legitimacy. This influential document, which served as a benchmark for judging progress in the (good) practices of donor countries in 2011, expresses a strong attachment to a Weberian vision of the state. Indeed, the preamble affirms that 'the long-term vision for international engagement in fragile states is to help national reformers to build effective, legitimate, and resilient state *institutions*', while the third principle (providing the most detailed discussion on state building) asserts that states are fragile when their 'structures lack political will and/or capacity to provide the basic functions' required by the population.[42] Interestingly the state is explicitly equated with its institutions, that is, with 'the executive branch of the central and local governments within a state but also the legislative and the judiciary arms of government'.[43] This so-called 'broad definition' is a perfect illustration of an institutionalist approach, demonstrating how 'building a state' becomes synonymous with 'institution building', an idea reaffirmed in the seventh principle.

The institutional approach is also emphasised in subsequent reports produced for the OECD. Following a functionalist framework, most reports include a list of the institutions necessary to meet basic needs or expectations through different services provided to the population. Generally this list includes security, justice, healthcare, education and economic development. As argued in the framing paper on legitimacy published in 2008, 'the core institutions of the state' include, 'by definition', the capability 'to maintain a monopoly on the use of force, to deliver a stable social contract, to protect citizens and, in most cases, to secure a functioning market'.[44] The rule of law and the management of the environment are also mentioned.[45] Meeting expectations and needs is therefore presented as the core function of strong states – or, as one report puts it, of 'better performing countries'.[46] In this approach the state is both *identified* and *justified* in relation to the services it provides; their absence or disappearance means the decline of the state. Reflecting the recent 'renaissance' of sovereignty as responsibility,[47] states have 'legal and normative responsibilities for assuring the security of their citizens, protecting property rights and providing public goods to enable the functioning of the market'.[48]

The state is therefore largely equated with the delivery of services provided by institutions: 'at the root of the definition of a modern state is that it is a set of *organisations* and *institutions* that ensure the rule of law within a given society'.[49] As a result, 'state fragility impairs the delivery of essential services to the people who need them'.[50] Consequently, in the 2011 policy guidance report (which draws together the conclusions of several years of thinking about legitimacy within the OECD), extreme state fragility is defined as 'the complete collapse of the functions of statehood',[51] and is associated with 'weaker policies and institutions'.[52] This approach reduces state building to a mere process of institution building, since the ability of the state to respond to the needs and expectations of its population is what makes a state a *state*. States are therefore 'reflected in their abilities [...] to perform functions, solve problems and achieve objectives'.[53] This functionalist vision of the state leads to the rather simplistic assertion that, 'in its simplest form, state building is the process of states functioning more effectively'.[54] The strength of the social contract between a state and its society is thus reduced to the satisfactory provision of services by the state.[55]

This institutionalist perspective can be logically translated into a specific conception of legitimacy. Following the Weberian perspective, certain OECD reports state that the 'effectiveness of service delivery' is the core component of 'the legitimacy of the political order'.[56] And if the state does not successfully ensure the provision of these services, 'the effect can be deleterious to state legitimacy'.[57] Moreover, 'states achieve legitimacy when they deliver services in accordance with the social contract'.[58] Consequently, when services are provided by sources outside the state, this has a negative impact on state legitimacy.[59]

However, in most OECD reports legitimacy is not reduced to its institutional definition. Four dimensions are generally identified, contributing to a more balanced view of legitimacy lying somewhere between purely institutional and purely social approaches. These four components of legitimacy are: (1) input (or process) legitimacy; (2) output (or performance) legitimacy; (3) traditional legitimacy (or legitimacy based on shared beliefs); and (4) international legitimacy.[60] Input legitimacy corresponds to how the state operates: legitimacy is reinforced when democracy is ensured and corruption and authoritative procedures are avoided. Output legitimacy corresponds to the Weberian approach in terms of the institutions and services provided to the population. The final element – international legitimacy – is usually considered to be of secondary importance (and is sometimes entirely omitted). The innovative aspect here is the introduction of the idea of 'traditional' legitimacy. This source of legitimacy is 'anchored in traditions, religion, ethnic identity, nationalism or even charismatic leaders' and therefore has 'little to do with performance or process'.[61] This alternative form of legitimacy introduces a historical and cultural sensibility into the otherwise radically institutionalist framework of the OECD.

The identification of this multi-dimensionality of legitimacy suggests that an institutional-only approach may prove insufficient – or even harmful – especially since the four types of legitimacy do not coexist in isolation from one another. Consequently, and in accordance with the social legitimacy approach, a position paper of 2010 argues that 'improving the quality of services will not necessarily increase state legitimacy'.[62] Viewing 'fragile states' as vacuums in which institutions can be built that will automatically or naturally become legitimate is counterproductive, as institutions will only prove effective (and thus legitimate) when 'understood in the context of locally prevailing ideas about the proper role of the state'.[63] The limits of an institutional approach are clearly highlighted: '*Effective political authority that is seen as legitimate cannot be created merely by trying to strengthen input sources of legitimacy (formal rules), or output sources (improved performance)*'.[64] Thus, the OECD seems to concur with the idea that 'the acceptable exercise of authority is something other than the production of good outcomes. For authority is not simply about outcomes but also about selfhood and relationships to others.'[65] Indeed, the formal institutions created by state-building interventions are not sufficient to create legitimacy, since 'people's perceptions of legitimacy are central to their willingness to engage with the state.'[66] One of the clearest expressions of this argument is found in an OECD discussion paper:

> Absent a careful understanding of the way in which the political and social fabric of society is expressed institutionally, investment in recreating or building new institutions that mimic the ideal Weberian form is often bound to fail.[67]

Although the reconstitution of basic services is still important, 'more is needed':[68] 'statebuilding approaches need to move beyond institution building towards fostering greater and deeper interaction between state and society'.[69] This idea of 'embedded' legitimacy (or support 'from within') means that the institutions 'cannot be divorced from the social and political setting' in which they act;[70] otherwise, they will run the risk of being considered 'formal' institutions,[71] ie ineffective and illegitimate institutions:

> Strengthening key state capabilities (police, the judiciary, public financial management, etc) from a technical standpoint alone is insufficient. To treat these merely as technical exercises denies the fundamentally political basis of statebuilding.[72]

A crucial move is thus made by arguing that 'state performance [alone] is no guarantee of legitimacy',[73] if the institutions behind this performance are not 'rooted in society'.[74] The performances expected, the services needed and the capacities necessary to satisfy them should therefore not be established in isolation from the historical and cultural contexts of each country.[75]

From concepts to policies: returning to institutionalist conceptions

The consequences of this evolution in the approach to legitimacy and state fragility are twofold. First, the concept of legitimacy itself becomes 'extremely complex because it has multiple sources, and [it] changes over time'.[76] Legitimacy is no longer seen as a unitary and internally coherent concept; in fact, the various dimensions of legitimacy can contradict each other,[77] especially since they vary according to time and place. But, more importantly, this emphasis on the local perceptions of legitimacy leads to the logical conclusion that state building is (at least partially) an endogenous process.[78] Consequently intervening countries will need to be 'realistic about their limited ability to understand, much less to shape, local patterns of legitimacy'.[79] In particular, the inclusion of 'traditional' legitimacy introduces a new element for intervening countries: 'Perhaps the dimension of state legitimacy the least well-understood by donors is that derived from appeals to accepted beliefs about the sources of authority in society and values widely held'.[80] This new, more complex approach to legitimacy 'makes it very difficult for external actors to understand and contribute to the process' of state-building;[81] indeed, it is unsurprising that the majority of intervening countries do not 'incorporate questions of legitimacy [understood here to include 'traditional' legitimacy] in any operational sense'.[82] Moreover, if legitimacy is intrinsically local, it follows that a clash between the local conception of legitimacy and that of the intervening countries is almost inevitable.[83] This gap between legitimacy as conceived by donors – or, as one report puts it, state legitimacy viewed as 'good governance'[84] – and the 'traditional' form of legitimacy is particularly problematic in the context of state building, which implies an encounter between 'competing sources of legitimacy'.[85] As this report explains, intervening countries usually come equipped with Western 'normative values' that can 'fundamentally' differ from local beliefs.[86] Undeniably 'the international community also has certain expectations of how states should perform',[87] which may go beyond or diverge from local expectations. Even more disconcerting, and based on the previous assertions, one report indicates that 'it is therefore important for donors not to assume that promotion of, or support for, reform that is aligned with international norms will necessarily increase internal legitimacy'.[88] This clearly indicates that the inclusion of 'traditional' legitimacy in the balance endangers the entire conceptual approach to state building developed in these reports.

The second consequence of this more nuanced vision of legitimacy is the creation of a circular argument that becomes difficult to operationalise. Indeed, the analysis revolves around the idea that 'capacity and legitimacy are distinct but interdependent';[89] in other words, institutions and social beliefs act together to reinforce legitimacy in fragile situations. Accordingly legitimacy comes to be seen as an ingredient in *and* an outcome of state building.[90] This is most clearly expressed in the following claim: 'Legitimacy aids the process of state building, and is reinforced as state building delivers benefits for people [...] As such, legitimacy is both a means and an end for successful state building'.[91] This conception of legitimacy suggests that, while state institutions can contribute to the strengthening of legitimacy (by means of the services they provide), legitimacy can also contribute to the quality of the services provided, since these services will be more readily accepted as legitimate. Here legitimacy is both the result of 'good' institutions – since the population will consider efficient institutions to be more acceptable and legitimate – and an ingredient in their establishment. While positively adding a level of complexity missing from most institutionalist analyses, and thus coming closer to depicting the reality of state building, this sociological approach also entails a vision of legitimacy as both *cause* and *effect*. This dual role means that 'capacity and legitimacy are mutually reinforcing, and can create virtuous or (in fragile situations) vicious circles'.[92] Although this is not regarded as problematic from a traditional academic perspective, it seems highly questionable from a 'policy-prescription' point of view. Where should intervening countries start – with legitimacy as an embedded belief or with legitimacy in terms of institutions and service delivery? What role and significance should be assigned to each approach? How can vicious circles be broken, and how can virtuous ones be started?

The process of complicating a concept of legitimacy that no longer flows from purely institutional sources and the related conclusion that legitimacy should be seen as both a means and an end for state building seem to have guided the OECD's analysis away from a sociological understanding of legitimacy, prompting a resurgence of the institutionalist conception of the state. In fact, in order to overcome these difficulties, the institutionalist approach has remained strongly influential, although in less obvious guises. This predominance of the institutionalist approach to legitimacy and the state is evident in the fact that 'state' and 'society' are still conceived as separate entities and that 'traditional' legitimacy, although included in the multidimensional approach to legitimacy, seems to serve a specific purpose, ie the strengthening of institutional legitimacy.

The first aspect of this predominance of the institutionalist form of legitimacy and the state is expressed in the persistent separation of state and society in OECD reports. This conception is at odds with sociological and ethno-cultural approaches that emphasise the impossibility of dissociating state and society, as they both form part of the same overall social structure. In these reports, however, it is asserted that 'the state needs to be both closely linked to and embedded in society, while at the same time maintaining sufficient autonomy to allow it to operate as the overarching authority.'[93] State and society are therefore viewed as strictly separate entities, and the task of state building is to 'reconnect' them. This conception brings us back to a Weberian model in which state building is equated with improvements in 'a state's relationship with society'.[94] Accordingly fragility is sometimes defined as a 'weak' relationship between the state and its citizens.[95] However, the OECD's perspective differs on one key aspect: this relationship between state and society is conceived of in terms of local perceptions, ie the 'factors and processes that produce a social contract between state and society'.[96] Hence, 'it is crucial to understand and support the social, political and economic processes through which relations between state and society are negotiated and constructed'.[97] Fundamentally, however, the dissociation between state and society remains a central characteristic of the OECD's approach to state building.

The second element reminiscent of an institutionalist perspective is related to the underlying justification for conceptualising legitimacy as a multidimensional concept that includes both a performance/institutional aspect and a 'traditional' aspect. This latter component of legitimacy, which can perhaps be better expressed by the idea of 'embedded' legitimacy, is included in part thanks to a sensitivity to pluralism and the desire to avoid ethnocentric bias but, more pragmatically, because the inclusion of local beliefs and the participation of the population produces better *institutional* results.[98] Services and institutions remain crucial, but they must be identified in the specific context of the 'fragile' state, meaning that 'a resilient state must be able to effectively deliver functions that match the expectations of societal groups'.[99] And if 'traditional systems' (such as informal structures of governance or traditional systems of justice) are considered to be crucial in state building, it is precisely because they can 'perform the same functions and generate the same outputs as formal state institutions'.[100] This insistence on institutions is also exemplified by the way 'traditional' forms of legitimacy are usually described: in one report the different sources of legitimacy are seen as competing with one another, but this is particularly true when 'traditional' legitimacy is involved.[101] In fact, there is an assumption that 'traditional' legitimacy is important but is more likely to lead to competing demands on and visions of the state, while performance legitimacy might be easier to deal with because it is supposedly more rational (although, here again, expectations vary across groups). In 2008 one report mentioned the fact that 'traditional' legitimacy might be 'more partial' and therefore of secondary importance in comparison to other forms of legitimacy.[102] As a result, in connection to the problem of circularity discussed above, the OECD's conception of legitimacy seems to overemphasise one dimension – namely, institutions and performance – over the others (especially the more socially and culturally oriented 'traditional' legitimacy).

Thus, the OECD has developed its own unique conception of legitimacy based on a prevailing institutionalist framework mixed with elements of social legitimacy. Abandoning institutionalism could actually prove dangerous to the role the organisation has assigned itself: one report considers international, uniform, 'good' practices and recommendations to be 'irrelevant or counterproductive' when legitimacy is defined in social terms,[103] while another finds that inclusion of 'traditional' legitimacy makes it 'difficult to come up with sound, replicable approaches that donors can take in programmes of development assistance'.[104] Preserving the institutionalist approach thus preserves the role that the OECD claims to play: that of provider of expertise on 'good' practices of intervention.

Reproducing worldviews: expertise and the standardisation of knowledge

This dominance of a specific vision of legitimacy can easily be explained if one adopts a view of the OECD as a unitary actor developing 'its' own opinions on these issues in order to maintain a coherent approach over time. But, like other organisations, not only does the OECD have a diverse staff, it also calls on external specialists in order to produce reports on state legitimacy. How, then, is this specific approach to state fragility created, maintained and replicated? We argue that it is possible to understand this phenomenon by examining how the organisation's main premises have become accepted and reproduced by the scholars involved in the process of writing reports for the OECD. We posit that an analysis of the production of policy reports can add an additional layer to the semantic debate over the meaning of state fragility. By taking into account the social conditions in which the cultural field of knowledge production operates – a field that can be defined as a series of institutions, rules, rituals, conventions, categories, designations, appointments and titles that constitute an objective hierarchy – we seek to understand how certain discourses and activities concerning 'fragile' states become accepted while others are discarded as illegitimate. Our analysis is focused on a relatively small epistemic community: the OECD staff and the 'experts' involved in writing the reports on state building in 'fragile' states. We want to emphasise that the existence and reproduction of this epistemic community through various mechanisms also preserve its theoretical orientations and preferences.

First of all, the world-view of the community emerges within the OECD as the result of interactions between the members and between members, the secretariat and the external contributors. As one of our interviewees remarked, this view is heavily influenced by those who invest time and money in the process of producing the reports.[105] It is not an overstatement to qualify this group as a 'community'; by the end of the 2000s this group had become an integrated community sharing common objectives and ideas, to the point that some members became disconnected from their own national administrations.[106] As with other epistemic communities, it is crucial that the shared beliefs (the world-view) of the community be maintained. This world-view is concisely described by Stephan Massing, who is responsible for the coordination between expert writers and OECD members, as translating research into policy discussions in order to 'give people tools, frameworks, terms and approaches that they can use in their work'.[107] However, this process of reproduction is not simply based on 'policy-relevance'; as Patrick Meagher indicates with regard to the process of writing policy reports, 'you've got to really constrain yourself within quite narrow confines to grapple with their terminology, their idea-set, and their understanding of the world'. Only by understanding 'how the organisation speaks' can one write a 'good' report.[108] As noted by Michael Barnett following his experience with the United Nations, reports must be written 'in a manner that conforms to the intended reader's organization of knowledge'; indeed, the 'culture' in which one works is the ultimate standard by which the 'effectiveness' or quality of one's work is judged.[109]

The production and reproduction of this world-view take place through various mechanisms. For instance, the creation of OECD-DAC policy reports can be described as collaborative and involving a great deal of interaction between OECD staff and the scholars selected as the main authors of the reports; this is one of the ways in which the community ensures the coherence of and respect for its world-view. After the potential contributors have been identified, selected and approached by OECD officials (in a process discussed below), the actual process of writing reports is an iterative procedure, with a constant back-and-forth between the organisation and the contributors in order to ensure that the right message is being conveyed. Initial drafts are sent to the organisation for comments and reviews, modified accordingly and sent back to OECD staffers for additional rounds of comments.[110] This 'joint process', in Stephan Massing's words,[111] includes many revisions and exchanges. In the process the OECD has a double role: reviewing the drafts produced by the writers, but also selecting (or 'filtering', according to one of the scholars who has participated in the process[112]) the comments and feedback sent to the authors. Massing describes his role as shaping the policy messages while making sure that the 'product' is in line with the organisation's expectations, since, *in fine*, 'the product is owned by the OECD'.[113] This process is not without certain tensions. For one participant in the process, 'the only thing that gave me pause was that they tended to push me in their direction'. The OECD staff 'wanted me to write the paper and they wanted to exert their influence on it, so there was a little bit of tension there'.[114] Another participant noted, 'you are free to explore, but you are in a political organisation. There are restrictions.'[115]

More subtle mechanisms are also at play to ensure the coherence and stability of the organisation's world-view – for instance, through the distinction between 'insiders' and 'outsiders'.[116] The selection of report writers is particularly exemplary in this regard. According to our interviewees, most writers are selected through direct and personal contact, and few reports are contracted out in an open competition (thus reducing the risks and the costs of dealing with outsiders). When asked why they were chosen by the OECD to write a report, several interviewees mentioned their previous work for the organisation,[117] or their past experience with similar policy institutions.[118] In the opinion of Bathylle Missika, OECD staffers prefer to work with scholars believed to be safe, ie those who do not represent a threat to the culture or identity of the organisation because they understand what the organisation wants (especially in terms of policy recommendations).[119] Stephan Massing feels that the selection is made based on the writer's ability to translate abstract concepts into policy recommendations.[120] Thus it does not surprise Patrick Meagher that 'they would choose a person based on the work that they've seen or the reputation that they have as being pragmatic or able to provide views that are not too distant from their policy preferences'.[121] As a consequence, being selected as an expert is dependent on one's 'ability to formulate questions and responses, to pose talking points, to use language, and to carry on conversations in ways that [are] consistent with the understandings and discourses' of the organisation.[122] In this context the members of the OECD generally have a good idea of who the report writers will be when they decide to work on a particular issue:[123] The process of deciding *what* to research and *who* the researcher will be are simultaneous.

One final notable aspect of how the specific culture of the OECD is preserved, transmitted and reproduced is the ability of the subcontracted experts to 'naturally' be aware of and adjust to the expectations of their client. This is what Pierre Bourdieu calls 'the internalisation of exteriority' (the norms of the organisation become a way of being and working for the insiders) and the 'exteriorisation of the interiority' (the practice of these norms by the insiders helps reproduce the organisation and its culture).[124] This echoes Barnett's experiences; as he describes the process, 'not only had I entered the bureaucratic world, but the bureaucratic world had entered me'.[125] Our initial hypothesis was that academics who work for the OECD must feel heavily constrained and uncomfortable with the process of writing a policy report. Over the course of the interviews we realised that this was simply not reflective of the experiences of the report writers we interviewed. The alignment between the specific expectations of the OECD and the scholars' willingness to comply with and reflect these requirements was harmonious in most cases. Implicit mechanisms ensure the preservation of these expectations and dispositions. As one scholar-practitioner told us, 'you can write what you want, but they might not use it or hire you again [...] If you want to continue working with the OECD, you have to understand the rules'.[126] Hence it seems simplistic to postulate that the OECD mechanisms involved in the production of its reports act as an obstacle to the writers involved; in fact, the writers themselves tend to willingly reproduce the organisation's expectations, thus confirming both the world-view of the organisation *and* their status as 'experts' (which is derived from the preservation of the epistemic community and its world-view). This indicates that the epistemic community is shaped by OECD's 'rules of the game'; however, it is also a mutually constitutive process where the main actors in this epistemic community – including organisations such as DFID and researchers such as Sue Unsworth, James Putzel and Bruce Jones – have also directly influenced and shaped the OECD's work on state fragility and state building over time.[127]

Conclusion

This article's main objective was to highlight the importance of issues of knowledge production in the context of an international organisation. The article has presented two distinct approaches to the state and state fragility, each with explicit sets of assumptions and explanatory mechanisms for understanding state fragility-related phenomena. The institutional approach, loosely inspired by the work of Max Weber, focuses on state capacity through an emphasis on institutional reconstruction and the monopolisation of legitimate violence. The social legitimacy approach, though recognising the importance of establishing a climate of security, concentrates on socio-political cohesion in the rebuilding process through an anthropologically or ethnologically oriented focus. While the institutional approach represents the orthodoxy in the field to a certain extent, and most policy organisations tend to abide by its main prescriptions, the OECD reports on fragile states have presented a more varied picture, drawing from both the institutional and the social legitimacy approaches. The article elaborated on this (welcome) complexity by taking an in-depth look at the most pivotal reports on state fragility. We found evidence of the inherent difficulty in operationalising state fragility through the social legitimacy approach; ultimately, our findings indicate that institutionalist premises still dominate the OECD approach to legitimacy. By complementing our analysis with interviews conducted with OECD staff and scholar-practitioners who have participated in the process of knowledge production, we have been able to make hypotheses regarding the social conditions in which this specific epistemic community works and how its particular world-view is (re)produced. The article specifically examined the selection process of practitioner-scholars and the writing process structured by the contractor–subcontractee relationship. We found an interesting illustration of Bourdieu's 'internalisation of exteriority', whereby the norms of the organisation become a way of being and working for insiders, and the 'exteriorisation of the interiority', in which the practice of these norms by insiders helps reproduce the organisation and its culture. This in turn opens up an interesting combined research and policy agenda on how marginal voices could be promoted in the OECD's discourse on fragile states, especially those voices affiliated with institutions and countries labelled 'fragile' by most indexes. However, this research agenda will have to investigate not only the substantive conceptual differences between insiders and outsiders, but also the sociological obstacles experienced by these outsiders – obstacles that would be defended by an epistemic community in order to preserve its identity and survival.

Acknowledgements

We would like to thank our colleagues, who have provided useful feedback on various drafts of this article. We would also like to specifically thank Philippe Beaulieu-Brossard, Nicolas Bouchet, Emmanuel Klimis, Félix Grenier and Stephan Massing for their comments, as well as the two anonymous reviewers who commented on an earlier draft, and Claire Bacher for her careful proofreading. We acknowledge the research support provided by the Research Assistant Scheme at the School of Government and Society (University of Birmingham), and we would like to thank in particular Fiona Hobson and Ayesha Harris for their help in the process.

Notes on Contributors

Nicolas Lemay-Hébert is Senior Lecturer in the International Development Department, University of Birmingham. His research interests include peace building and state building, humanitarian interventions in post-conflict or post-disaster contexts, the political economy of international interventions, and local narratives of resistance to international intervention. He has published various articles in *International Studies Perspectives*, *International Peacekeeping*, *Third World Quarterly*, *Democratization* and the *Journal of Intervention and Statebuilding*, among others. His most recent book is *Semantics of Statebuilding: Language, Meanings and Sovereignty* (2014; co-edited with N. Onuf, V. Rakic, and P. Bojanic).

Xavier Mathieu is a PhD student in the Department of Politics, University of Sheffield. His research focuses on the concept of sovereignty, hierarchy in international relations, state building and performative approaches to the study of international politics. He is currently completing his thesis on the impact that the 'Great Discoveries' and new ideas of civilization and barbarism had on the concept of sovereignty in early modern Europe.

Notes

1. Herbst, "Let Them Fail"; and Luttwak, "Give War a Chance."
2. Doornbos, "State Collapse and Fresh Starts"; Eisenstadt, "Beyond Collapse"; and Mehler and Ribaux, *Crisis Prevention*.
3. Lemay-Hébert, "The Semantics of Statebuilding and Nationbuilding"; and Lemay-Hébert, "Statebuilding without Nation-building?"
4. Buzan, *People, States and Fear*, 64; and Holsti, *The State, War, and the State of War*, 98.
5. Lemay-Hébert, "Rethinking Weberian Approaches to Statebuilding."
6. Martens and Jakobi, "Introduction," 2.
7. OECD, *Principles for Good International Engagement in Fragile States*.
8. Interestingly, various disciplines view this 'frontier' differently. According to a former French representative in charge of the questions of state fragility at the OECD, the authors subcontracted are generally political scientists, legal experts or economists. In contrast, anthropologists, sociologists and historians generally tend to refuse to partake in (and exclude themselves from) these networks of 'scholar-practi-

tioners' as they consider this work to be normative and producing only partial knowledge. This illustrates how the supposedly stable 'frontier' between academia and the policy world depends on the prevalent ethos of each discipline. Interview with a former French representative, Paris, 15 July 2013.

9. As Haas argues, 'members of epistemic communities not only hold in common a set of principled and causal beliefs but also have shared notions of validity and a shared policy enterprise. Their authoritative claim to policy-relevant knowledge in a particular domain is based on their recognized expertise within that domain.' Haas, "Introduction," 16. See also Adler and Haas, "Conclusion."
10. Lemay-Hébert et al., "Introduction."
11. Schein, *Organizational Culture and Leadership*.
12. Paris, "Ordering the World," 58.
13. Weber, "Politics as a Vocation," 78.
14. See, for instance, Migdal, *Strong Societies and Weak States*; and Stepan, *The State and Society*.
15. Hobson and Seabrooke, "Reimagining Weber," 258.
16. Beetham, *Max Weber*, 151; Hobson, "Debate," 288; and Palumbo and Scott, "Weber, Durkheim," 387.
17. Lemay-Hébert, "Statebuilding without Nation-building?"; and Zaum, *The Sovereignty Paradox*, 29.
18. Helman and Ratner, "Saving Failed States"; Rotberg, "The Failure and Collapse of Nation-states"; and Fukuyama, *State-building*.
19. Helman and Ratner, "Saving Failed States," 5.
20. Rotberg, "The Failure and Collapse of Nation-states," 2.
21. Mcloughlin, *Topic Guide on Fragile States*, 9.
22. Jackson, *Quasi-states*; Keohane, "Political Authority after Intervention"; and Krasner, "Sharing Sovereignty."
23. Ottaway, "Rebuilding State Institutions."
24. Kaplan, "The Coming Anarchy."
25. Lynch, *Engaging Eurasia's Separatist States*, 17.
26. Ghani and Lockhart, *Fixing Failed States*, 22.
27. Ghani and Lockhart, "Rethinking Nation-building."
28. Annan, "Two Concepts of Sovereignty."
29. Clapham, "Degrees of Statehood"; Clapham, "Sovereignty and the Third World State"; and Deng et al., *Sovereignty as Responsibility*.
30. Durkheim, *Professional Ethics and Civic Morals*, 79–80; Durkheim, *The Division of Labor in Society*, 79; and Durkheim, "The Concept of State," 54.
31. Durkheim, *The Division of Labor in Society*, 80.
32. Holsti, *The State, War, and the State of War*, 82.
33. Buzan, *People, States and Fear*, 64.
34. Giddens, *The Nation-state and Violence*, 17.
35. De Wall, "Fixing the Political Marketplace."
36. Gourevitch, "The Unfailing of the State," 260.
37. Durkheim, *Suicide*, 382.
38. Our distinction between institutionalist and social legitimacy approaches overlaps with Morten's analysis of legitimacy in the state-building literature. The Weberian approach is similar to what he calls a 'normative–institutionalist' view, while the social legitimacy approach shares characteristics with his 'empirical–societal' category. Andersen, "Legitimacy in State-building."
39. Boutros-Ghali, "Concluding Statement," 9.
40. DFID, *Why We Need to Work More Effectively in Fragile States*, 7.
41. Interview with a former French representative, Paris, 15 July 2013.
42. OECD, *Principles for Good International Engagement*, Preamble (emphasis added), Third Principle.
43. Ibid., footnote 1.
44. OECD, *Concepts and Dilemmas of State Building*, 28.
45. OECD, *Do No Harm*, 88.
46. OECD, *International Engagement in Fragile States*, 19.
47. ICISS, *Responsibility to Protect*. See also Glanville, "The Antecedents of 'Sovereignty as Responsibility'."
48. OECD, *Concepts and Dilemmas of State Building*, 11, 33.
49. OECD, *Do No Harm*, 94 (emphasis added).
50. OECD, *Service Delivery in Fragile Situations*, 39.
51. OECD, *Supporting Statebuilding*, 25.
52. OECD, *Ensuring Fragile States are not Left Behind*, 10.
53. OECD, *Monitoring the Principles for Good International Engagement*, 22.
54. OECD, *State Building in Fragile Situations*, para. 2.
55. OECD, *Supporting Statebuilding*, 31, 72.
56. OECD, *Service Delivery in Fragile Situations*, 15.
57. OECD, *Concepts and Dilemmas of State Building*, 46.
58. Ibid., 40.
59. OECD, *Do No Harm*, 69.

60. OECD, *Concepts and Dilemmas of State Building*, 17; OECD, *State Building in Fragile Situations*, para. 11; OECD, *The State's Legitimacy in Fragile Situations*; OECD, *Do No Harm*, 48; and OECD, *Supporting Statebuilding*, 36.
61. OECD, *Do No Harm*, 48, 50.
62. OECD, *The State's Legitimacy in Fragile Situations*, 24.
63. Ibid., 27. See also Lemay-Hébert, "The 'Empty-shell' Approach."
64. OECD, *The State's Legitimacy in Fragile Situations*, 52 (emphasis in the original).
65. Koskenniemi, "Conclusion," 240.
66. OECD, *The State's Legitimacy in Fragile Situations*, 19.
67. OECD, *Concepts and Dilemmas of State Building*, 39.
68. OECD, *Service Delivery in Fragile Situations*, 13.
69. OECD, *International Engagement in Fragile States*, 27.
70. OECD, *Service Delivery in Fragile Situations*, 23.
71. OECD, *Concepts and Dilemmas of State Building*, 14.
72. OECD, *Supporting Statebuilding*, 36. This 'rediscovered' political basis of state building is particularly noteworthy and has been expressed by other reports as well. See OECD, *Monitoring the Principles for Good International Engagement*, 41.
73. OECD, *Monitoring the Principles for Good International Engagement*, 22.
74. OECD, *State Building in Fragile Situations*, para. 22.
75. OECD, *Concepts and Dilemmas of State Building*, 16.
76. OECD, *The State's Legitimacy in Fragile Situations*, 13.
77. OECD, *Supporting Statebuilding*, 25, 30.
78. OECD, *The State's Legitimacy in Fragile Situations*, 52; and OECD, *Supporting Statebuilding*, 42.
79. OECD, *The State's Legitimacy in Fragile Situations*, 13.
80. OECD, *Do No Harm*, 50.
81. OECD, *The State's Legitimacy in Fragile Situations*, 37.
82. OECD, *Concepts and Dilemmas of State Building*, 16.
83. OECD, *The State's Legitimacy in Fragile Situations*, 17–18.
84. OECD, *Do No Harm*, 123.
85. OECD, *The State's Legitimacy in Fragile Situations*, 27.
86. Ibid., 51 and 53.
87. OECD, *State Building in Fragile Situations*, para. 5.
88. OECD, *The State's Legitimacy in Fragile Situations*, 29.
89. Ibid., 20.
90. OECD, *Concepts and Dilemmas of State Building*, 14.
91. OECD, *State Building in Fragile Situations*, para. 10.
92. OECD, *Supporting Statebuilding*, 37.
93. OECD, *The State's Legitimacy in Fragile Situations*, 20. See also OECD, *Supporting Statebuilding*, 42, 64.
94. OECD, *Do No Harm*, 44.
95. OECD, *Supporting Statebuilding*, 21.
96. OECD, *Concepts and Dilemmas of State Building*, 12.
97. OECD, *Supporting Statebuilding*, 15.
98. See, for instance, OECD, *Concepts and Dilemmas of State Building*, 21.
99. OECD, *State Building in Fragile Situations*, para. 8.
100. OECD, *Concepts and Dilemmas of State Building*, 36.
101. OECD, *Supporting Statebuilding*, 37.
102. OECD, *Service Delivery in Fragile Situations*, 15.
103. OECD, *Supporting Statebuilding*, 43.
104. OECD, *Do No Harm*, 120.
105. More specifically certain countries and organisations (such as DFID) seem to dominate state-building debates. These actors have a clear interest in influencing the development of the concepts and practices that they support. Interview with a former French representative, Paris, 15 July 2013.
106. Our interviewee qualified the group as an 'elitist epistemic community'. Interview with a former French representative.
107. Interview with Stephan Massing, OECD-DAC Secretariat, Paris, 30 November 2012.
108. Phone interview with Patrick Meagher, independent consultant, 11 December 2012.
109. Barnett, "The UN Security Council," 555.
110. Interview with Bathylle Missika, OECD Development Centre, formerly with the DAC Secretariat, Paris, 28 November 2012.
111. Interview with Stephan Massing.
112. Phone interview with Sue Unsworth, The Policy Practice, 23 November 2012.
113. Interview with Stephan Massing.
114. Phone interview with Patrick Meagher.
115. Interview with Sumedh Rao, Governance and Social Development Resource Centre, Birmingham, 25 April 2013.

116. Barnett, "The UN Security Council," 555.
117. Email interview with a consultant (under conditions of anonymity), 16 November 2012; and phone interview with Sue Unsworth.
118. Phone interview with Patrick Meagher; and phone interview with Sue Unsworth.
119. Interview with Bathylle Missika.
120. Interview with a Team Leader at the OECD-DAC, Paris, 30 November 2012; and interview with Stephan Massing.
121. Phone interview with Patrick Meagher.
122. Barnett, "The UN Security Council," 555.
123. Interview with a former French representative.
124. Bourdieu, *Esquisse d'une théorie de la pratique*, 256.
125. Barnett, "The UN Security Council," 557.
126. Interview with Sumedh Rao.
127. Phone interview with Stephan Massing, 9 September 2013.

Bibliography

Adler, Emmanuel, and Peter Haas. "Conclusion: Epistemic Communities, World Order, and the Creation of a Reflective Research Program." *International Organization* 46, no. 1 (1992): 367–390.

Andersen, Morten Skumsrud. "Legitimacy in State-building: A Review of the IR Literature." *International Political Sociology* 6, no. 2 (2012): 205–219.

Annan, Kofi. 1999. "Two Concepts of Sovereignty." *The Economist*, 18 September.

Barnett, Michael. "The UN Security Council, Indifference, and Genocide in Rwanda." *Cultural Anthropology* 12, no. 4 (1997): 551–578.

Beetham, David. *Max Weber and the Theory of Modern Politics*. Cambridge: Polity Press, 1985.

Bourdieu, Pierre. *Esquisse d'une théorie de la pratique*. Paris: Seuil, 2000.

Boutros-Ghali, Boutros. "Concluding Statement of the UN Congress on Public International Law: Towards the Twenty-First Century, International Law as a Language for International Relations." New York, 13–17 March 1995.

Buzan, Barry. *People, States and Fear: An Agenda for International Security Studies in the Post-Cold War Era*. New York: Harvester Wheatsheaf, 1991.

Clapham, Christopher. "Degrees of Statehood." *Review of International Studies* 24, no. 2 (1998): 143–157.

Clapham, Christopher. "Sovereignty and the Third World State." *Political Studies* 47, no. 3 (1999): 522–537.

Deng, Francis M., Sadikiel Kimaro, Terrence Lyons, Donald Rothchild and I. William Zartman. *Sovereignty as Responsibility: Conflict Management in Africa*. Washington, DC: Brookings Institution Press, 1996.

De Wall, Alex. "Fixing the Political Marketplace: How Can We Make Peace without Functioning State Institutions?" Fifteenth Christen Michelsen Lecture, Bergen, 15 October 2009.

DFID. *Why We Need to Work More Effectively in Fragile States*. London: DFID, 2005.

Doornbos, Martin. "State Collapse and Fresh Starts: Some Critical Reflections." In *State Failure, Collapse & Reconstruction*, edited by Jennifer Milliken, 45–62. Oxford: Blackwell, 2003.

Durkheim, Émile. "The Concept of State." In *Durkheim on Politics and the State*, edited by Anthony Giddens, 32–62. Cambridge: Polity Press, 1986.

Durkheim, Émile. *The Division of Labor in Society*. New York: Free Press, 1964.

Durkheim, Émile. *Professional Ethics and Civic Morals*. London: Routledge, 1957.

Durkheim, Émile. *Suicide: A Study in Sociology*. New York: Simon and Schuster, 1997.

Eisenstadt, Samuel. "Beyond Collapse." In *The Collapse of Ancient States and Civilizations*, edited by Norman Yoffee, and George Cowgill, 236–243. Tucson: University of Arizona Press, 1988.

Fukuyama, Francis. *State-building: Governance and World Order in the 21st Century*. New York: Cornell University Press, 2004.

Ghani, Ashraf, and Clare Lockhart. *Fixing Failed States: A Framework for Rebuilding a Fractured World*. Oxford: Oxford University Press, 2008.

Ghani, Ashraf, and Clare Lockhart. "Rethinking Nation-Building." *ODI Opinions* 63 (2006). http://www.odi.org.uk/opinion/507-rethinking-nation-building.

Giddens, Anthony. *The Nation-state and Violence*. Cambridge: Polity Press, 1985.

Glanville, Luke. "The Antecedents of 'Sovereignty as Responsibility'." *European Journal of International Relations* 17 (2011): 233–255.

Gourevitch, Alexander. "The Unfailing of the State." *Journal of International Affairs* 58, no. 1 (2004): 255–260.

Haas, Peter M. "Introduction: Epistemic Communities and International Policy Coordination." *International Organization* 46, no. 1 (1992): 1–35.

Helman, Gerald, and Steven Ratner. "Saving Failed States." *Foreign Policy* 89 (1992–93): 1–20.

Herbst, Jeffrey. "Let Them Fail: State Failure in Theory and Practice – Implications for Policy." In *When States Fail: Causes and Consequences*, edited by Robert Rotberg, 302–318. Princeton, NJ: Princeton University Press, 2004.

Hobson, John. "Debate: The 'Second Wave' of Weberian Historical Sociology." *Review of International Political Economy* 5, no. 2 (1998): 284–320.
Hobson, John, and Leonard Seabrooke. "Reimagining Weber: Constructing International Society and the Social Balance of Power." *European Journal of International Relations* 7, no. 2 (2001): 239–274.
Holsti, Kalevi. *The State, War, and the State of War*. Cambridge: Cambridge University Press, 1996.
ICISS. *Responsibility to Protect*. Ottawa: International Development Research Centre, 2001.
Jackson, Robert H. *Quasi-states: Sovereignty, International Relations and the Third World*. Cambridge: Cambridge University Press, 1990.
Kaplan, Robert. "The Coming Anarchy: A New Kind of War." *Atlantic Monthly*, February 1994. http://www.theatlantic.com/doc/199402/anarchy/7.
Keohane, Robert O. "Political Authority after Intervention: Gradations in Sovereignty." In *Humanitarian Intervention: Ethical, Legal, and Political Dilemmas*, edited by Holzgrefe, J. L. and Robert O. Keohane, 275–298. Cambridge: Cambridge University Press, 2003.
Koskenniemi, Martti. "Conclusion: Vocabularies of Sovereignty – Powers of a Paradox." In *Sovereignty in Fragments: The Past, Present and Future of a Contested Concept*, edited by Hent Kalmo, and Quentin Skinner, 222–242. Cambridge: Cambridge University Press, 2010.
Krasner, Stephen D. "Sharing Sovereignty: New Institutions for Collapsed and Failing States." *International Security* 29, no. 2 (2004): 85–120.
Lemay-Hébert, Nicolas. "The 'Empty-Shell' Approach: The Setup Process of International Administrations in Timor-Leste and Kosovo, its Consequences and Lessons." *International Studies Perspectives* 12, no. 2 (2011): 190–211.
Lemay-Hébert, Nicolas. "Rethinking Weberian Approaches to Statebuilding." In *Routledge Handbook of International Statebuilding*, edited by David Chandler, and Timothy Sisk, 3–14. London: Routledge, 2013.
Lemay-Hébert, Nicolas. "The Semantics of Statebuilding and Nationbuilding: Looking Beyond Neo-Weberian Approaches." In *The Semantics of Statebuilding: Language, Meanings and Sovereignty*, edited by Nicolas Lemay-Hébert, Nicholas Onuf, Vojin Rakic, and Petar Bojanic, 89–105. London: Routledge, 2014.
Lemay-Hébert, Nicolas. "Statebuilding without Nation-Building? Legitimacy, State Failure and the Limits of the Institutionalist Approach." *Journal of Intervention and Statebuilding* 3, no. 1 (2009): 21–45.
Lemay-Hébert, Nicolas, Nicholas Onuf, and Vojin Rakic. "Introduction: Disputing Weberian Semantics." In *The Semantics of Statebuilding: Language, Meanings and Sovereignty*, edited by Nicolas Lemay-Hébert, Nicholas Onuf, Vojin Rakic, and Petar Bojanic, 1–18. London: Routledge, 2014.
Luttwak, Edward. "Give War a Chance." *Foreign Affairs* 78, no. 4 (1999): 36–44.
Lynch, Dov. *Engaging Eurasia's Separatist States: Unresolved Conflicts and De Facto States*. Washington, DC: United States Institute of Peace Press, 2004.
Martens, Kerstin, and Anja P. Jakobi. "Introduction: The OECD as an Actor in International Politics." In *Mechanisms of OECD Governance: International Incentives for National Policy-Making?*, edited by K. Martens, and A. P. Jakobi, 1–25. Oxford: Oxford University Press, 2010.
Mcloughlin, Claire. *Topic Guide on Fragile States*. Birmingham: Governance and Social Development Resource Centre, 2010.
Mehler, Andreas, and Claude Ribaux. *Crisis Prevention and Conflict Management in Technical Cooperation: An Overview of the National and International Debate*. Wiesbaden: UniversumVerlangsanstalt/Deutsche Gesellschaft für Technische Zusammenarbeit, 2000.
Migdal, Joel. *Strong Societies and Weak States: State-Society Relations and State Capabilities in the Third World*. Princeton, NJ: Princeton University Press, 1988.
OECD. *Concepts and Dilemmas of State Building in Fragile Situations: From Fragility to Resilience*. OECD-DAC Discussion Paper. Paris, OECD, 2008.
OECD. *Do No Harm: International Support for Statebuilding*. Paris: OECD, 2010.
OECD. *Ensuring Fragile States are not Left Behind: 2011 Report on Financial Resource Flows*. Paris: OECD, 2011.
OECD. *International Engagement in Fragile States: Can't We Do Better?* Paris: OECD, 2011.
OECD. *Monitoring the Principles for Good International Engagement in Fragile States and Situations*. Paris: OECD, 2010.
OECD. *Principles for Good International Engagement in Fragile States and Situations*. Paris: OECD, 2007.
OECD. *Service Delivery in Fragile Situations: Key Concepts, Findings and Lessons*. OECD Discussion Paper. Paris: OECD, 2008.
OECD. *State Building in Fragile Situations: Initial Findings*. Paris: OECD, 2008.
OECD. *The State's Legitimacy in Fragile Situations: Unpacking Complexity*, Paris: OECD, 2010.
OECD. *Supporting Statebuilding in Situations of Conflict and Fragility: Policy Guidance*. Paris: OECD, 2011.
Ottaway, Marina. "Rebuilding State Institutions in Collapsed States." In *State Failure, Collapse and Reconstruction*, edited by Jennifer Milliken, 245–266. Oxford: Blackwell, 2003.
Palumbo, A., and A. Scott. "Weber, Durkheim and the Sociology of the Modern State." In *The Cambridge History of Twentieth-century Political Thought*, edited by T. Ball, and R. Bellamy, 368–391. Cambridge: Cambridge University Press, 2008.
Paris, Roland. "Ordering the World: Academic Research and Policymaking on Fragile States." *International Studies Review* 13 (2011): 58–71.

Rotberg, Robert. "The Failure and Collapse of Nation-states: Breakdown, Prevention, and Repair." In *When States Fail: Causes and Consequences*, edited by Robert Rotberg, 1–45. Princeton, NJ: Princeton University Press, 2004.
Schein, Edgar. *Organizational Culture and Leadership*, 4th ed. San Francisco, CA: Jossey-Bass, 2010.
Stepan, Alfred. *The State and Society: Peru in Comparative Perspective*. Princeton, NJ: Princeton University Press, 1978.
Weber, Max. "Politics as a Vocation." In *From Max Weber: Essays in Sociology*, edited by Hans Gerth, and C. Wright Mills, 77–128. New York: Oxford University Press, 1948.
Zaum, Dominik. *The Sovereignty Paradox: Norms and Politics of International Statebuilding*. Oxford: Oxford University Press, 2007.

The European Union's ambiguous concept of 'state fragility'

Sonja Grimm

Department of Politics and Public Administration, University of Konstanz, Konstanz, Germany

Although scholars and practitioners alike perceive 'state fragility' to be a key challenge for security and development, there are significant variations in the definition of this phenomenon. This article analyses the European Union's notion of 'state fragility'. Based on a document analysis covering the years 2001–12 and expert interviews conducted in November 2012, the article reveals that the EU has not (yet) decided on a clear-cut definition of 'state fragility'. Three factors explain this lack of decisiveness: the EU's complex institutional framework, which impedes policy coherence; developments at the international level that require the EU's compliance; and the organisation's diplomatic efforts to maintain cooperative relationships with aid-recipient countries that have been labelled 'fragile'. The result is conceptual ambiguity that potentially reduces the EU's capacity to respond to fragile situations.

Introduction

Especially since the events of 9/11 'state fragility' has been perceived by scholars and practitioners alike as a major threat to security and a problem for development.[1] Despite some convergences and overlaps, there are significant variations in how various donor governments and international agencies define 'state fragility' and in which countries they include in their lists of 'fragile' states.[2] Disparities in working definitions can be found even between different departments in the same government: security agencies typically emphasise the threat aspect, while development cooperation agencies focus on relationships or functions, and diplomats tend to avoid the concept altogether.[3] To increase conceptual clarity and to explore the notion of 'state fragility' found in one of the major global players in international affairs, this article investigates the EU's notion of 'state fragility' in detail, asking: how does the European Union define state fragility, and how can the development of the EU's concept of state fragility be explained?

The EU has been chosen for this study because of its financial and normative importance. The organisation controls substantial material resources and is among the largest donors of official development assistance (ODA). In 2010 the EU and its member states spent €53.5 billion on aid, corresponding to 0.44% of the member states' combined gross national income (GNI). In this way the EU collectively accounted for 58% of net ODA to developing countries and for 65% of the global €26 billion ODA increase from 2004 to 2010.[4] Its main executive body, the European Commission, influences the spending of roughly one-fifth of this aid, as it both coordinates the foreign aid spending of the member states and acts as an independent aid donor.[5] In addition to its financial power, the EU also pursues a strong normative agenda in its foreign affairs related to the promotion of democracy, human rights, good governance and the rule of law.[6] As an organisation it claims added value in the form of its capacity to implement best practices 'that build high international credibility in promoting human rights, pursuing democratisation, including electoral observation, and improving governance'.[7] Clearly, what the EU decides and how it behaves have an impact on both the donors who align their strategy to the EU's and on the recipient states that negotiate terms of cooperation with the EU.[8]

Given its financial and moral importance, it is astonishing that there have been no studies (with the exception of Hout's) in security, development or state-building research to explicitly address the Union's policy towards fragile states, nor any that examine the underlying 'state fragility' concept.[9] This contribution will close this gap. Going beyond Hout, the analysis focuses on elaborating the Union's notion of 'state fragility', seeking to explain its development. However, the article will not discuss the specific policy instruments employed by the EU to deal with fragile states, nor the effectiveness of EU policies in 'fragile' contexts.

The analysis is built upon an examination of the documents published by the EU bodies most directly concerned with fragile states, including the European Commission's Directorates-General Development and Cooperation – EuropeAid (DEVCO) and Humanitarian Aid (ECHO), the European Parliament, the Council of the European Union, the European Council and (since 2010) the European External Action Service (EEAS). The investigation covers the period from 2001 (when the international interest in state fragility spiked as a result of 9/11) to 2012. The document analysis is complemented by interviews conducted in Brussels in November 2012 with representatives of DEVCO, EEAS and several think-tanks active in the field of EU development cooperation.[10]

Based on these data, the article reveals that the EU has not (yet) decided upon a clear-cut definition of 'state fragility', despite substantial EU internal discussions on the topic. Three factors explain this lack: first, the EU's complex institutional framework, which impedes policy coherence; second, developments at the international level that require the EU's compliance; and, third, the EU's diplomatic efforts to maintain cooperative relationships with aid-recipient countries that have been labelled 'fragile'. The result is conceptual ambiguity that potentially reduces the EU's capacity to respond to fragile situations. To substantiate this argument, the next two sections introduce the complexities involved in defining 'state fragility' and describe the institutional framework of the EU. Subsequently the way the main EU bodies understand 'state fragility' is analysed and explained. The final section concludes.

Defining the concept, causes and consequences of state fragility

Since the emergence of the term, scholars and practitioners alike have struggled to reach a consensus on how 'state fragility' should be conceptualised (for details on this process, see Nay in this issue). To first define what is meant by a 'functioning state', scholars in the institutionalist tradition refer to the Weberian notion of a state as a hierarchical structure of authoritative decision making that enjoys external and internal sovereignty. Weber characterised the state as 'a human community that successfully claims the monopoly of the legitimate use of physical force within a given territory'.[11] In his view the continued existence of modern Western states is dependent on the constant progression of their bureaucratic foundations over time. Consequently, Weber saw administration and the provision of security as the benchmarks by which states can be judged (see Lemay-Hebert and Mathieu in this issue). From this perspective, security is the central criterion of state strength. Other criteria have been added by various authors to further refine the description of the state's capability to organise society. According to Fabra Mata and Ziaja, what most of these definitions have in common is that they include one or more central attributes of the state, such as: (1) effectiveness (how well state functions necessary for the security and well-being of citizens are performed); (2) authority (understood as the enforcement of a monopoly on the legitimate use of force); and (3) legitimacy (public, non-coercive acceptance of the state).[12] In a subsequent analytical step these criteria can be used to identify a state's malfunctions and to classify it on a continuum between the poles of 'consolidated' and 'failed', with 'fragile' falling somewhere in the middle (the thresholds for classification are subject to contention).[13]

Critical scholars have begun to challenge the analytical validity of the 'fragile state' concept as defined above, as well as the underlying state concept.[14] Hagmann and Hoehne, Nuruzzaman, and Nay suggest that using the Weberian notion of a state may imply transferring a basically 'Western' understanding of 'statehood' to parts of the world in which different understandings of how communities organise themselves prevail. Scholars argue that this conceptual vagueness does not help policy makers create efficient tools to overcome fragility;[15] in a worst-case scenario it might even allow powerful countries to deprive certain states of the privileges of sovereignty, opening the door to interventions by the West.[16]

Not only are the criteria for what constitutes a 'fragile state' disputed, so too are the causes of state fragility. Scholars disagree over whether state fragility is (1) the result of internal malfunctions;[17] (2) the result of the structure of the global political economy and fragile states' position in this economy;[18] or (3) the result of external interference and various transnational forces.[19] With respect to identifying the consequences of state fragility, scholars have primarily assumed its effects on development and security to be negative (although more research is needed to substantiate these claims). Where development is concerned, state fragility is considered to be at the core of many internal and regional development problems, such as the failure to reduce poverty, to achieve the UN Millennium Development Goals (see, for example, the self-description of the g7+, a recently founded group of states calling themselves 'fragile'[20]) or to comply with the goals of foreign aid donors. Where security is concerned, it is often claimed that fragile states are an ideal breeding ground for domestic and international terrorism, organised crime (eg human and drug trafficking), violent conflict and regional instability, emphasising the potential threats to a fragile state's neighbours and the wider global community.[21]

The EU, security, development and 'state fragility'

How might the EU be expected to define 'state fragility'?

Given that it is an organisation consisting of sovereign nation-states, one might expect that the EU, like many other governmental donors, would apply the Weberian concept of 'statehood' explored above to differentiate 'consolidated' states from 'fragile' states. Categories such as effectiveness, authority and legitimacy would thus somehow be reflected in EU documents describing the phenomenon. With regard to the causes of fragility, it is likely that the EU would subscribe to explanations that view state fragility as the result of the internal malfunctions of a state, as such an organisation would scarcely be likely to call into question its own contribution to the structure of the global political economy, nor would it blame itself for the negative impacts of its external interventions in sovereign states. Instead, a more diplomatic approach should be observable. With respect to the consequences of fragility, it is more difficult to develop a hypothesis about which approach the EU will follow. Recent research has revealed the emergence of a so-called 'security–development nexus', as well as a 'whole-of-government approach', in the Union's external relations. Especially since 9/11 the Union has sought to integrate development aspects into security policy and security aspects into development assistance, efforts that are likely to also influence the Union's notion of 'state fragility'.[22]

How can the development of the EU's concept of 'state fragility' be explained?

In order to explain EU policy making, it should be noted that 'the EU' is not a singular actor.[23] The European Council (representing heads of states and governments), the European Parliament (representing European citizens), the Council of the European Union (representing the ministerial bureaucracies of the member states) and the European Commission (the EU's executive branch) all generally participate in EU policy making.[24]

Depending on the topic, EU policy making may be driven by intergovernmental and/or supranational logics. Since its foundation the Union's foreign and security policies have been determined in an intergovernmental fashion, in which decisions are taken consensually by the member states.[25] The Union's development policy is a mix of intergovernmental approaches, whereby the EU coordinates the policies of its member states, and supranational approaches, in which the EU acts as an independent organisation (primarily through the Commission), taking the interests of the three main EU bodies (Commission, Council and Parliament) into account.[26] Following the Treaty of Lisbon, the creation of the office of High Representative of the Union for Foreign Affairs and Security Policy (a sort of 'foreign minister' for the EU), together with the EEAS (the EU's new diplomatic service), has added an additional layer of institutional complexity; these bodies are intended to coordinate and represent the Union's Common Foreign and Security Policy (including its external assistance instruments).[27] Complying with the demands to achieve policy coherence internally and to 'speak with one voice' externally would require supra-nationalising the EU's foreign and security policy (eg extending qualified majority voting on foreign and security policy issues). However, even after the Lisbon reforms, decisions on these issues have been taken consensually.[28] This means that basic decisions on war and peace are still taken unanimously by the member states via the Council), while the initiative for development policy lies with the Commission, and more recently also with the High Representative and the EEAS; national development policies exist in parallel.

This mixture of responsibilities and competences requires substantial efforts of coordination between EU bodies and with the member states, which should also influence the Union's notion of 'state fragility'. It is to be expected that the different EU bodies will be motivated by different policy goals. The positions of the Council are likely to be more security-oriented, whereas those taken by the Commission (DEVCO and ECHO) would be expected to be oriented towards development and humanitarian assistance; the positions of the Parliament would presumably reflect human rights and parliamentary independence.[29] According to Carbone, achieving policy coherence should be a fundamental concern, but will also represent a challenge for the EU, given its complex institutional framework.[30]

The EU's internal struggle to achieve coherence on 'state fragility'

For over a decade now, the main EU bodies have produced a significant corpus of texts that encompass both security and development facets of state fragility. In 2001 the European Commission set the tone for the general EU framework in the areas of conflict, security and fragility, while leaving room for divergent conceptualisations in the other main EU bodies. Without specifically referring to 'state fragility', the Commission observed that the situation of countries in 'structural crisis' receiving aid from ECHO 'can be aggravated by weak, emerging or disintegrating state institutions'.[31] In addition, in a 2003 Communication on governance, the Commission linked weak statehood to weak governance capacity, limited service delivery and the lack of commitment to good governance.[32] In contrast, in its 2003 Security Strategy, the European Council defined 'fragility' as a consequence of bad governance, civil conflict and the easy availability of small arms, all of which can weaken state and social structures. Domestic and external security problems were perceived as the major consequences of fragility.[33] 'State failure', the most extreme form of weak governance, was listed third (after terrorism and the proliferation of nuclear weapons) among the key threats to the Union.[34] At that time, the European Council was expressing ideas similar to those of the other two bodies, highlighting the lack of good governance as a key factor in underdevelopment and fragility.[35] However, it also placed emphasis on the circumstances of a country's citizens and the protection of citizens' rights – especially human, civil and gender rights – in fragile states (without offering a definition),[36] as well as the rights of people to decide independently and democratically how to overcome poverty and fragility.[37]

The differences between these main EU bodies apply not only to the specific concept of 'state fragility', but also to the EU development approach in general. As recently as December 2005, with the 'European Consensus on Development', the EU bodies outlined for the first time a shared vision intended to guide the Union's policies and activities in the field of development.[38] With regard to managing and overcoming state fragility, the Council, Commission and Parliament jointly declare in this document that:

> the EU will improve its response to difficult partnerships and fragile states, where a third of the world's poor live. The EU will strengthen its efforts in conflict prevention work and will support the prevention of state fragility through governance reforms, rule of law, anti-corruption measures and the building of viable state institutions in order to help them fulfil a range of basic functions and meet the needs of their citizens. The EU will work through state systems and strategies, where possible, to increase capacity in fragile states. The EU advocates remaining engaged, even in the most difficult situations, to prevent the emergence of failed states.[39]

The focus of this approach is clearly on top-down institution- and capacity building, as well as on crisis prevention. However, this statement should be considered in context. Among the common principles explored in Chapter 4 of the document, 'state fragility' ranks only fifth, after – in the EU's interpretation – more urgent problems such as 'ownership/partnership' (Chapter 4.1), 'in-depth political dialogue' (Chapter 4.2), 'participation of civil society' (Chapter 4.3) and 'gender equality' (Chapter 4.4). Furthermore, the Commission, Council and Parliament promise to develop an early warning system and to support democratic governance and institutional capacity building in fragile countries. The bodies also recognise the necessity of implementing the OECD's 'Principles for Good International Engagement in Fragile States and Situations'.[40] As a major policy goal – using the same wording proposed by the OECD – they seek 'to increase ownership and continue to build legitimate, effective and resilient state institutions and an active and organised civil society, in partnership with the country concerned'.[41] In line with the OECD principles, the 2007 document expresses the ambition to better coordinate and more flexibly use EU instruments, while indicating the need to harmonise the interventions of EU member states in fragile states.

Since the 2005 Consensus the EU bodies have placed special emphasis on the improvement of governance quality, institution- and capacity building in 'situations of fragility' or 'fragile states', as stated in several documents that express support for the Consensus.[42]

In 2006, the EU adopted a new approach to governance with a specific initiative implemented within the framework of the 10th European Development Fund (EDF) programming for the African, Caribbean and Pacific (ACP) group of states. This approach is based on dialogue and incentives, rather than on sanctions and conditionality. The Governance Action Plans (GAPS), including the commitments of ACP partners to improve governance, are linked to Country Strategy Papers. The GAPS constitute a guarantee of mutual commitment that forms the basis for ongoing political dialogue with partner countries on governance reforms.[43] Here, the EU bodies follow the contractual approach of the

World Bank's Poverty Reduction Strategy Papers, a similarly cooperative approach based on mutual agreement and partnership instead of threats and negative rewards.

In response to a peer-reviewed report of the OECD's Development Assistance Committee (DAC) in 2007, which criticised the Commission for not possessing a 'specific policy document to guide a Community approach to conflict and fragile states programming',[44] in October 2007 the Commission adopted its Communication 'Towards an EU Response to Situations of Fragility – Engaging in Difficult Environments for Sustainable Development, Stability and Peace'.[45] In this Communication, the Commission declares both 'the notion and the terminology' to be 'important to frame the debate on fragility'. However, it also demonstrates its awareness of the concerns of partner countries that 'tend to perceive the term "fragile states" as a "stigma" and, potentially, as a new form of conditionality, which may involve more or less formal "sanctions/suspension of cooperation"'.[46] Moreover, the Commission criticises the term 'fragile state' as 'donor-driven' rather than 'partnership-driven'.[47] To overcome this obstacle, the Commission proposes avoiding any reference to 'states' from the outset. Instead, and in line with OECD principles, it states a preference 'to focus on preventing and addressing effectively structural or contingent "situations" of fragility, which expose a country, a region within a country or even a particular community, to excessive strains and threats'.[48] The Communication asserts that the EU must remain engaged, even in the most difficult situations in which 'the social contract is broken' as a result of a 'state's incapacity or unwillingness to deal with its basic functions, obligations and responsibilities'.[49] The basic strategic approach outlined in the Communication does not propose any new instrument; rather, it encourages the EU bodies and the member states to take better advantage of the many policy frameworks and tools already at their disposal, and to ensure that these instruments are used in a 'holistic, coordinated, complementary and coherent manner'.[50]

The Commission's Communication was welcomed by the follow-up 'Conclusions of the Council' and a resolution by the European Parliament in the same year.[51] However, the promise of a coherent approach to overcoming situations of fragility was not realised: the 2007 Communication has never been given final approval by the Council, nor has an action plan been enacted.[52] The various EU bodies have pursued different preferences, a fact that became apparent in their first responses to the Commission's initiative. The Council of the European Union highlighted the problem of the lack of political legitimacy resulting from weak governance and limited service delivery.[53] Although it generally adheres to the World Bank's classification of 'fragile states',[54] the Parliament noted in its response that 'state fragility is more an empirical concept than a normative one' and that 'the responsibility for determining when states are no longer "fragile" should be that of their citizens'.[55] Thus, the Parliament has refused to agree to a precise definition of 'state fragility', instead leaving it to the citizens affected by fragility to describe the situations in which they live.

The Lisbon Treaty, which laid the groundwork for joint external action, entered into force on 1 December 2009, raising expectations with regard to the enhancement of EU policy coherence in external affairs. The EEAS was created and included a specific division for Conflict Prevention, Peacebuilding, and

Mediation Instruments. At the same time, DEVCO established a Unit for Fragility and Crisis Management.[56] This institutional strengthening on the topic can be seen as a new push for increased awareness within the EU of fragility issues and for further efforts to improve coherence in development policy. However, whether this will eventually include a new conceptualisation and a more refined understanding of 'state fragility' remains to be seen.

At the time of writing, the EU bodies are about to negotiate the new aid budget for the period 2014–20, additionally clarifying the division of competences among the bodies involved.[57] In its draft proposal for a new Development Cooperation Instrument (DCI), the Commission highlights the need to focus on the '[strengthening of] the rule of law and governance' in 'crises, post-crisis and fragility situations', a topic that was somewhat neglected in the programming of the previous DCI.[58] The Commission seeks to ensure 'flexible mechanisms to facilitate a more effective EU response to rapidly evolving situations in crisis, post-crisis and fragile states'.[59] In this way the Commission is also motivated by developments at the international level, especially the International Dialogue on Peace- and Statebuilding established in 2008.[60] This International Dialogue seeks to 'bring together countries affected by conflict and fragility and their international partners to identify, agree and realise more effective ways of supporting transitions out of fragility and building peaceful states'.[61] In response to these processes, in 2011, the Council adopted an 'Operational Framework on Aid Effectiveness', reaffirming the agreements under the Paris Declaration, and the EU Guidelines for the Accra Agenda for Action (2008), again highlighting the need for more effective aid spending and better coordination among EU bodies and Member States.[62]

Analysing and explaining the EU's concept of state fragility

How does the EU define 'state fragility'?

In the documents presented and analysed above tentative descriptions rather than clear-cut definitions of 'state fragility' are found. Except in the 2007 Commission Communication no in-depth discussion of the concept of 'fragility' or 'fragile state' is provided. However, it can be determined that all EU bodies more or less explicitly adhere to the Weberian notion of 'statehood', understanding 'state fragility' as the result of internal malfunctions (such as governance deficits and limited service delivery) that call into question the authority and legitimacy of the state. But in further descriptions of the phenomenon, the causes and consequences of 'state fragility' are often intermixed: following DEVCO's lead, the Commission frequently highlights development issues and emphasises the lack of good governance and service delivery as obstacles to sustainable development. The Council focuses on the security concerns resulting from state failure, where such failure triggers regional instability or threatens international and EU security. The Parliament instead emphasises citizens' perceptions as a marker for 'state fragility' and the need for state building, while the EEAS places emphasis on crisis prevention and mediation.

The question of how and where to identify fragility remains unanswered. In contrast to other aid donors (such as the World Bank, USAID and the OECD),[63] the EU still does not employ an assessment or measurement tool to clearly identify and rank cases of fragility. It relies instead upon publically available fragility and development indices, such as those published by the United Nations, the World Bank and the OECD – even though, as a DEVCO official indicates, the organisation is aware of the deficiencies in these databases, as 'all indices are flawed in many ways' (interviewee 2). Other than blatantly obvious cases of state failure in Somalia, Sudan and South Sudan, and Afghanistan, the EU bodies do not name countries that might qualify as 'weak' or 'fragile' in official documents, nor does any of the EU bodies publish a list of such countries.[64] Research on the EU for this paper confirms what Cahill stated in 2007: 'Labeling a state as "weak" or "failed" can be a politically sensitive subject so most governments keep this list private in order to not offend potential partners'.[65] All interviewees highlighted how the EU took care to avoid stigmatising potential partners as 'weak' or 'fragile' in its attempt to enhance equal partnerships 'at eye level'.[66] However, they also indicated that the EU sets clear country priorities internally.[67] In the interviews, the state disintegration of Sudan and South Sudan and the conflict-ridden situation in the Central African Republic (CAR) were mentioned several times as important cases of fragility that deserved EU attention.

In summary, despite its obvious interest in circumventing the use of the term 'fragility' in order to avoid offending potential partners, the EU cannot completely avoid describing situations in which it is not satisfied with the quality of governance, the capacity to deliver services or with regional or international security. In fact, in the words of a DEVCO official, the term 'state fragility' is 'a euphemism for "poor performer"'.[68] However this phenomenon may be labelled, there remains a need to identify poor performance in governance and security issues in order to facilitate the development of 'context-sensitive approaches' to resolve these problems.[69] The newest draft regulations for the 2014–20 budget seem to heed this observation and seek greater flexibility. However, the concept of 'fragility' has become even more vague: under the proposal any type of domestic crisis would be subsumed under a new category for states in 'crisis, post-crisis and fragile situation',[70] regardless of the conflict's root causes or the current political, social and economic status of the country.

How can the lack of a clear concept of 'state fragility' be explained?

As elaborated above, EU policy making on 'state fragility' suffers – like all EU foreign and security policies – from the idiosyncrasies of the EU's internal decision making and the challenging process of continuous institutional reform. The failure to adopt the 2007 Commission Communication on state fragility is a striking example of the competing logics of supranational (led by the Commission for development issues) and intergovernmental (led by the Council for security issues) policy making. The outcome of this clash of logics depends heavily on the internal coordination processes that attempt to reach a consensus between the various EU bodies and the member states, here with regard to a commonly shared understanding of 'fragility' and the adequate responses to it.

Additionally, the EU's conception and treatment of fragility are affected by events and developments at the international level, including the post-9/11 discourse on security and the war on terror, the Millennium Development Goals and the International Dialogue on Peace- and Statebuilding. As a major aid donor the EU would like to influence the development of globally shared policy-positions concerning fragile states, even though it often struggles to catch up with and align itself to the process because of the lack of policy coherence analysed above. None of the EU documents responding to international high-level meetings on aid (and aid effectiveness) or the International Dialogue on Peace- and Statebuilding offers anything new or innovative, nor do any display the 'added value' of the EU as an independent aid donor with special expertise in the fields of governance, democracy and human rights. Instead of taking advantage of its financial and moral power in an outward-directed communication, the documents read more like internal communications to EU bodies and member states, a vivid reminder of the EU's need for coordination to enable it more powerfully to influence agenda setting and the formulation and implementation of aid policies. This observation was clearly confirmed by all interviewees.

However, this is not yet the full story. Although it has often been criticised for its technocratic approach, the EU attempts to respect country-specific developments, giving consideration to the concerns and needs of aid-recipient countries. In four cases (Afghanistan, Sudan and South Sudan, the Democratic Republic of the Congo (DRC) and the CAR[71]), an inspection of EU country assessment and strategy papers, reports, Council resolutions and joint resolutions of the Commission, the Council and the Parliament reveals a very tentative and diplomatic assessment of the situation, generally circumventing the labels of 'fragility' or 'failure'. The documents indicate that the Union's approach to these country partners is characterised by an effort to harmonise a variety of competing objectives: first, the objective to mainstream the EU's external relations in order to develop more generally applicable approaches towards partners in different regions of the world; second, the attempt to increase flexibility towards 'states in fragile, crisis and post-crisis, including conflict affected, situations'[72] by using a country-sensitive approach; third, the desire to avoid offending potential partners by labelling them 'fragile'.

In the selected documents, all EU bodies demonstrate a preference for language describing 'threats' to human security or 'challenges' for development over 'state fragility' and 'state failure'. When used, the terms 'fragile' or 'weak' qualify only a limited governance capacity at the national level or in specific parts of the country.[73] At times the terms are used to characterise specific temporal situations of 'weakness', such as a situation involving a 'fragile economy', 'fragile security' or 'regional instability'.[74] When the terms appear in the documents, the EU immediately emphasises that the situations are not permanent; rather, they can be improved through a cooperative approach supporting the incumbent government. As a partner in the contract, the incumbent government should 'own' the process.[75] In fact, the documents generally employ neutral language in describing poor-performing countries with a history of conflict.

Conclusions

The analysis presented here of the official publications, documents, conclusions, communications and strategy papers of EU bodies, as well as the interviews conducted with EU officials and experts, allow three conclusions concerning the Union's notion of 'state fragility'. First, EU bodies still have trouble agreeing on a definition of the phenomenon, even though the problem of 'state fragility' was identified in 2003 as a major challenge for EU security. The 2007 Communication by the Commission was the first document to explicitly conceptualise the EU's specific understanding of 'state fragility', revealing the Union's awareness of the needs and concerns of partner countries. However, this Communication has never been adopted, depriving the Union's notion of 'state fragility' of conceptual clarity. Second, the internal lack of coherence between EU bodies and between the EU and its member states, as well as the ongoing process of institutional reform, make it difficult for the EU to define a consistent position on state fragility; however, developments in the international aid community also require EU policy adoption – a challenging prospect, given that external coherence is unlikely to be achieved without internal coherence. Third, EU external communications are motivated by a desire to respect the integrity of their country partners; specifically they seek to avoid stigmatising them as 'fragile'. Whether this is a wise strategy is a matter of debate. No government would want to be devalued by such a label; however, without clearly stating the problems, it is impossible to develop meaningful and sustainable country-sensitive strategies to overcome deficits in governance, socioeconomic development and security.

If the EU is serious in its belief that that a lack of governance capacity is a key factor underlying 'fragility', it cannot continue to uphold its preference for top-down contractual approaches to state building, since the executive bodies that are accused of shortcomings are also the partners in the state-building contracts. These malfunctioning bodies are unlikely to be able to overcome the 'situations of fragility' that emerge as a result of governance and capacity deficits. No solution to this dilemma has yet been proposed.

A great deal remains to be done. In particular, the EU should take advantage of the knowledge available from both internal and external sources. It needs to more precisely define the term 'fragility' in order to better assess the root causes of the phenomenon, define the goals of support and set achievable benchmarks for partner countries, while maintaining its goals regarding flexibility. Furthermore, it should clarify the added value resulting from EU development cooperation. These steps could enable the EU to translate its financial power into political influence, allowing it to assume a role as a leading donor in fragile contexts.

Acknowledgements

I am very grateful to all the interview partners from EU bodies and think-tanks who were kind enough to share their insights with me. Furthermore, I wish to thank my colleagues who have contributed to this special issue, as their support during the preparation of this manuscript has been extremely helpful. The comments of two anonymous reviewers on an earlier draft of this text included very constructive suggestions that improved the contribution considerably. Special thanks go to Julia Leininger, who introduced me to the EU development landscape. Last but not least, I thank Juliane Erler, Teresa Christine Hagedorn and Katarina Lavric for their research assistance and Claire Bacher for her careful proofreading. Financial support by the Young Scholar Fund of the University of Konstanz is gratefully acknowledged. All remaining errors are mine alone.

Notes on Contributor

Sonja Grimm is Senior Lecturer in the Department of Politics and Public Administration, University of Konstanz. She has published various studies on the transition to democracy in post-conflict societies and on international democracy promotion and has previously co-edited special issues of *Democratization* on "War and Democratization: Legality, Legitimacy, and Effectiveness" (15, no. 3 (2008) with Wolfgang Merkel) and "Do all Good Things go Together? Conflicting Objectives in Democracy Promotion" (19, no. 3 (2012) with Julia Leininger and Tina Freyburg). More about her can be found at www.sonja-grimm.eu.

Notes

1. Stern and Öjendal, "Mapping the Security–Development Nexus"; and Chandler, "The Security–Development Nexus."
2. Fabra Mata and Ziaja, *User's Guide*; and Ziaja, "What do Fragility Indices Measure?"
3. Engberg-Pedersen et al., "Fragile Situations," 23.
4. European Commission, "Annual Report 2012," 25.
5. Grimm, "Zur Wirksamkeit Europäischer Entwicklungspolitik," 382.
6. Amichai et al., eds, *Promoting Democracy*; Kotzian et al., "Instruments"; and Manners, "Normative Power Europe Reconsidered."
7. European Commission, "Increasing the Impact of EU Development Policy," 4.
8. See also the European Union's self-description. Accessed August 1, 2013. http://ec.europa.eu/europeaid/how/ensure-aid-effectiveness/busan_en.htm.
9. Hout, "Between Development and Security."
10. The aim of the interviews was to obtain knowledge about how EU officials define and use the term 'state fragility'. The relative openness of the interviews allowed the identification of the priorities set by EU officials, as well as revealing the concerns EU officials had regarding EU policy making towards fragile states. All interviewees were guaranteed anonymity. Information stemming from these interviews is cited by numbering the interviewees according to the chronological order of their interviews.
11. Weber, "Politics as a Vocation," 78.
12. Fabra Mata and Ziaja, *User's Guide*, 6.
13. François and Sud, "Promoting Stability," 143.
14. Call, "Beyond the 'Failed State'"; Putzel, "Why Development Actors Need a Better Definition"; Hagmann and Hoehne, "Failures of the State Failure Debate"; and Niemann, "War Making and State Making."
15. Hagmann and Hoehne, "Failures of the State Failure Debate," 45; Nuruzzaman, "Revisiting the Category of Fragile and Failed States"; and Nay, "Fragile and Failed States."
16. Chandler, *Empire in Denial*, 64; and Boas and Jennings, "Failed States and State Failure," 475–485.
17. Rotberg, *When States Fail*; Cahill, "Donor Engagement in Fragile States"; and Fabra Mata and Ziaja, *User's Guide.*
18. Engberg-Pedersen et al., "Fragile Situations," 11; and Clapham, "The Challenge to the State."
19. Hagmann and Hoehne, "Failures of the State Failure Debate," 45; and Nuruzzaman, "Revisiting the Category of Fragile and Failed States."
20. g7+ Secretariat, "Introducing the g7+."
21. Iqbal and Starr, "Bad Neighbours"; and Patrick, "Weak States and Global Threats."
22. Youngs, "Fusing Security and Development"; Bagoyoko and Gibert, "The Linkage between Security, Government and Development"; and Zwolski, "The EU and a Holistic Security Approach."
23. For an overview, see Risse-Kappen, "Exploring the Nature of the Beast."
24. For further details, see Hix and Høyland, *The Political System of the European Union*; and Carbone, "Mission Impossible."
25. Risse, "Identity Matters," 89.
26. Grimm, "Zur Wirksamkeit Europäischer Entwicklungspolitik," 382. It should also be noted that development cooperation is just one foreign policy field among many, and it is generally regarded as less important than trade, agriculture and security policy. See Grimm and Leininger, "Not All Good Things Go Together."
27. Zwolski, "The EU and a Holistic Security Approach."
28. The Lisbon Treaty on European Union offers the option of 'permanent structured co-operation' (Article 42(6)), allowing nine or more member states to press ahead on an EU project.
29. Bagoyoko and Gibert, "The Linkage between Security, Government and Development," 791–794.
30. Carbone, "Mission Impossible."
31. European Commission, "Communication from the Commission on Conflict Prevention," 8.
32. European Commission, "Governance and Development," para. 72.
33. Council of the European Union, *A Secure Europe in a Better World*, 6.

34. Ibid., 4.
35. European Parliament, "Resolution as of 17 November 2005," paras 8–9.
36. Ibid., paras 9, 11.
37. Ibid., para. 28.
38. European Commission, "Room Document," 1; Council of the European Union et al., "The European Consensus on Development"; Council of the European Union, "Governance on the European Consensus for Development"; and European Parliament, "Resolution as of 17 November 2005."
39. Council of the European Union et al., "The European Consensus on Development," para. 20.
40. The OECD 'Principles for Good International Engagement in Fragile States and Situations' were originally drafted in January 2005. They were finally endorsed at an OECD-DAC high-level meeting in 2007. Council of the European Union et al., "The European Consensus on Development," para. 89.
41. Ibid., para. 90; and OECD, *Principles for Good International Engagement.*
42. For example, Council of the European Union, "Governance on the European Consensus for Development," para. 21.
43. European Commission, "Room Document," 4.
44. OECD-DAC, "European Union," 66.
45. European Commission, "Towards an EU Response to Situations of Fragility."
46. European Commission, "EU Response to Situations of Fragility in Developing Countries," 3.
47. Ibid.
48. Ibid.
49. European Commission, "Room Document," 2–3.
50. Ibid.
51. Council of the European Union, "Security and Development"; and European Parliament, "Resolution of 15 November."
52. Interviewee 2; and European Commission, "Increasing the Impact of EU Development Policy," 6.
53. European Commission, "Towards an EU Response to Situations of Fragility," 8.
54. European Parliament, "Resolution of 15 November 2007," para. A.
55. Ibid., para. B.
56. Interviewees 3 and 4.
57. This process is being guided by European Commission and High Representative for Foreign Affairs and Security, "Global Europe", and by several draft proposals provided by the Commission for the reorganisation of development financing instruments: "Preparation of the Multiannual Financial Framework"; "Proposal for a 'Regulation of the European Parliament'" (PREP), Com(2011) 840 Final; PREP, Com(2011) 842 Final; and PREP, Com(2011) 845 Final.
58. European Commission, PREP, Com(2011) 840 Final, 4.
59. Ibid., 5.
60. OECD, "International Dialogue on Peacebuilding and Statebuilding," 1.
61. Ibid.
62. Council of the European Union, "Operational Framework on Aid Effectiveness"; OECD, *Paris Declaration on Aid Effectiveness*; and European Commission, "Preparation of the Multiannual Financial Framework," 7.
63. For an overview, see Ziaja, "What do Fragility Indices Measure?"; and Nay, and Lemay-Hébert and Mathieu in this issue.
64. Interviewees 2, 3 and 4.
65. Cahill, "Donor Engagement in Fragile States," 10.
66. Interviewees 2 and 3.
67. Interviewees 2, 3 and 4.
68. Interviewee 2.
69. Interviewee 2. Similar opinions were expressed by interviewees 3 and 4.
70. European Commission, PREP, Com(2011) 840 Final, art. 12.
71. Afghanistan, Sudan and South Sudan, and the DRC are singled out, because they appear on most donor lists as obvious cases of fragility. Thus, as a donor, the EU would be unable to avoid being confronted by the causes and consequences of 'state fragility' or even state failure. The CAR is included because all interviewees indicated the EU's special interest in this country.
72. European Commission and High Representative for Foreign Affairs and Security Policy, "Global Europe," 8.
73. Council of the European Union, "Council Conclusions on Sudan and South Sudan," 3; and European Commission, *Country Strategy Paper*, 33.
74. Republic of Sudan and European Community, *Strategy Paper*, 9; Républic Centrafricaine and Communauté européenne, *Stratégie de Coopération*, 6, 8; and European Commission, *Country Strategy Paper*, 7. In the 2008–13 programme the CAR is described as a 'fragile post-conflict country close to implosion due to its decades long structural crisis'. Républic Centrafricaine and Communauté européenne, *Document de Stratégie*, 8. The integrative strategy is described as a response for a country 'in the category "fragile"'. Ibid., 30.
75. See, for example, Républic Centrafricaine and Communauté européenne, *Document de Stratégie*, 30.

Bibliography

Amichai, Magen, Thomas Risse, and Michael A. McFaul, eds. *Promoting Democracy and the Rule of Law*. Basingstoke: Macmillan, 2009.

Bagoyoko, Niagale, and Marie V. Gibert. "The Linkage between Security, Governance and Development: The European Union in Africa." *Journal of Development Studies* 45, no. 5 (2009): 789–814.

Boas, Morten, and Kathleen M. Jennings. "Failed States and State Failure: Threats or Opportunities?" *Globalizations* 4, no. 4 (2007): 475–485.

Cahill, Devin M. "Donor Engagement in Fragile States: A Case Study of Donors in the Democratic Republic of Congo and the OECD Principles for Good International Engagement in Fragile States." In *IPIS/Fatal Transactions Background Paper*, edited by Didier Verbruggen and Jan Cappelle. Antwerp: IPIS/Fatal Transactions International Secretariat, 2007.

Call, Charles T. "Beyond the 'Failed State': Toward Conceptual Alternatives." *European Journal of International Relations* 17, no. 2 (2011): 303–326.

Carbone, Maurizio. "Mission Impossible: The European Union and Policy Coherence for Development." *Journal of European Integration* 30, no. 3 (2008): 323–342.

Chandler, David. *Empire in Denial: The Politics of State-Building*. London: Pluto Press, 2006.

Chandler, David. "The Security-Development Nexus and the Rise of 'Anti-Foreign Policy'." *Journal of International Relations and Development* 10, no. 4 (2007): 362–386.

Clapham, Christopher. "The Challenge to the State in a Globalized World." *Development and Change* 33, no. 5 (2002): 775–795.

Council of the European Union. "Council Conclusions on Sudan and South Sudan." 3142th Foreign Affairs Council Meeting. Brussels, 23 January 2012.

Council of the European Union. "Governance on the European Consensus for Development: Towards a Harmonised Approach within the European Union." 14024/06. Luxembourg, 16 October 2006.

Council of the European Union. "Operational Framework on Aid Effectiveness." 18239/10. Brussels, 11 January 2011.

Council of the European European Union. *A Secure Europe in a Better World: European Security Strategy*. Brussels: Council of the European Union, 2003.

Council of the European Union. "Security and Development." Conclusions of the Council and the Representatives of the Governments of the Member States Meeting within the Council. 15097/07. Brussels, 19 November 2007.

Council of the European Union, European Parliament, and European Commission. "The European Consensus on Development." 14820/05. Brussels, 24 February 2006.

Engberg-Pedersen, Lars, Louise Andersen, Finn Stepputat, and Dietrich Jung. "Fragile Situations: Background Papers." *DIIS Report 2008/11*. Copenhagen: Danish Institute for International Studies, 2008.

European Commission. "Annual Report 2012 on the European Union's Development and External Assistance Policies and their Implementation in 2011." Staff working document, SWD(2012) 242 Final. Brussels, 6 August 2012.

European Commission. "Communication from the Commission on Conflict Prevention." Com(2001) 211 Final. Brussels, 11 April 2001.

European Commission. *Country Strategy Paper Islamic Republic of Afghanistan 2007–2013*. Brussels: European Comission, 2007.

European Commission. "EU Response to Situations of Fragility in Developing Countries: Engaging in Difficult Environments for Long-term Development." Report of the External Debate. Issues Paper. European Comission/Directorate-General Development and Relations with African, Caribbean, and Pacific States. Brussels, 2007.

European Commission. "Governance and Development." Communication from the Commission to the Council, the European Parliament and the European Economic and Social Committee. Com(2003) 615 Final. Brussels, 20 October 2003.

European Commission. "Increasing the Impact of EU Development Policy: An Agenda for Change." Communication from the Commission to the European Parliament, the Council, the European Economic and Social Committee and the Committee of the Regions. Com(2011) 637 Final. Brussels, 13 October 2011.

European Commission. "Preparation of the Multiannual Financial Framework Regarding the Financing of EU Cooperation for African, Caribbean and Pacific States and Overseas Countries and Territories for the 2014–2020 Period (11th European Development Fund)." Communication from the Commission to the European Parliament and the Council. Com(2011) 837 Final. Brussels, 7 December 2011.

European Commission. "Proposal for a 'Regulation of the European Parliament and of the Council Establishing Common Rules and Procedures for the Implementation of the Union's Instruments for External Action'." Com(2011) 842 Final. Brussels, 7 December 2011.

European Commission. "Proposal for a 'Regulation of the European Parliament and of the Council Establishing a Financing Instrument for Development Cooperation'." Com(2011) 840 Final. Brussels, 7 December 2011.

European Commission. "Proposal for a 'Regulation of the European Parliament and of the Council Establishing an Instrument for Stability'." Com(2011) 845 Final. Brussels, 7 December 2011.

European Commission. "'Room Document': Synthesis of the Main Policy Work on Fragility Currently Ongoing at EU Level." Brussels, 2009.

European Commission. "Towards an EU Response to Situations of Fragility: Engaging in Difficult Environments for Sustainable Development, Stability and Peace." Communication from the Commission to the Council, the European Parliament, the European Economic and Social Committee and the Committee of the Regions. Com(2007) 643 Final. Brussels, 25 October 2007.

European Commission, and High Representative for Foreign Affairs and Security Policy. "Global Europe : A New Approach to Financing EU External Action." Joint Communication to the European Parliament and the Council. Com(2011) 865 Final. Brussels, 7 December 2011.

European Parliament. "Resolution as of 17 November 2005 on the Proposal for a Joint Declaration by the Council, the European Parliament and the Commission on the European Union Development Policy 'the European Consensus'." Strasbourg, 2005.

European Parliament. "Resolution of 15 November 2007 on the EU Response to Situations of Fragility in Developing Countries." Strasbourg, 2007.

Fabra Mata, Javier, Sebastian Ziaja. *User's Guide on Measuring Fragility*. Bonn/Oslo: German Development Institute/United Nations Development Programme, 2009.

François, Monika, and Inder Sud. "Promoting Stability and Development in Fragile and Failed States." *Development Policy Review* 24, no. 2 (2006): 141–160.

g7+ Secretariat. "Introducing the g7+: Goodbye Conflict, Welcome Development." Dilli: g7+ Secretariat at Ministry of Finance, Timor-Leste, 2013.

Grimm, Sonja, and Julia Leininger. "Not All Good Things Go Together: Conflicting Objectives in Democracy Promotion." *Democratization* 19, no. 3 (2012): 391–414.

Grimm, Sven. "Zur Wirksamkeit Europäischer Entwicklungspolitik." In *Wirksamere Entwicklungspolitik: Befunde, Reformen, Instrumente*, edited by Jörg Faust, and Susanne Neubert, 381–402. Baden-Baden: Nomos, 2010.

Hagmann, Tobias, and Markus V. Hoehne. "Failures of the State Failure Debate: Evidence from the Somali Territories." *Journal of International Development* 21, no. 1 (2009): 42–57.

Hix, Simon, and Bjørn Høyland. *The Political System of the European Union*. Basingstoke: Palgrave Macmillan, 2011.

Hout, Wil. "Between Development and Security: The European Union, Governance and Fragile States." *Third World Quarterly* 31, no. 1 (2010): 141–157.

Iqbal, Zaryab, and Harvey Starr. "Bad Neighbours: Failed States and their Consequences." *Conflict Management and Peace Science* 25, no. 4 (2008): 315–331.

Kotzian, Peter, Michèle Knodt, and Sigita Urdze. "Instruments of the EU's External Democracy Promotion." *Journal of Common Market Studies* 49, no. 5 (2011): 99–118.

Manners, Ian. "Normative Power Europe Reconsidered: Beyond the Crossroads." *Journal of European Public Policy* 13, no. 2 (2006): 182–199.

Nay, Olivier. "Fragile and Failed States: Critical Perspectives on Conceptual Hybrids." *International Political Science Review* 34, no. 3 (2013): 326–341.

Niemann, Michael. "War Making and State Making in Central Africa." *Africa Today* 53, no. 3 (2007): 21–39.

Nuruzzaman, Mohammed. "Revisiting the Category of Fragile and Failed States in International Relations." *International Studies* 46, no. 3 (2009): 271–294.

OECD-DAC. "European Union: Development Assistance Committee Peer-Review." Paris, 2007.

OECD. "International Dialogue on Peacebuilding and Statebuilding." Factsheet. Paris, 2012.

OECD. *Paris Declaration on Aid Effectiveness*. Final Declaration of the High Level Forum on Aid Effectiveness, Paris: OECD, 2005.

OECD. *Principles for Good International Engagement in Fragile States and Situations*. Paris: Organisation for Economic Co-operation and Development, 2007.

Patrick, Stewart. "Weak States and Global Threats: Fact or Fiction?" *Washington Quaterly* 29, no. 2 (2006): 27–53.

Putzel, James. "Why Development Actors Need a Better Definition of 'State Fragility'." In *Policy Directions*. London: Crisis States Research Centre/London School of Economics, 2010.

Républic Centrafricaine and Communauté européenne. *Document de Stratégie Pays et Programme Indicatif National 2008–2013*. Brussels: European Commission, 2007.

Républic Centrafricaine and Communauté européenne. *Stratégie de Coopération et Programme Indicatif 2002–2007*. Brussels: European Commission, 2003.

Republic of Sudan and European Community. *Strategy Paper and National Indicative Strategy for the Period 2005–2007*. Brussels: European Commission/Directorate-General Development, 2005.

Risse-Kappen, Thomas. "Exploring the Nature of the Beast: International Relations Theory and Comparative Policy Analysis Meet the European Union." *Journal of Common Market Studies* 34, no. 1 (1996): 53–80.

Risse, Thomas. "Identity Matters: Exploring the Ambivalence of EU Foreign Policy." *Global Policy* 3, no. Supplement 1 (2012): 87–95.

Rotberg, Robert I., ed. *When States Fail: Causes and Consequences*. Princeton, NJ: Princeton University Press, 2004.

Stern, Maria, and Joakim Öjendal. "Mapping the Security-Development Nexus: Conflict, Complexity, Cacophony, Convergence?" *Security Dialogue* 41, no. 1 (2010): 5–29.

Weber, Max. "Politics as a Vocation." In *Max Weber: Essays in Sociology*, edited by Hans Gerth, and C. Wright Mills, 77–128. New York: Oxford University Press, 1948.

Youngs, Richard. "Fusing Security and Development: Just Another Euro-platitude?" *Journal of European Integration* 30, no. 3 (2008): 419–437.

Ziaja, Sebastian. "What Do Fragility Indices Measure? Assessing Measurement Procedures and Statistical Proximity." *Zeitschrift für Vergleichende Politikwissenschaft* 6, no. 1 (2012): 39–64.

Zwolski, Kamil. "The EU and a Holistic Security Approach after Lisbon: Competing Norms and the Power of the Dominant Discourse." *Journal of European Public Policy* 19, no. 7 (2012): 988–1005.

Measuring and managing 'state fragility': the production of statistics by the World Bank, Timor-Leste and the g7+

Isabel Rocha De Siqueira

Department of War Studies, King's College London, UK

Indicators are currently being widely used in international policy making to substantiate analyses and justify decisions on the basis of their alleged scientific objectivity. This article analyses the role of indicators and statistics in the labelling and managing of 'fragile states', examining the powerful consequences of these classifications but also discussing the untraceable nature of numbers and the difficulties in attributing ownership of numerical claims and assigning responsibility for their many unforeseen impacts. Focusing on the education sector in Timor-Leste and on the World Bank's Country Policy and Institutional Assessment (CPIA) programme, the article shows how accountability and ownership are negotiated within the context of the g7+ group of self-labelled 'fragile states', encouraging an examination of the power relations involved.

Indicators and the power of numbers

One of the first statistical analyses to focus on 'fragile states' was compiled by the CIA-sponsored State Failure Task Force, established in 1994 and later hosted by the Center for Global Policy at George Mason University.[1] Since then the work of quantifying and categorising 'state fragility' has only intensified. Many social, economic and institutional aspects of 'fragile states' are now being constantly measured and monitored by agencies seeking to identify the roots of 'fragility' and improve the delivery of public goods. Over the past two decades these practices have often culminated in indices of 'fragile states', such as the 'Failed States Index', the *Index of State Weakness in the Developing World* and the *State Fragility Index*.[2] The perceived inaccuracies and political problems inherent in these statistics do not halt this quest for classification, as might have been expected, but actually encourage ongoing work aimed at improvement and refinement.[3]

Various names have been applied to this recent widespread focus on the measurement and management of 'fragile states'; 'regulatory biopolitics' and 'governance by indicators' are among the proposed concepts that have attempted to describe the growth of technologies linked to the indirect measurement of national performance.[4] Both terms suggest that the process of classification has gone through powerful technological revolutions. Today we have the technical tools to perform complex data assessments and compilations that were previously unimaginable, and the tantalising prospect of simplifying social phenomena has resulted in a growing tendency to measure everything, from epidemics to conflict probabilities. However, the indicators and indices of 'state fragility' are more than instruments used to control, contain and mould; rather, they have power in themselves, as they are reproduced and applied in ways not originally envisaged, with consequences that are often different or more powerful than anticipated.[5] Indices of 'state fragility' have direct influence over the allocation of resources for many aid organisations; in addition, the data reproduced in rankings are used by citizens to hold their governments accountable, and the statistics collected for the indices are also influential in governmental policy making. As these numbers are reproduced and reworked, they 'hold':[6] they become a bureaucratic routine as much as a reality. As rankings classify states according to 'degrees of fragility', a multiple 'ontological slippage' shifts the focus to the adjectivation rather than the reality of 'state fragility' itself [7] – indicating the power of social and practical taxonomies Bourdieu describes.[8] Thus assumed and naturalised, this qualified and quantified existence becomes 'real in its consequences'.[9] 'Fragile states' thereby become a reality of international politics without ceasing to be a scientific, social and political construction.[10]

Even though they have been criticised, these numbers have become entrenched in everyday policy making. Despite the high costs incurred by data acquisition and the necessary mastery of analysis techniques, statistical and technical knowledge reinforce their importance by 'adding layers or tiers of quantified evaluation' to the social and political analysis of 'state fragility'.[11] As Latour claims with regard to scientific facts, 'state fragility' classifications are 'many well-equipped men's words' tightly wrapped together by means of an enormous number of human and technical associations.[12] So much has been done with these schemes that any opposition has become impractical and too costly. It takes time for staff and equipment to assimilate new software and for knowledge to be acquired, and investments have to offer a return. Moreover, when a system has finally become practically usable, comfort and predictability dictate the options. Indicators can become powerful by the subtle imposition inherent in this cost: at the end of the day a 'material culture of [numerical] bureaucracy' is so ingrained in our understanding of the world that writing down numbers and making them official is but a secondary step in an already established mode of thinking.[13]

This article is indebted to other sociological works in IR that have examined the implications and construction of taken-for-granted political tools and practices.[14] It explores questions on why numbers on 'state fragility' hold[15] – despite criticism and the immense expert knowledge required to compile and interpret them – and what their consequences may be. In addressing this question, I take as the object of my study the statistics produced in the education sector in Timor-Leste by international agencies and by the national government. The article analyses how these statistics influence and are influenced by the numbers generated for the World Bank's Country Policy and Institutional Assessment (CPIA) exercise, illustrating the difficulties in attributing ownership of numbers and accountability for their implications.[16] These difficulties are considered in an examination of the g7+'s newly established Fragility Assessments, in view of the changes in accountability and ownership they may represent.[17] If numbers can have important implications in international politics but are generally untraceable, what do the statistics produced by 'fragile states' themselves represent in terms of the accountability and ownership of these processes? My purpose in analysing the numbers on 'state fragility' is not to identify miscalculations, as this has been extensively done elsewhere.[18] The focus here is on understanding whether and how the g7+ represents a departure from current practices of categorising 'state fragility'.

The findings suggest accountability and ownership processes are being shifted, perhaps not as radically as some scholars might hope,[19] but in significant ways. The changes are not truly radical primarily because the 'fragile' label is not being abandoned, refined or subdivided, as some researchers advocate, but instead is being used for self-classification. Second, numbers on fragility remain powerfully consequential but also highly untraceable, rendering author-attribution a fruitless exercise, as I will argue. Nonetheless, the observed changes in accountability and ownership are important: donors are increasingly held accountable and are expected to become experts in the development solutions they advance – a change that critics of interventions in 'fragile states' have long championed. These findings indicate that the classification of 'fragile states' is a more complex practice than a simplistic 'Western versus Fragile States' view may suggest.

The next section analyses some of the important implications of fragility rankings using the example of the World Bank's CPIA.[20] These impacts are exemplified in the third section through an analysis of the World Bank/Global Partnership for Education (GPE) project in Timor-Leste, the country that co-founded and now chairs the g7+.[21] The section discusses the statistics involved in measuring and categorising Timorese achievements in the context of the GPE project, focusing attention on how these numbers can easily become non-attributable. The country's leadership of the g7+ is central in the article's fourth section, which looks into the groups' promotion of alternative Fragility Assessments and its declared intention of using the exercise to gain ownership over development processes.[22] Final comments will then reflect on the power of the numbers being analysed and on the practices associated with the new g7+ measurement exercises, in order to understand what changes, if any, can be seen in the ownership and accountability involved in development practices dealing with 'fragile states'.

The discussion will be specific to the education sector in Timor-Leste, a focus that is highly relevant to the debate in this special issue. The knowledge necessary for the expert production of complex statistical analyses of government performance is intrinsically related to the ability to cultivate human capital in the country and it is also linked to the capacity to maintain outside influence at a minimum on technical matters that will dictate policy. The article's focus on the GPE project in Timor-Leste provides an insightful snapshot. Among other criteria, GPE's grants are allocated to states that are considered 'fragile'; the project in Timor-Leste has prioritised 'management strengthening' in terms of both human capacity and available systems.[23] The example clearly shows the impact of numbers beyond their expected reach, as the CPIA both subtly influences and is influenced by numbers generated in the context of the GPE project – impacts that were not anticipated and are hardly attributable, but that are also key in defining 'state fragility'.

The classification of 'state fragility': CPIA ratings

The World Bank's CPIA is perhaps the most widely reproduced index of 'state fragility' in terms of its implications for policy decisions.[24] Based on four clusters and 16 indicators, the CPIA attributes scores according to countries' performances in policy and institutional areas.[25] It is important to highlight both CPIA's distance from its initially proposed uses and its impact on aid allocation. Staff at the World Bank state that the CPIA was 'never created' to categorise or define 'fragile states' *per se*.[26] Nonetheless, the system's banding of 'fragile states' below the 3.2 score threshold has been largely accepted as a practical (and numerical) definition of 'state fragility'.[27] The CPIA ratings are intended to guide the resource allocation of the World Bank's International Development Association (IDA), for which 29 countries classified as 'fragile' are eligible.[28] In the distribution of these resources countries are analysed according to a formula that heavily relies on the CPIA score and on countries' performances in the Bank's projects (Portfolio Performance rating).[29] In addition, the CPIA is also the basis for decisions taken by the African Development Bank (AFDB), the Asian Development Bank (ADB), Scandinavian governments, the UK and France. Moreover, 'even where not used explicitly, CPIA rankings serve to signal "good performers" to other aid agencies'.[30] Resources are limited but the demand is not, enhancing the relevance of this formula. As a natural unfolding, the system's many powerful implications lead to frequent attempts to either perfect or abolish it, based on critiques of its accuracy, theoretical background and applicability.[31]

Important questions can be raised: how are the indicators chosen? How are data collected and by whom? What conceptual guideposts are provided for subjective ratings, and how are they used? However, beyond frequent attempts to render the exercise more consistent across countries and more transparent by releasing more data,[32] the CPIA is no closer to being discarded or radically changed. As with many indices of state fragility, criticism seems to encourage never-ending revisions and attempts at improvement which, rather than weakening the data only intensify their circulation. This can be attributed both to the producers' acknowledgment of existing problems and to the growing use of the same (measurable) results-oriented rationale by 'fragile states' themselves, despite perceived inaccuracies or undesired consequences. The producers' acknowledgment of the limits of the statistics motivates the bureaucratic machine to constantly try to improve numbers and processes;[33] this in itself has the powerful result of integrating critics into the established system. Because the system determines important resource allocations and there is no indication of its potential elimination or replacement, frequent exercises to refine the CPIA are seen as windows of opportunity to advocate changes in the formula. Instead of discarding or radically changing the CPIA and similar quantified classification schemes, as frequently defended in academic texts,[34] international actors, including the representatives of 'fragile states', have effectively engaged in attempts to rework and improve formulae, rearticulating the system but in certain ways also maintaining the order of things.[35]

In this endless re-elaboration donors' analyses are constantly peppered with *meae culpae* that call attention to the difficulties of data collection and the limits of analysis.[36] Numbers on 'fragility' are seen as works in progress, or provisional numbers, as Lampland puts it: created and used with a specific purpose, but not intended to accurately reflect the social.[37] In the politics of classifying 'fragile states', authors and reports generally acknowledge these limits: it seems that 'for those who use numbers day in and day out, the observation that numbers are temporary devices is banal'.[38] However, their temporary character does not stop them from circulating, making accountability for such statistics virtually impossible. There is a tacit consensus on the use of 'good enough data',[39] and imperfections that affect the allocation of development resources are rarely attributable, as the next section will show.

The case of education: data collection in Timor-Leste

The education sector in Timor-Leste provides an eloquent example of the blurred power relations in the politics of classifying 'fragile states'. It points to the difficult distinction between the classifiers and the classified with respect to 'fragile states', a blur that is created in large part exactly by the mixture of roles in the production of the very numbers that will ultimately categorise 'fragility'. This section shows how the classification of 'fragility' is essentially based on minor bureaucratic practices of data compilation, statistical monitoring and evaluation, whose ownership and consequences are almost untraceable, although not less significant. It is argued that the problem lies not in getting the numbers to perfectly reflect reality, but in how the accountability for these data and their impacts can be shifted and negotiated. I discuss the difficulties the World Bank has faced in collecting and analysing data in the education sector in Timor-Leste in comparison with the challenges confronted by the Timorese government in the same area when applying for additional international funding. This comparison serves to highlight the impossibility of tracing numbers back to any origins, raising the issue of shared competences *and* responsibilities in the process of classifying 'fragility'.

Between 2000 and 2010, although the World Bank's resources in Timor-Leste were highly concentrated on education,[40] its work in the sector was evaluated as 'moderately unsatisfactory'. The report by the Bank's Independent Evaluation Group (IEG) pointed to the lack of any attempt to measure learning skills in a 'structured way'.[41] The Bank has been involved in education projects in Timor-Leste since 2001, starting with the emergency reconstruction of schools and the production of basic classroom material during the United Nations Transitional Administration (UNTAET, 1999–2002). However, at the end of 2010 the IEG estimated that 'a full cohort of the population' was still functionally illiterate.[42] The Bank's staff have linked these problems to the difficult country context. The end of the Indonesian occupation in 1999 resulted in the destruction by militias of around 80% of the country's education infrastructure. The Bank's focus was thus directed towards rebuilding schools, hiring teachers and increasing children's educational access. In this context actual learning performance, it is said, might have been considered less of a priority.[43]

If such difficulties were experienced by senior Bank staff, it is no surprise that the new government, faced with an overwhelmingly daunting scenario, asked for the Bank's support in applying for additional help from a multi-donor trust fund, the GPE. In order to obtain these grants, the Timorese government had to propose projects based on measurable targets and demonstrate its capacity to implement them; its progress would then be evaluated by the Bank (as the Supervisor Entity) starting in 2005.[44]

Timor-Leste's classification as a 'fragile state' by the CPIA made it eligible for GPE funding,[45] but final approval and the decision on the amount to be allocated was dependent on the GPE's Needs and Performance Framework (NPF),[46] a process that identifies a country`s needs and performance through measurable indicators. Although the World Bank is the Supervisor Entity for the GPE programme in Timor-Leste, the core of the programme framework is intended to be the responsibility of the government, which decides on the specific national priorities and targets for the education sector and also endorses the indicators selected for each target, based on the country's National Education Sector Plan (NESP).[47] Thus, the process towards implementing a GPE Education Plan involves the collection, production and analysis of statistics for the application process and for the monitoring and evaluation during implementation, a requirement of the GPE fund. However, the mastery of numbers and the technical tools required for such activities are often extremely hard to find in 'fragile states'' offices just after crises; as a result, their governments tend to seek advice and external technical expertise. In Timor-Leste, for example, after the country's 2006 internal conflict, 60% of the Timorese Ministry of Finance's personnel had achieved only third-grade level in mathematics, according to the minister herself.[48] Moreover, the household surveys conducted by the Statistics Office until 2010 were considered unsatisfactory by the government, which requested the World Bank's assistance and training in the use of new software.[49]

Considering the issues related to human capacity, one problem with the GPE application process is in the paradox of having to apply for a grant using a complex form involving statistics and measurable targets, when requesting in part the funding needed to qualify analysts for such work in an area in which, as noted, the work conducted by the Bank itself has been evaluated as not completely satisfactory.

The application using the NPF form requires complex data compilation in the form's Need Index and Performance Index (Figure 1; see below).[50] Mastering these calculations is crucial in determining the resources a country will receive: To establish the value of the grant, the country is scored based on its needs, performance and population size.[51]

The GPE partners fill in gaps with data from international systems, such as the CPIA, and national documents such as the NESP, Joint Sector Reviews and grant applications. However, even when this entire process functions as a joint enterprise, the disparities in terms of human resources and knowledge can create many difficulties. One World Bank country team member in Timor-Leste noted

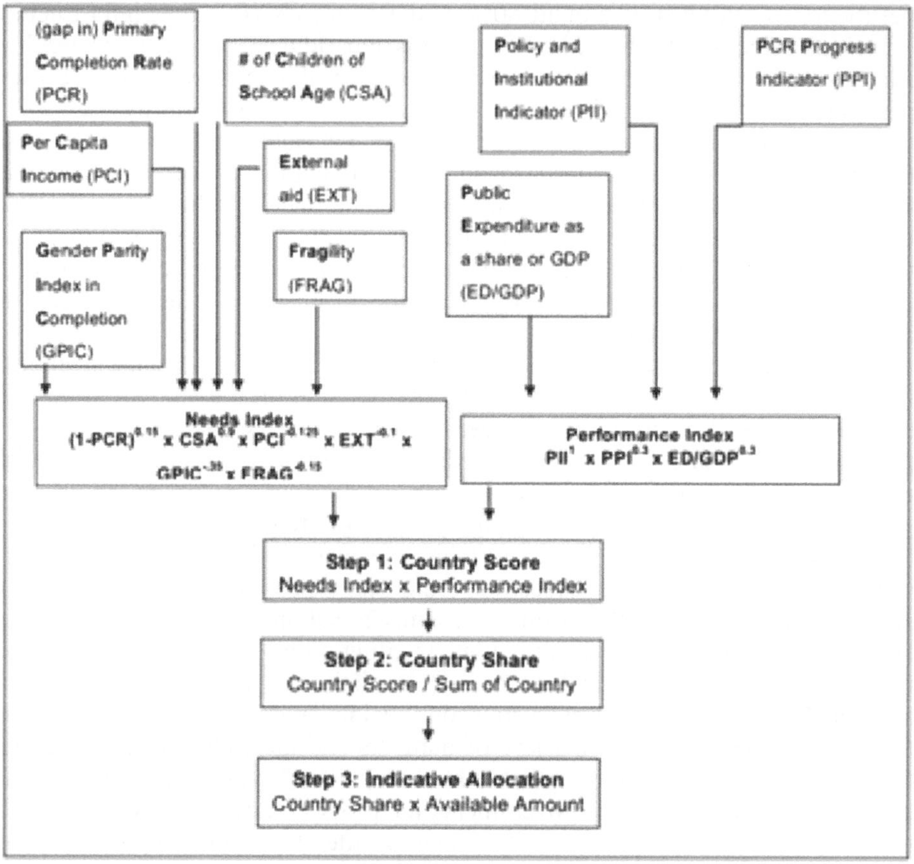

Figure 1. The GPE's 'method for determining allocations'.
Source: Global Partnership for Education. 'Revised Needs and Performance Framework.' BOD/2012/01-DOC 01. January 2012.

the complexity of balancing the Bank's demands for accurate statistics and the need to produce documents that would be fully understood by and useful for the government, as opposed to 'shelf reports'.[52] On the other hand, the workload can also become onerous for the counterparts in donor organisations responsible for advising the government's staff on the production of data, supervising the analysis and producing their own separate reports for the Bank. In fact, it seems staff members barely have enough time to visit all the countries in their portfolio: in the Pacific Islands region one employee might be in charge of 13 countries, which raises questions about the ratings subjectively produced by country team members for the CPIA exercise.[53] Despite this, the Bank's environment is characterised as one of hard work and rigorous peer-review. It is doubtless in the context of matching rigour and the virtual impossibility of producing perfect numbers that 'good enough data' became an acceptable reality for the creation of 'good enough targets'.

In this sense the case of the GPE is highly significant. The funded plan is monitored and evaluated through the Results Framework, whose objective is to check on the implementation of the targets defined by local partners.[54] However, it is not recommended that the Results Framework be used to compare different countries, as national sources 'may differ from the data available through international sources because of differences in definitions, methods of calculation, or the underlying data'.[55] This attests to the difficulty of finding common forms of measurement in a situation of basic social and economic discrepancies; nevertheless, this does not stop the numbers from circulating beyond their intended boundaries. 'Good enough data' are welcome to the extent that they fill important gaps; they become unwelcome only when better data are made available. Either way, data are always necessary - the 'new oil', as one interviewee described it.[56] Between their production, refinement and distribution, however, the data become almost untraceable. In the case of the GPE programme in Timor-Leste, the data produced in local joint meetings required the experts provided by the Bank not only to advise but also to collect and analyse material. It seems impossible to differentiate between purely national numbers and numbers produced by mixed teams. Moreover, the projects supervised by the Bank as part of the GPE programme in Timor-Leste will ultimately be judged as satisfactory or not in the IEG report on the Bank's work in the country. This evaluation may influence the country's portfolio rating, which is taken into account for the IDA allocation and the classification of 'fragile states'.[57] Insufficient data or the incomplete or unsatisfactory establishment and monitoring of targets might render a project 'problematic' – that is, the project might be rated as 'moderately unsatisfactory', precisely the rating received by the education sector in Timor-Leste, as discussed above.[58] Because the numbers produced in the application and in the monitoring and evaluation of country programmes can be untraceable, the resulting judgment of a project's success might also be based on mixed sources. In the case of the World Bank's/GPE's education projects in Timor-Leste, failures might arise as much from the national staff's difficulties in collecting data and monitoring new policies as from donors' incomplete implementation of self-established targets. The primary numbers collected for the GPE projects might therefore contribute, albeit in a small part, to the aggregation that will finally classify Timor-Leste as 'fragile' and determine the resources to be allocated. The bureaucracy is huge and intertwined. In this context how can we trace the paths taken by numbers and indicators? And if we cannot, what are the impacts of this impossibility in our readings of power in the development aid to 'fragile states'?

In this way, the very basic statistics produced by minor bureaucratic processes can have powerful consequences in the labelling of 'fragile states' and the assistance provided to them. In the case of Timor-Leste the numbers were produced by the government based on national plans, but relied heavily on international expertise; in addition, statistical gaps were filled with reference to international databases.[59] It is thus nearly impossible to assign accountability to one sector or group, in the Bank or in the Timorese government, for the numbers, measures and targets established, not to mention the successes and failures. The Bank is held accountable for results based on numbers that have not necessarily been produced or supported by its staff; Timorese staff can indirectly contribute to establishing processes and thresholds to which they will later see themselves unfortunately tied. At the least this observation blurs the processes of accountability and introduces caveats in the understanding of practices of power in such dynamics: the responsibility rests on many different shoulders, as do the burdens of rigorous data collection and analysis, albeit unequally distributed. In their independent wander, statistics on education that are not necessarily traceable to any sources could have powerful unforeseen impacts on resource allocation.

The fact is that such inaccuracies cannot be eradicated and might be impossible to avoid: the various databases are interconnected with one another, generating important political consequences for all those involved in classifying 'state fragility'. However, perhaps contrary to academic common sense, the alternative being proposed by the g7+ group of self-classified 'fragile states' does not focus on radically changing classification processes, but rather on the ownership of the measuring exercises and on shifting the accountability for established targets and aid intervention to donors, at least more broadly than in current practice. The following section describes the new measurement tools advanced by the g7+, analysing how the proposed assessments might change the current dynamics of accountability and ownership in the classification of 'state fragility'.

The g7+'s Fragility Assessment

The g7+ group, which has pioneered an alternative assessment of 'state fragility', was founded in 2010; it is currently chaired by the Timorese government, led by the Minister of Finance, Emilia Pires. The group, composed of self-categorised 'fragile states', has become a recognised participant in discussions over aid effectiveness in the international arena.[60] It has obtained widespread support for its New Deal, which proposes a 'new approach' to 'fragile states'.[61] Most importantly, the group has also developed its own Fragility Assessment, which is intended to take into account the specific characteristics of each country.[62] If researchers needed more direct answers with regard to how 'fragile states' might respond to the labels being attached to them, the g7+'s Fragility Assessments provide eloquent insights. The group's demands have circumvented the labels, no matter how problematic they might seem from an academic perspective: 'we are not trying to change it [the fragile state label], but to redefine it and use *our* definition by assessing ourselves'.[63] Fragile states' governments have focused on what the labelling entails, the authority of the practice as such. Their proposal has been not radical change, but rather the use of established institutions and tools to do precisely what these institutions and tools do: measure 'state fragility'.[64]

The g7+'s Fragility Assessment analyses five clusters of indicators: legitimate politics, security, justice, economic foundation, and revenue and services. With the exception of security,[65] these clusters are not much different from those seen in other indices, such as the CPIA; they are evaluated according to the five stages of the Fragility Spectrum also created by the group: crisis, rebuild/reform, transition, transformation and resilience. Scores are assigned using a scale from 1 to 5 for each cluster, but, for now, there is no overall score.[66] The development of the assessment indicators was entrusted to a mixed working group including donors and g7+ representatives. The assessment involves common indicators and some country-level indicators, based on a 'bottom-up approach' centred on pilot studies of the Fragility Assessment and the Fragility Spectrum in seven member countries, including Timor-Leste. The idea is to develop simple indicators that can be realistically measured by the members' statistical capacity and that are thoroughly discussed with internal stakeholders.[67] Outside advice and support is intended to be restricted to logistics, networking and background papers on the topics discussed in the meetings.[68]

The pilot test of the Fragility Assessment and Spectrum was a first attempt at developing the proposed new system of ownership:

> Each pilot country adopted a distinct approach to developing their fragility assessments, field-testing their spectrums, and identifying appropriate indicators, while maintaining the fundamental principles of a country-owned, country-led process that was participatory in nature.[69]

Alongside this self-measurement of 'state fragility' the g7+ has also been vocal in criticising and proposing changes in current forms of interventions in 'fragile states'. In fact, the advocated shift in accountability in development aid was one of the first indications of the group's initial plans. When the government of Timor-Leste volunteered to take part in the *Monitoring of the Principles for Good International Engagement in Fragile States* in 2009,[70] instead of measuring the improvements in the country's indicators in general, the exercise measured donors' success in implementing the proposed principles. This subtle change, or rather the way it was made, is said to have caused some discomfort at the time and the report was somehow negotiated.[71] In a similar vein, in 2010, the Timorese response to the IEG programme evaluation of the World Bank's work in the country was presented in an appended letter written by the Minister of Finance, Emilia Pires. In the government's view there was much to thank the Bank for, and several points were mentioned in that regard, but the letter also noted a lack of 'detailed data and qualified analysis to contribute to some conclusions' – 'like all documents produced by international donors'. The World Bank was criticised for not providing cross-sectoral analysis, even when demanding that a 'fragile nation' (in the document's words) undertake an exercise that the Bank itself, over the course of a decade and with the support of 26 other donors, had been unable to adequately address.[72] Perhaps tellingly, at the Fourth High Level Forum on Aid Effectiveness in Busan in 2010, Timor-Leste, together with the Democratic Republic of Congo and Liberia, led a parallel closed meeting for the representatives of 'fragile states', resulting in the establishment of the g7+. The group was founded with the main stated goal of developing a country-led and country-owned new paradigm for aid intervention, adapting the way in which this aid would be 'managed, designed and delivered' in 'fragile states'.[73]

Although the basic premises behind the measuring and labelling of 'state fragility' have not been contested, the new proposals by the g7+ seem to seek to redirect ownership and leadership by making use of national capacity. As noted above, for now the movement does not advocate the elimination of the current practices and institutions that classify 'fragile states' but rather the gradual appropriation of this classification system. It is still too soon to analyse the actual impacts of the Fragility Assessments, but the most important aspect is not the potential independence of these analyses. As the previous sections have sought to highlight, the numbers and indicators will still be highly untraceable, and attributing accountability can frequently be a fruitless exercise, not least because of the mixed composition of the working groups and the assistance of donors and international organisations. These numbers are too widely dispersed to allow true ownership over formulae and their impacts. Therefore, the question should not turn on how much ownership the g7+ will have of their own measurements as 'fragile states', but rather on how the very exercise of measuring can shift accountability practices towards the donors, demanding greater expertise in development processes and, most importantly, more effective use of the power of intervention. However, this will come at a price to 'fragile states' as well, as they must increasingly embrace greater responsibility for their own labelling and categorisation.

Caveats, nuances and a blur: some concluding thoughts

There is no question regarding the intrinsic power of 'fragility' indices and labels, not least because of their impact on the allocation of resources, as discussed. However, there should also be no doubt that the 'fragile states' themselves (or some of them) are now playing the game in the form of the g7+ and its corroboration of the widespread urge to measure and classify. It is power that makes it necessary to play, as a 'different way of thinking would prohibit any form of action'.[74] This is the power of practicality inherent in taxonomies: the more these statistical schemes become entrenched in international bureaucracy by means of their self-perpetuating process of 'improvement in use', the more difficult they are to change.[75] Hence, the g7+ does not 'speak out' *against* the established practice of 'fragility' quantification; instead, its new proposals aim to establish a better hold of 'numerical claims'.[76] As discussed, the g7+ seeks to accomplish this not by opposing donors, but rather by joining the 'multitude of allies', becoming one more association in the chain of people, techniques and events that define and characterise 'state fragility'.[77]

The classification of and intervention in 'fragile states' are shared enterprises involving many different international and domestic actors who mix and negotiate in a bureaucratic routine, attempting to achieve a balance between efficiency and accuracy, and practicality and feasibility. In this balance numbers, indicators and classifications are constantly produced and improved, and their impact goes far beyond the original established goals. The classification of 'fragile states' is, thus, as much a routinised political construction as a fight over the proper measures of what is perceived as an objective reality. It is crucial to understand that there is power in this politics of classification by the very impacts the labels make possible; however, that power is everywhere in the loose production of data discussed and exemplified here. Therefore, it is necessary to consider the g7+ representatives' achievements in slowly and partially shifting accountability to donors and ownership to themselves, but is also important to acknowledge, for good or for worse, the role of 'fragile states' in the game of measuring, encoding and categorising.

Acknowledgements

An earlier version of this article was presented at the ISA 2013 conference, in San Francisco. I would like to thank all participants for their contributions, as well as the editors of this special issue, reviewers, interviewees, and Didier Bigo, Bruno Magalhães and Emma McCluskey for their helpful comments. I also acknowledge the scholarship provided by CAPES-Brasil and the support offered by the Department of War Studies, King's College London.

Notes on Contributor

Isabel Rocha de Siqueira is a PhD student in the Department of War Studies, King's College London. Her thesis focuses on the politics of classifying 'fragile states' and the relation between the g7+ group of self-labelled 'fragile states', the OECD and the World Bank, borrowing insights from International Political Sociology (IPS), sociology of quantification and critical studies on conflict, security and development. She co-founded the IPS group at Kings, now part of the Research Centre in International Relations, and has presented several papers on current and past research. Please see also http://www.kcl.ac.uk/sspp/departments/warstudies/people/phd/siqueira.aspx.

Notes

1. Esty et al., *Working Papers*.
2. *Foreign Policy*, "Failed States Index." Accessed August 13, 2013, http://www.foreignpolicy.com/failed_states_index_2012_interactive; Rice and Patrick, *Index of State Weakness*; and Marshall and Cole, *State Fragility Index*.
3. For a discussion, see Hansen and Muhlen-Schulte, "The Power of Numbers."
4. Duffield, *Development, Security and Unending War*, 5; Davis et al., *Governance by Indicators*; and Davis et al., "Indicators."
5. Davis et al., "Indicators."
6. From the discussion on the role of statistics in making things that hold through objectification – 'a bond between science and practice'. Desrosières, *The Politics of Large Numbers*, 9. See also Latour, *Science in Action*, 12–13.
7. Bourdieu, *In Other Words*, 55.
8. Ibid.
9. Bowker and Star, *Sorting Things Out*, 53. The authors were inspired by the Thomas Theorem. Thomas and Thomas, "Situations."
10. For a discusssion, see Bhuta, "Governmentalizing Sovereignty," 136.
11. Espeland et al., "The Dynamism of Indicators," 87.
12. Latour, *Science in Action*, 62. For a discussion, see also Espeland et al., "A Sociology of Quantification," 411.
13. Bowker and Star, *Sorting Things Out*, 137.
14. For a broader theoretical discussion, see Bigo, "Pierre Bourdieu." For examples, see Madsen, "Reflexivity"; and Neumann, "Returning Practice to the Linguistic Turn."
15. For a discussion, see Latour, *Science in Action*, 93.
16. Ownership: 'Developing countries set their own strategies for poverty reduction, improve their institutions and tackle corruption'; 'Countries have more say over their development processes through wider participation in development policy formulation, stronger leadership on aid co-ordination and more use of country systems for aid delivery'. Accountability: 'Donors and partners are accountable for development results'. See OECD, *Paris Declaration and Accra Agenda for Action*. Accessed October 13, 2013, http://www.oecd.org/dac/effectiveness/parisdeclarationandaccraagendaforaction.htm#Paris.
17. International Dialogue Secretariat, "Progress Report."
18. For an example, see Fabra Mata and Ziaja, *User's Guide*.
19. Bilgin and Morton, "Historicising Representations of 'Failed States'"; Bilgin and Morton, "From 'Rogue' to 'Failed' States"; Dolek, "The Myth of Failed States in Africa"; and Call, "The Fallacy of the 'Failed State'."
20. See http://web.worldbank.org/wbsite/external/topics/environment/extdatasta/0,,contentmdk:21115900~menupk:2935553~pagepk:64168445~pipk:64168309~thesitepk:2875751,00.html, accessed October 14, 2013.
21. g7+, "Dili Declaration."
22. Ibid. See also g7+, "About." Accessed July 25, 2013, http://www.g7plus.org/.
23. Among recent documents, see World Bank, "Project Information Document."
24. Grävingholt et al., *State Fragility*; and Independent Evaluation Group (IEG), *The World Bank's Country Policy and Institutional Assessment*.
25. The four clusters are Economic Management, Structural Policies, Policies for Social Inclusion/Equity, and Public Sector Management and Institutions. Indicators in each cluster are rated from 1 to 6 by regional staff, using individual judgments based on conceptual guides. Scores are averaged to provide cluster scores and a total score for each country. The system is under constant evaluation by the IEG in order to update and clarify proxies and cluster conceptualisation. The volume of concessional lending and grants

follows a formula that includes weighted clusters and the portfolio performance ratings. See World Bank, "IDA's Performance Based Allocation System," 2010, Annex 3.

26. Interview with Rui Coutinho, World Bank headquarters, Washington, DC, 12 April 2013. Coutinho is the senior economic policy adviser at the World Bank's Operations Policy Committee, which oversees the CPIA process.
27. Department for International Development (DFID), *Why We Need to Work More Effectively*, 7; African Development Bank (AFDB), "Strategy for Enhanced Engagement," note 4. (Although criticising some of its aspects, the AFDB affirms that the 'CPIA remains as the best available, simplest and most transparent single measure'.) Until 2008 the CPIA was also the only basis for the OECD's list of 'fragile states'. Now it is complemented by other rankings. See International Network on Conflict and Fragility (INCAF), "Ensuring Fragile States," note 3.
28. World Bank, "Harmonized List of Fragile Situations FY13." Accessed July 26, 2013, http://siteresources.worldbank.org/EXTLICUS/Resources/511777-1269623894864/FCSHarmonizedListFY13.pdf.
29. World Bank, "IDA's Performance Based Allocation," 2010, 33.
30. AFDB, "Country Resource Allocation." Accessed August 19, 2013, http://www.afdb.org/en/about-us/african-development-fund-adf/country-resource-allocation; Asian Development Bank, "Asian Development Bank's Support"; and Fabra Mata and Ziaja, *User's Guide*, box 1.
31. Gelb et al., "Implementing Performance-based Aid in Africa"; Guillaumont, "Adapting Aid Allocation Criteria"; Kararach et al., "Is There a Case?"; and IEG, *The World Bank's Country Policy and Institutional Assessment*. See also AFDB, "Strategy for Enhanced Engagement," 5.
32. Interview with Neil Fantom, World Bank headquarters, Washington, DC, 9 April 2013. Fantom is manager at the World Bank, the leader of the Open Data Initiative and the supervisor of *World Development Indicators*.
33. The frequent IEG evaluations of the CPIA, which take place every four to five years, are an example.
34. Bilgin and Morton, "Historicizing Representations of 'Failed States'"; Bilgin and Morton, "From 'Rogue' to 'Failed' States?"; Hameiri, "Failed States or a Failed Paradigm?"; Dolek, "The Myth of Failed States in Africa"; and Call, "The Fallacy of the 'Failed State'."
35. Alexander, *The Country Policy and Institutional Assessment*; and Kararach et al., "Is There a Case?"
36. For a known example, see Global Partnership for Education, *Results for Learning Report*, box 1.1
37. Lampland, "False Numbers," 13.
38. Ibid.
39. Interview with Stephen Close via Skype, 8 March 2013. Close is a Human Development Specialist at the World Bank, where he works on Education Sector Policy and Pacific Islands. He is the former task team leader for the Education Sector Support Project in Timor-Leste.
40. IEG, *Timor-Leste Country Program Evaluation*, 17, note 27.
41. Ibid., 37, 38.
42. Ibid., 39.
43. Interview with Luis Constantino via Skype, 15 May 2013. Constantino has been the World Bank's Country Manager in Timor-Leste since 2011. Interview with Stephen Close, 8 March 2013.
44. Global Partnership for Education (GPE), *Timor-Leste*. Accessed August 19, 2013, www.globalpartnership.org/timor-leste.
45. http://www.globalpartnership.org/finance-and-funding/gpe-fund/program-implementation-grant/indicative-allocations/, accessed October 15, 2013.
46. GPE, "Indicative Allocations." Accessed May 15, 2013, http://www.globalpartnership.org/finance-and-funding/gpe-fund/program-implementation-grant/indicative-allocations/; and GPE, "Revised Needs and Performance." Accessed May 30, 2013, http://www.globalpartnership.org/media/Final%20NPF%20Note%20January%202012.pdf.
47. GPE, *Results for Learning Report*.
48. "The Revolutionary: Minister of Finance Emilia Pires is Leading a Global Movement," *Timor Leste Now*. Special advertising section in *Foreign Policy*. Accessed July 25, 2013, http://www.foreignpolicy.com/timor/content/g7+/the_revolutionary.php. On the crisis, see Porter and Rab, "Timor Leste's Recovery."
49. Interview with Epifânio Martins, World Bank headquarters, Washington, DC, 12 April 2013. Martins works in the Timorese Ministry of Finance, having been hired just after Timorese independence. He was receiving training at the Bank at the time of the interview. The software in question is ADePT, a programme developed by the Bank itself.
50. GPE, "Revised Needs and Performance." Accessed May 30, 2013, http://www.globalpartnership.org/media/Final%20NPF%20Note%20January%202012.pdf
51. Idem.
52. Interview with Stephen Close, 8 March 2013.
53. For the subjective ratings, see World Bank, "Country Policy and Institutional Assessments," 4. The difficulties faced by staff members were discussed in an anonymous interview via Skype with a member of the country team in the East Asia and Pacific Islands region, March 2013.
54. GPE, *Results for Learning Report*, 7.
55. Ibid., 321.

56. Interview with Neil Fantom, April 2013.
57. IEG, *Timor-Leste Country Program Evaluation*, 132.
58. World Bank, "IDA's Performance-based Allocation System", 2007, 16.
59. One example is the UNESCO Institute for Statistics in Montreal, the source for the GPE's statistics on Youth Literacy Rates in its Education Sector Indicators. GPE, "Timor Leste: Education Sector Indicators." Accessed August 19, 2013, http.//country.globalpartnership.org/country_export/pdf/country/TL.
60. International Dialogue on Peacebuilding and Statebuilding, "Home." Accessed July 25, 2013, www.pbsbdialogue.org/.
61. g7+, "Who Has Endorsed the New Deal?" Accessed August 19, 2013, http://www.g7plus.org/new-deal-endorsement/.
62. 'g7+, "Work Program." Accessed July 25, 2013, http://www.g7plus.org/work-programme/.
63. Interview with Habib ur Rehman Mayar, OECD headquarters, Paris, 6 June 2013. My emphasis. Mayar is a Senior Policy Specialist in the g7+ Secretariat, Dili.
64. Interview with Leigh Mitchell via Skype, 19 April 2013. Mitchell participated in the process as a World Bank staff member working inside the Timorese Ministry of Finance, and he corroborated this view. An important caveat applies, however: for now, the g7+ expresses no intention of generating any rankings of its member countries. Interview with Habib ur Rehman Mayar, 6 June 2013.
65. Interview with Sarah Cliffe, 17 July 2013. Cliffe was Chief of Mission for the World Bank in Timor-Leste from 1999 to 2002, and led the Bank's Fragile and Conflict-affected Countries Group from 2002 to 2007. In her view the security element was added to the fragile states agenda by the g7+ in response to the lack of indicators for security in the Millennium Development Goals.
66. International Dialogue Secretariat, "Progress Report."
67. Ibid.
68. Interview with Ozong Agborsangaya-Fiteu, 10 April 2013. Agborsangaya-Fiteu is a Senior Operations Officer in the World Bank Institute's Fragile and Conflict-affected States Unit, where she also acts as focal point for the g7+. Also phone interview with Claire Leigh, 8 July 2013. Leigh is ODI's Head of the International Partnerships within the Budget Strengthening Initiative, leading ODI's support for the g7+.
69. International Dialogue on Peacebuilding and Statebuilding, "Piloting the Fragility Spectrum," 6.
70. OECD, *Monitoring the Principles for Good International Engagement Country Report 6: Democratic Republic of Timor-Leste.*
71. Interview with Leigh Mitchell, 19 April 2013.
72. IEG, *Timor-Leste Country Program Evaluation*, 191–192.
73. g7+, "About."
74. Desrosières, *The Politics of Large Numbers*, 11.
75. See Bourdieu, *In Other Words*, 73.
76. Lampland, "False Numbers," 1.
77. See Latour, *Science in Action*, 138–139.

Bibliography

African Development Bank (AFDB). "Strategy for Enhanced Engagement in Fragile States." Operations Policies and Compliance Department, AFDB. Tunis, January 2008.

Alexander, Nancy. *The Country Policy and Institutional Assessment (CPIA) and Allocation of IDA Resources: Suggestions for Improvements to Benefit African Countries*. Washington, DC: Heinrich Böll Foundation, 2010.

Asian Development Bank (ADB). "Asian Development Bank's Support to Fragile and Conflict-affected Situations." Independent Evaluation Department, ADB. October 2010.

Bhuta, Nehal "Governmentalizing Sovereignty: Indexes of State Fragility and the Calculability of Political Order." In *Indicators as Technologies of Global Governance*, edited by Benedict Kingsbury, Sally Engle Merry and Kevin E. Davis. Oxford: Oxford University Press, 2012, pp. 132-162.

Bigo, Didier. "Pierre Bourdieu and International Relations: Power of Practices, Practices of Power." *International Political Sociology* 5, no. 3 (2011): 225–258.

Bilgin, Pinar, and Adam David Morton. "From 'Rogue' to 'Failed' States? The Fallacy of Short-Termism." *Politics* 24, no. 3 (2004): 169–180.

Bilgin, Pinar, and Adam David Morton. "Historicising Representations of 'Failed States': Beyond the Cold-war Annexation of the Social Sciences?" *Third World Quarterly* 23, no. 1 (2002): 55–80.

Bourdieu, Pierre. *In Other Words: Essays Towards a Refelexive Sociology*. Stanford, CA: Stanford University Press, 1990.

Bowker, Geoffrey C., and Susan Leigh Star. *Sorting Things Out: Classification and its Consequences*. Cambridge, MA: MIT Press, 2000.

Call, Charles. "The Fallacy of the 'Failed State'." *Third World Quarterly* 29, no. 8 (2008): 1491–1507.

Davis, Kevin, Angelina, Fisher, Benedict Kingsbury, and Sally Engle Merry, eds. *Governance by Indicators: Global Power through Classification and Rankings*. Oxford: Oxford University Press, 2012.

Davis, Kevin, Benedict Kingsbury, and Sally Engle Merry. "Indicators as a Technology of Global Governance." *Law & Society Review* 46, no. 1 (2012): 71–104.
Department for International Development (DFID). *Why We Need to Work More Effectively in Fragile States*. London: DFID, 2005.
Desrosières, Alain. *The Politics of Large Numbers: A History of Statistical Reasoning*. Cambridge, MA: Harvard University Press, 1998.
Dolek, Caglar. "The Myth of Failed States in Africa: A Question on Atomistic Social Ontology." *Journal of Turkish Weekly* 28 April 2008.
Duffield, Mark. *Development, Security and Undending War: Governing the World of Peoples*. Cambridge: Polity Press, 2007.
Espeland, Nelson Wendy, and Michael Sauder. "The Dynamism of Indicators." In *Governance by Indicators: Global Power through Classification and Rankings*, edited by Benedict Kingsbury, Sally Engle Merry, and Kevin E. Davis, 86–109. Oxford: Oxford University Press, 2012.
Espeland, Nelson Wendy, and Mitchell L. Stevens. "A Sociology of Quantification." *European Journal of Sociology* 49, no. 3 (2008): 401–436.
Esty, Daniel C., Jack Goldstone, Ted Robert Gurr, Pamela Surko, and Alan Unger. *Working Papers: State Failure Task Force Report*. McLean, VA: Science Applications International, 30 November 1995.
Fabra Mata, Javier, and Sebastian Ziaja. *User's Guide on Measuring Fragility*. Bonn/Oslo: German Development Institute/United Nations Development Programme, 2009.
g7+. "Dili Declaration." Dili, 2010.
Gelb, Alan, Brian Ngo, and Xiao Ye. *Implementing Performance-based Aid in Africa: The Country Policy and Institutional Assessment*. Africa Region Working Paper Series 77, Wasington, DC: World Bank, 2004.
Global Partnership for Education (GPE). *Results for Learning Report 2012: Fostering Evidence-based Dialogue to Monitor Access and Quality in Education*. Washington, DC: World Bank, 2012.
Grävingholt, Jörn, Sebastian Ziaja, and Merle Kreibaum. State Fragility: Towards a Multi-dimensional Empirical Typology. Bonn: German Development Institute, 2012.
Guillaumont, Patrick. Adapting Aid Allocation Criteria to Development Goals. In Development Cooperation Forum. New York: United Nations Economic and Social Council, 2008.
Hameiri, Shahar. "Failed States or a Failed Paradigm? State Capacity and the Limits of Institutionalism." *Journal of International Relations and Development* 10, no. 2 (2007): 122–149.
Hansen, Hans Krausen, and Arthur Muhlen-Schulte. "The Power of Numbers in Global Governance." *Journal of International Relations and Development* 15, no. 4 (2012): 455–465.
Independent Evaluation Group (IEG). *Timor-Leste Country Program Evaluation*, 2000–2010. Washington, DC: World Bank, 2011.
IEG. *The World Bank's Country Policy and Institutional Assessment: An IEG Evaluation*. Washington, DC: World Bank, 2012.
International Dialogue on Peacebuilding and Statebuilding Working Group on Indicators. "Piloting the Fragility Spectrum and Identifying Country-specific Peacebuilding and Statebuilding Indicators: Interim Guidance Note." 2012. Accessed 30 May, 2013, http://www.interpeace.org/publications/doc_download/320-piloting-the-fragility-spectrum-interim-guidance-note-english.
International Dialogue Secretariat. "Progress Report on Fragility Assessments and Indicators." OECD–INCAF, Paris, 4 December 2012. Accessed 30 May, 2013, http://www.newdeal4peace.org/wp-content/uploads/2012/12/progress-report-on-fa-and-indicators-en.pdf.
International Network on Conflict and Fragility (INCAF). "Ensuring Fragile States are not Left Behind." OECD Development Assistance Committee, Paris, 2010.
Kararach, George, Abbi Kedir, Frannie Léautier, and Victor Murinde. "Is There a Case for Reforming the Country Policy and Institutional Assessment (CPIA) as an Aid Allocation Tool?" *Africa Capacity Development Brief* 3, no. 4 (December 2012).
Lampland, Martha. "False Numbers as Formalizing Practices." In *Contingency and Dissent in Science*, edited by Damien Fennel, 1–48. London: Centre for the Philosophy of Natural and Social Science, London School of Economics, 2009.
Latour, Bruno. *Science in Action*. Cambridge, MA: Harvard University Press, 1987.
Madsen, Mikael Rask. "Reflexivity and the Construction of the International Object: The Case of Human Rights." *International Political Sociology* 5, no. 3 (2011): 259–275.
Marshall, Monty G., and Benjamin Cole. *State Fragility Index and Matrix*. Center for Systemic Peace, 2011. Accessed May 30, 2013, http://www.systemicpeace.org/SFImatrix2011c.pdf.
Neumann, Iver B. "Returning Practice to the Linguistic Turn: The Case of Diplomacy." *Millennium: Journal of International Studies* 31, no. 3 (2002): 627–651.
OECD. *Monitoring the Principles for Good International Engagement in Fragile States and Situations*. Country Report 6: Democratic Republic of Timor-Leste. Paris: OECD, 2010.
Porter, Doug, and Habib Rab. "Timor Leste's Recovery from the 2006 Crisis: Some Lessons." World Bank, 2 November 2010.
Rice, Susan E., and Stewart Patrick. *Index of State Weakness in the Developing World*. Washington, DC: Foreign Policy/Brookings Institution, 2008.

Thomas, W.I., and D.S. Thomas. "Situations Defined as Real are Real in Their Consequences." 1917. Reprinted in *Social Psychology through Symbolic Interaction*, edited by G.P. Stone and H.A. Faberman. Waltham: Xerox Publishers, 1970.

World Bank. "Country Policy and Institutional Assessments: 2009 Assessment Questionaire." Operations Policy and Country Services, 10 September 2009.

World Bank. IDA's Performance-based Allocation System: Options for Simplifying the Formula and Reducing Volatility. Internatational Development Association Resource Mobilization Department, Washington, DC, February 2007.

World Bank. IDA's Performance Based Allocation System: Review of the Current System and Key Issues for IDA16. Washington: International Development Association Resource Mobilization Department, Washington, DC, May 2010.

World Bank. "Project Information Document (PID) – Concept Stage: *FTI* Management Strengthening Program 2011–12." Report No. AB6731.

How Sudan's 'rogue' state label shaped US responses to the Darfur conflict: what's the problem and who's in charge?

Maria Gabrielsen Jumbert

Peace Research Institute Oslo, Norway

Few conflicts have been subject to as much international attention and efforts at resolution as the conflict in Darfur between 2004 and 2009. In spite of these attempts, the situation in Darfur today can at best be qualified as an unresolved conflict. This article closely examines the ways in which the Sudanese state has been perceived and qualified in order to determine how the conflict was understood and how the state was approached by outsiders. As is shown, despite frequent descriptions of the nation as a 'fragile' or 'failed' state, throughout the conflict Sudan has primarily been approached as a 'rogue' state. The article argues that this distinction has led to the prioritisation of certain strategies based on 'protection' and 'punishment' over attempts to resolve the underlying causes of the conflict, something a more sophisticated understanding of the Sudanese state's internal weaknesses and instability might have allowed.

Introduction

Sudan has been plagued by civil wars and domestic conflicts ever since its independence in 1956. The last fully fledged war broke out in Darfur in 2003 and came to international attention in the spring of 2004. As a result of comparisons to the conflict in Rwanda 10 years earlier and descriptions of the war as the 'twenty-first century's first genocide', Sudan quickly became the subject of widespread activist mobilisation – first and foremost in the USA but also in several European countries – and of high-level diplomatic engagement. What effects can the perception of state capacity and responsibility in such conflicts have on the type of international involvement that is triggered? More specifically, how do the varying discourses on state 'fragility' and the more defiant variant of state 'rogueness' (to be investigated more closely in this article) shape the international responses to such conflicts? This article addresses these questions by examining in particular how the US responses to the Darfur conflict were shaped by varying and sometimes contrasting perceptions and qualifications of the Sudanese state.

The conflicts in South Sudan and Darfur both progressed from being widely ignored by the 'international community' to becoming highly internationalised. The central explanatory factors behind the timing, level and type of international responses to these conflicts are the mobilisation of activists, the broader international contexts and the way the conflicts have been qualified.[1] The qualification component will be examined in detail here, with the underlying assumption that how a conflict is understood and thereby qualified by external actors with various mandates to respond to such crises plays a significant role in the type of international response that is triggered.[2] The case of Sudan is relevant here for two main reasons. First, Sudan has been the subject of a number of international 'responses' to its internal problems, ranging from development aid, humanitarian assistance and diplomatic support for its peace negotiations to international and regional peace keepers – not to mention the various international sanctions and different forms of pressure and threats that have been applied. By positioning these reactions in the larger debate concerning fragile states (defined as incapable or unwilling to govern according to certain standards), an investigation of the relationship between these responses and the dominant perceptions of the Sudanese state might also tell us something about the way the fragile-state discourse functions. Second, despite appearing on various lists and rankings of 'fragile' and 'failed' states, Sudan was generally approached as a 'rogue' state throughout the Darfur conflict. Although these concepts may have a similar function of legitimising external interference, the term 'rogue' carries a different connotation, as it emphasises the state's defiant posture and often presumes a certain level of control. As will be argued here, how a state is qualified can have consequences for the ensuing international response.

The article will focus on the specific approach of the USA to Sudan during the Darfur crisis for three main reasons. First of all, as in many other cases of external interventions in internal armed conflicts, the USA acted as a forerunner and tone-setter for other international responses to the crisis. Second, public engagement on Darfur was particularly strong in the USA, which pressured the administration to keep the issue high on its agenda and shaped the responses it formulated. Third, the USA has maintained an often paradoxical but special relationship with Sudan over the past two to three decades. Indeed, it is within US policy towards Sudan that the broader contradictions in the international responses to Darfur are most evident.

To begin with the article describes the outbreak of the conflict and the first attempts to resolve the crisis. It then turns to an examination of how Sudan has been characterised as a 'fragile' or 'failed' state in various policy studies and aid organisation reports, although the label of 'rogue' state has had the greatest impact on US responses to the conflict. After a review of the special and tumultuous relations between Washington and Khartoum, the article shows how the 'rogue' label has coloured two of the most important responses to the conflict: the efforts to send peacekeepers to the region and the UN Security Council referral of the crisis to the International Criminal Court (ICC). In the final section the 'rogue state' image of Sudan is contrasted with a perspective emphasising the country's weaknesses and internal instability; arguably this latter view would have more effectively revealed the underlying causes of the conflict, which are still unresolved.

Outbreak of the Darfur conflict and international attempts to resolve it

The conflict in Darfur started in February 2003, when the Darfur Liberation Front (later the Sudan Liberation Army, SLA) attacked Gulu, the capital of the district of Jebel Marra, followed by an unprecedented attack on government forces in El Fasher on 25 April.[3] The Sudanese army was profoundly humiliated by these strikes and by later additional setbacks in other confrontations with the rebels. The Darfur rebel uprising represented a particularly tough blow for Khartoum, as the region had traditionally provided a pool of manpower for the nation's military ventures elsewhere in the country; this made it more difficult to deploy regular forces to crush the insurgency. Consequently the Darfur problem was handed over to Sudanese military intelligence, which devised a counter-insurgency strategy based on air attacks, military intelligence and the local Janjaweed militia.[4] The government persistently denied its support of the Janjaweed; however, the Arab militia continued to receive arms, artillery and communications equipment from government sources and soon gained the upper hand in Darfur. Similar strategies had been used during the war in the south with the Muraheleen militias, as well as in the conflict in the Nuba mountains in the 1990s; both cases led to massive human rights violations and displacements. By early 2004 thousands of people, mostly from the country's non-Arab tribes, had been killed and over a million were displaced.[5]

The international spotlight was turned on Darfur in April 2004, following declarations of concern from high-ranking UN officials and US lobbyists, which compared what was happening in Darfur to Rwanda on the eve of the 10th anniversary of the genocide in the Great Lakes region.[6] The UN negotiated an agreement with Khartoum on humanitarian access in July 2004.[7] Starting in the autumn, peace talks were held in Abuja under the auspices of the African Union (AU), gathering together the main Darfuri rebel groups and representatives from the Sudanese government. The Darfur Peace Agreement (DPA) was finally signed in May 2006; however, it was widely considered to be flawed even before its implementation began, as only one of the three rebel leaders had signed it.[8] It had little legitimacy within Darfuri civil society and the discrepancies in signing only caused further internal fighting among the various rebel groups.[9] In the period that followed, the Western powers engaged with the issue (primarily the USA and the UK but also countries such as France and Germany) no longer saw a need to improve the political solution to the conflict, focusing instead on sending a UN peace-keeping mission to the region. The year following the signing of the DPA was chiefly characterised by a tug-of-war between Khartoum and the UN and Western powers, involving an attempt to make the country accept a UN-led peace-keeping mission in place of the underequipped, AU-backed African Mission in Sudan (AMIS). In June 2007, after much international pressure, the Sudanese government finally accepted a joint proposal from the UN and the AU for the deployment of a hybrid mission in Darfur. This paved the way for the adoption of Resolution 1769 on 31 July, which entailed the deployment of 26,000 soldiers within the UN African Union Mission in Darfur (UNAMID).[10] On 31 December 2007 UNAMID formally took over from AMIS.

In parallel the Darfur crisis was placed on the judicial agenda as the result of a series of events. First of all, the International Commission of Inquiry into Darfur concluded that, although the intent of genocide could not be proved, the commission could not exclude the possibility that 'acts with genocidal intent' may have been committed on an individual basis.[11] 'Whether this was the case in Darfur, however, is a determination that only a competent court can make on a case-by-case basis',[12] the authors of the report stated. This assertion was noted by French diplomats, who drafted the proposal for UN Resolution 1593, which on 31 March 2005 referred the situation in Darfur to the ICC prosecutor.[13] The prosecutor's announcement of his decision to indict the Sudanese president in the summer of 2008 had a tremendous effect on the other international initiatives attempting to put an end to the conflict.[14]

While the activist movements for Darfur were gaining momentum in summer 2004 (with the foundation of the Save Darfur coalition in the USA), the government in Khartoum was in the final phase of its peace negotiations with the Sudan People's Liberation Movement (SPLM) to end the civil war between North and South Sudan. While Khartoum has generally been represented by international activists as incapable and unwilling to negotiate, at that time it was actually responding to international pressure by seeking to put an end to the years of war in South Sudan.[15] Significant concessions were granted to the South Sudanese, thanks in part to the mediators' leverage, but also to the Sudanese government's desire to emerge from international isolation and improve its relations with the West (especially with the USA). However, over the years any normalisation of relations became an increasingly distant prospect because of the Darfur crisis.

Sudan as seen through the 'fragile' and 'rogue' state labels

As outlined in the introduction to this issue, the concept of 'fragile' states is one of a range of more or less similar concepts – including 'weak', 'collapsed' and 'quasi-' states – some of which have a more academic basis, while others are more policy-oriented. It is primarily the political salience of this concept and its derivatives that we are interested in here. In 2013 the OECD defined 'fragile' states as follows: 'A fragile region or state has a weak capacity to carry out basic governance functions, and lacks the ability to develop mutually constructive relations with society. Fragile states are also more vulnerable to internal or external shocks such as economic crises or natural disasters'.[16] A total of 47 states were identified as fragile by the OECD in 2013; among these, Sudan is listed as one of the countries of particular concern, as it faces a combination of diminishing aid and slow growth. Sudan was among the top 10 recipients of official development assistance in both 2005 and 2010, and the country received a record high share of the total humanitarian assistance to fragile states in 2005.[17] In a report commissioned by the Canadian International Development Agency (written by David Carment and Yiagadeesen Samy from Carleton University) Sudan is identified as one of the nations currently caught in a 'fragility trap', a category consisting of those states that have appeared most frequently in the list of the top 20 fragile states over the past 30 years.[18] In short, Sudan has been classified as among the worst-off even among fragile states, beginning in the period before it started producing and exporting oil and extending beyond the secession of South Sudan, which deprived the country of a large share of its oil resources.

One derivative of the concept of 'fragile' states is the notion of 'failed' states. Although this is more controversial than the 'fragile' state concept, it is also more widely used in policy and media contexts. In a ranking prepared by the Fund for Peace (an independent Washington-based think-tank), which has been published every year since 2005 by the magazine *Foreign Policy*, Sudan is ranked third on the 2013 Failed States Index, the same rank it has achieved four years in a row. In the 2013 ranking it is joined for the first time by South Sudan, which is ranked fourth.[19] This ranking draws on 12 different political, social and economic indicators. Sudan scores high on all indicators, and especially high on 'Massive Movement of Refugees or Internally Displaced Persons', 'Vengeance-seeking Group Grievance', 'Security Apparatus', 'Rise of Factionalized Elites' and 'Intervention of External Actors' (between 9.8 and 10 points out of 10). Since scholarly work on the concept of 'fragile states' has often criticised the way the term seems to function as a means of discrediting the state in question and legitimising various forms of intervention,[20] it is interesting to see here that the *level* of external interventions is being used as an indicator of state failure. The OECD report emphasises that fragile states deserve particular attention, not only because they are home to most of the greatest poverty and development challenges, but also because they present the highest risk of violent conflict. It is therefore argued that investing in and providing foreign assistance to fragile states represent a form of prevention, invoking Collier and Hoeffler's contribution to this debate.[21] From this perspective fragile states have governance structures that are too weak to allow them to maintain a monopoly on violence, increasing the risk of a general disintegration and fragmentation of society and almost inevitably leading to the spread of violence.

However, in the international mobilisation and diplomatic activity intended to halt the conflict and violence in Darfur, Sudan has generally been approached as a so-called 'rogue' state, that is, as a state that is defiant and disrespectful of international norms, but nevertheless a strong state with direct control over and responsibility for violence. The concept of 'rogue states', first formulated by the Clinton administration in 1994, is essentially a politically motivated qualification; the term was officially abandoned in favour of the more toned-down concept of 'states of concern' in 2000,[22] although its political saliency has enabled it to survive in media and policy reports. The list of 'rogue states' generally corresponds to and is often used as a synonym for the US State Department's list of State Sponsors of Terrorism, first established in 1979.[23] However, this list is more formal, as a country's addition to it requires the approval of the Secretary of State and will be followed by a series of economic sanctions. The concept of 'rogue states' is both more controversial and more loosely applied. One common denominator of the different usages seems to be that they designate certain states as not complying with international norms; as Rose defines them, they are 'a class of states that combines the seeming irrationality and fanaticism of terror groups with the military assets of states'.[24] Irrationality and military strength are certainly two key aspects of this concept which have coloured the US-led international responses to Darfur: Sudan has been approached as a state that possesses sufficient control over military assets to be held responsible for the conflict, yet is seen as irrational enough to make negotiations seem pointless.

The idea of Sudan's 'rogueness' is formally related to its inclusion on the State Department's list of State Sponsors of Terrorism. The perception has further manifested itself in the debate over the possible genocide in Darfur, and more specifically among those who believe such genocide occurred. The question of a potential genocide in Darfur first emerged when the region was compared with Rwanda in April 2004. Proving the genocidal aspect of the war crimes committed required the politicians, NGOs and opinion leaders who believed this to be the case to show that there was a form of state control over the violence in order to demonstrate its 'intent'.[25] As Scott Straus points out, two primary reasons motivated activists and other observers of the crisis in Darfur to insist on the qualification of 'genocide'. First, they believed that the situation corresponded to the definition of genocide because 'the violence targeted an ethnic group for destruction, was systematic and intentional, and was state supported'.[26] Indeed, a common thread throughout the narratives of the Darfur conflict formulated by the advocacy movement was that the violence was state-controlled, and therefore the state was the only one that could stop it.[27] Second, proponents of the use of the term 'genocide' believed that it was a prerequisite for any international intervention to stop the violence. As Salih Booker and Ann-Louise Colgan (from Africa Action, an advocacy group specialising in Africa-related issues) wrote in *The Nation*, 'We should have learned from Rwanda that to stop genocide, Washington must first say the word'.[28] This reflects not only the idea that certain qualifications lead to certain responses, but also the approach that became dominant in the grassroots mobilisation for Darfur in the USA: organisations felt that it was important to impress this qualification of the crisis upon their elected representatives in order to trigger a sense of responsibility, compelling them to 'do something' – at least, that is what the groups hoped would happen. This resulted in a pressure-based approach involving threats of sanctions against the regime in Sudan, rather than support for the 'fragile' state structures to facilitate the management of the country's internal chaos; such support might have been the expected response if it was only the 'fragile state' qualification that had been considered. This interpretation of the nature of the problem in Darfur has been largely neglected in the analysis of the Darfur conflict.

The 'genocide' qualification was easy to impose, not only because of the evidence (or the interpretation thereof) on the ground, but also because of the already existing perceptions and qualifications of the regime in Khartoum. As Alex de Waal wrote in 2004 about Darfur, referring to the violence perpetrated in earlier conflicts in South Sudan and in the Nuba mountains, 'it is genocide by force of habit';[29] however, he would later qualify his claim regarding the genocide in Darfur.[30] Although the comparison with Rwanda on the eve of the 10th anniversary of the genocide there played a crucial role, it would have been difficult to sustain the genocide narrative about Darfur if there had been no historical precedent or deep-rooted perception of Sudan as a rogue state capable of committing terrible acts against its own civilian population.

Khartoum's unstable relations with Washington

In the 1980s Sudan was an ally of the USA in its policy of containment, representing a useful buffer zone against Libya in the west and Ethiopia in the east. However, the new Islamist military regime that seized power in 1989 attracted US attention and disfavour when it chose to declare its support for Saddam Hussein after his invasion of Kuwait in 1991.[31] The fact that in the 1990s Sudan became a refuge for a wide range of leading Islamist figures, as well as presumed terrorists, increased the Americans' new concerns regarding the country. During the summer of 1992 the Sudanese army assassinated two Sudanese employees of USAID, who were accused of cooperating with the SPLA in South Sudan.[32] Matters worsened after the attack on the World Trade Center in New York on 24 June 1993: five of the arrested suspects were carrying Sudanese passports.[33] It was following this attack that Sudan was first included on the US list of State Sponsors of Terrorism. In February 1996 the US Embassy in Khartoum was closed; there has been no US ambassador there ever since, only an interim Chargé d'Affaires following the start of the Naivasha peace talks in 2002.[34] Despite the country's recent history, which included hosting Osama Bin Laden throughout a large part of the 1990s, Sudan was not mentioned among the countries in George W Bush's 'axis of evil' in 2001.[35]

A new opening towards cooperation between the two governments was made in 2001 during the first months of the Bush administration, with the first manifestation being an increase in collaborative efforts between the secret services of the two countries.[36] In the meantime the new Assistant Secretary of State for African Affairs, Walter H Kansteiner, who had worked in African Affairs at the State Department during a previous Republican administration, was focusing on investments in emerging markets. He is described by former colleagues as having returned to the State Department with a strong orientation towards furthering US business interests.[37] His team resolved to try a new approach with Sudan, as the previous administration's policy had not made much progress. They also identified Sudan as a case in which they could potentially be forced to react in ways counter to their interests as a result of pressure from certain constituencies (mainly the Black Caucus and the Christian right) unless they thought through and carefully prepared their preferred approach.

Consequently they decided to propose that the Sudanese engage in new attempts at cooperation and negotiations with the South Sudanese, while threatening to resort to even harsher sanctions and tougher pressure if the cooperative efforts failed. In a speech in Washington on 3 May 2001 Bush publicly denounced the crimes and atrocities perpetrated by the Khartoum regime.[38] According to a former State Department official, a secret meeting was arranged outside Nairobi shortly afterwards with a delegation from the Sudanese government (including the foreign minister and a senior general) and a delegation from the Africa bureau team of the US State Department.[39] The options were presented and the Sudanese were given a week to consider the offer; they were informed that, if they did not respond, it would be taken as a sign that they had opted for the confrontational path. The Sudanese reportedly answered 48 hours later, favouring the negotiation option; first talks with the parties were organised that summer. As Kansteiner stated in testimony before the Senate Foreign Relations Committee Subcommittee on African Affairs a little over a year later, 'The government [of Sudan] appears to have calculated that it could not be against us'.[40] The 9/11 terrorist attacks added more force to the US threats, and the Sudanese government further stepped up its collaboration with the CIA.[41]

Over the next few years, until the signing of the Comprehensive Peace Agreement in January 2005, the USA closely monitored the negotiations between the government of Sudan and the SPLM. A major motivating factor enabling the Sudanese government to move forward with the negotiations was the prospect of normalised relations with the USA, through the lifting of sanctions and removal from the list of State Sponsors of Terrorism. However, these hopes were dashed by the outbreak of fully fledged war in Darfur in 2003 and the massive protests triggered by that conflict, both inside the USA and internationally. Among the first in the USA to learn about this outbreak of violence in Darfur were the then heads of USAID, the group's administrator Andrew Natsios and the assistant administrator Roger Winter.[42] As they would later explain, they had already told Ali Osman Taha, the Sudanese vice-president, that, despite earlier promises to normalise relations on the condition of a peace agreement in the South, this would no longer be sufficient. They made it clear to Taha that normalisation would also depend on the resolution of the Darfur conflict.[43] It remains uncertain to what extent Khartoum understood the new conditions being set for normalisation: they were voiced by high-ranking officials of the USAID humanitarian agency but not by officials from US intelligence organisations or the State Department – ie not by those who would, at least in Khartoum's perspective, be the only representatives capable of lifting the sanctions on Sudan. In addition, the fact that the international diplomats involved in Sudan seemingly dealt with South Sudan separately from Darfur may explain why Khartoum thought it could get away with conducting two very different 'policies' in the two regions. The disappointment of the political elite in Khartoum, who had been banking on a new era of reconciliation with the USA, could be measured in their subsequent reticence to accept any form of interference in Darfur – whether by journalists, who provided more material to the activists, or by peacekeepers, as the activists demanded.

Not unexpectedly the Sudanese government firmly rejected the allegations that genocide had been underway in the Darfur region since 2003, and strongly opposed the efforts to place negotiations under UN auspices and mount a UN peacekeeping operation – both of which were seen as attempts to launch a Western intervention in Darfur. Khartoum expended extensive effort on keeping the resolution process within an African framework. A comprehensive rhetoric of anti-imperialism and anti-interventionism supporting 'African solutions to African problems' was developed and has been skilfully deployed ever since. In a telephone interview with the *Voice of America News* in 2004 Foreign Minister Mustafa Ismail claimed that 'The people of Sudan are against any foreign intervention'.[44] The tone was noticeably tougher two years later in June 2006, when President al-Bashir called the prospect of a UN peacekeeping mission in Darfur a 'neo-colonialist' intervention. 'These are colonial forces and we will not accept colonial forces coming into the country' (*Mail & Guardian Online*, June 21, 2006) al-Bashir stated when a joint UN–AU mission met in Sudan to plan for the UN peacekeeping force.

Despite having been an important and loyal collaborator in the US war on terror, Sudan has not been removed from the US Department's list of State Sponsors of Terrorism. Its renouncement of international terrorist networks and its active collaboration in US counter-terrorism efforts could indicate that it no longer merits a place on that list. However, its continued inclusion has allowed the USA to maintain leverage over Sudan when pressing for an end to the conflict in Darfur or for compliance with other requests related to governance and human rights. In any case it would have been impossible for the US government to lift these sanctions in the midst of the public indignation over the alleged war crimes in Darfur. The cooperation between the CIA and Sudanese intelligence services has been kept out of the public eye, in part because of the sensitivity of the work, but also because such joint efforts would not be viewed positively in the USA.

The 'rogue state responsible for genocide' narrative: how it affected the responses to the Darfur conflict

The Sudanese regime in power and the state apparatus it controls have been accused of responsibility for the alleged genocide in Darfur. In both NGO reports and assessments made by the ICC it is generally the culpability of the president that is asserted, which is in line with the Court's definition of the individual responsibility of heads of state when it comes to war crimes.[45] It is first and foremost the perception of Omar al-Bashir and his ruling elite as having perfect control over the state apparatus that has led to an approach to the conflict based primarily on threats of sanctions unless the violence is stopped by this same state apparatus. In the following section the 'genocide' qualification of the conflict and the 'rogue' state label will be examined to determine how they affected the efforts to send peacekeepers to the region and the referral to the ICC.

UNAMID's peacekeeping effort: intervening to protect and pacify

It is not difficult to understand how the situation in Darfur, portrayed as a conflict in which a strong state was attacking its own civilian population, which lacked any means to defend itself, rapidly became a major interest for the advocates of the responsibility to protect (R2P). The debate on R2P was well underway when the international community became aware of the Darfur conflict in 2004.[46] And when the R2P principle was adopted during the UN World Summit in New York in September 2005, the Darfur crisis was already high on the political agendas of the UN and those countries most involved in the R2P process. The Darfur crisis quickly came to be seen as a litmus test for the relevance and ability of the R2P to serve as a guiding principle for the international community in its search for more appropriate and efficient ways of responding to such internal crises.[47] The underlying concept of the R2P is that, when internal violence reaches a certain level, and when the state is either unwilling or incapable of stopping this violence, the responsibility shifts to the 'international community'.[48] This idea has been omnipresent throughout the US activist campaign for Darfur under the Save Darfur banner. As David Lanz wrote in 2009, 'There is therefore a tendency to portray the people affected by conflict as helpless victims, who need to be saved from the outside – hence the name *Save* Darfur'.[49] The focus on the need to 'save' Darfur thus effectively reinforced the calls for a peace-keeping force. In short, the 'rogue state responsible for genocide' narrative had two underlying concepts: first, that there was a need to save the victimised population and, second, that the state – or in this case the head of state – had to be punished for the crimes committed rather than made a partner in negotiations.

However, the public and activist pressure on the question of peacekeepers was intense, and this had a direct effect on the shaping of policy priorities in Washington, as well as in other Western capitals. As a State Department official explains, an estimated 90% of the time he and his colleagues spent on Sudan in the period 2006–07 was occupied by issues of peace keeping.[50] The pressure from the activist constituency to send peace keepers was so strong that it became the priority issue for members of Congress, who in turn set the order of priorities for the executives at the State Department. These latter officials, closely following the situation on the ground, expressed a desire to invest more effort in facilitating a re-launch of the peace talks. However, the pressure to focus on the peace-keeping issue overshadowed any other idea, especially less concrete and less visible ones, as a former UN official explains.[51] Demands for a peacekeeping force were not actually focused on installing a force to *keep* the peace, as many observers rightly pointed out: there was no peace to keep.[52] They should instead be understood as a continuation of earlier demands for military interventions or a no-fly zone to stop the perpetrators of violence,[53] in combination with the realisation that any such 'intervention' without UN backing would be unrealistic. The request that the 'international community' intervene to stop the genocide (as voiced by the Save Darfur coalition and its various advocates) was thus a response to a 'genocide' that had to be stopped, as well as a reflection of the situation in Rwanda and regret that the UN had not intervened there.

The ICC process as convenient for the USA: justice without intervention

Another process of qualification involving the conflict in Darfur and the determination of the appropriate solutions to be applied has been the criminalisation of the violence and the 'judiciarisation' of the solutions. Sara Dezalay describes how the law has increasingly become an instrument utilised to respond to conflicts,[54] not only as a framework for understanding current armed conflicts, but also as an efficient method of circumventing the state and of legitimising different forms of international intervention. This process has accompanied rather than competed with the protection approach; however, in the later years of heightened international focus on Darfur – namely, before 2009–10, when the attention shifted to the secession process for South Sudan – the judicial approach to the conflict took centre stage. The international arrest mandate issued by the ICC against President Bashir in March 2009 came at a moment in which little progress was being made on other fronts, as the deployment of UNAMID troops was going slowly and the first new talks since May 2006 had just been launched in Doha the previous month. It was symbolically the strongest international action against the Sudanese regime that Western leaders could imagine, and thus eventually served the function of lending greater weight to the endless threats against Khartoum. US politicians used this option strategically, telling their constituencies that their protests had been taken seriously, all the while freeing themselves from any responsibility in the ICC process – to which the US is not a state party – *vis-à-vis* Khartoum.[55]

Underlying this international justice agenda is an increasingly accepted (though still contested by various international actors) international norm prescribing that certain war crimes and crimes against humanity be prosecuted in an international court and not through national mechanisms or in national courts considered incapable of dealing with the crimes committed.[56] The existing international conventions on war crimes, crimes against humanity and genocide upon which the Rome Statute is based define certain crimes as 'international' on the basis of their 'gravity'.[57] The ICC is intended to intervene only in cases in which national jurisdictions are for various reasons incapable of dealing with the crimes allegedly committed.[58] Indeed, the Sudanese government's main response to the indictment has been to try to establish a national judicial procedure to judge the war criminals, thus arguing for the disengagement of the ICC. In an attempt to bridge these opposing approaches, the AU presented a proposal to establish hybrid courts that would include international judges in the Sudanese trials; however, Khartoum has persisted in refusing any externalisation or foreign meddling in the process (*Sudan Tribune*, July 25, 2011).

The invocation of the ICC led to a widening gap between the 'peace' approach and the 'justice' approach to the Darfur conflict.[59] Proponents of the former argued that the arrest warrant for President Bashir represented an obstacle to peace negotiations, while proponents of the latter argued that peace without justice was worthless, focusing the culpability for the atrocities on the actions of the president. The fundamental issue revolves around the confusing messages conveyed by the USA and other international actors to the different stakeholders in the conflict.[60] The pressure to resume negotiations (that is, maintenance of a transactional relationship with the Sudanese state), while simultaneously seeking to judge the representatives of the same state, proved to be only minimally productive on all fronts. This resulted in a no-win situation in which the different approaches to the conflict ended up as rivals, preventing any priority from progressing.

Beyond state 'rogueness': exposing Sudan's internal weaknesses

A closer examination of the Sudanese state reveals a system that does not retain the level of control assumed by the ICC, either in its state apparatus or in the various political groupings within the ruling elite. The domestic conflicts in Sudan are often described as resulting from grievances in the marginalised peripheries and the concentration of power and wealth at the centre.[61] Mansour Khalid discusses the 'hegemony' of the central government over the rest of the country, a government that is both 'omnipotent' (wielding unlimited power) and 'omniscient' (knowing all there is to know). However, the problems in the peripheries are based on the lack of rule and control rather than a strong state ruling by force, as Øystein H Rolandsen explains.[62] He describes Sudan's eroding state capacity as diluted into party structures, informal structures and militias in the peripheries, ruling through suppression more than anything else. Alex de Waal describes the Sudanese state as 'turbulent', a combination of 'hyper-dominant' and 'unstable'. He identifies 'the inability of any one elite faction to establish unchallenged political dominance over the state' as a central feature of the Sudanese state: the 'center possesses sufficient economic, social, cultural, and political infrastructure that it can support not one but multiple elite groups'.[63] This is seen as the main reason behind the state's incapacity to govern its peripheries or to achieve any sustainable peace, as it has prevented the state from becoming powerful enough to play a stabilising role when needed. Had these analyses of the role of the Sudanese state been considered, they could have pointed towards more useful conflict-resolution approaches for the parties involved.

The US approach to Sudan, based on the perception of it being a rogue state, has had two primary effects. First, it has revealed the ineffectiveness of constant pressure on Khartoum to put an end to the violence; the underlying assumption regarding this pressure was that the state could stop the bloodshed if it only wanted to, as Democratic Representative Tom Lantos wrote in early May 2004 (*Boston Globe*, May 4, 2004) and as George W Bush stated in his address to the UN in September of the same year.[64] There is undoubtedly some diplomatic strategy here: this is what the US government is expected to say to the Sudanese. However, if this posing is not followed by other response mechanisms or diplomacy aimed at understanding the underlying causes of the situation, it has little chance of having any significant effect. The unfortunate result of threats of sanctions that were not always followed through (but also of carrots that were never given) was a disruption in the bargaining and transactional relation with Khartoum, whereby the 'rogue' state simply did not allow the pressure to affect its behaviour. In fact, this disruption has in many ways encouraged Khartoum to adopt a more defiant attitude. Further, the US approach to the Darfur conflict has not prioritised a thorough understanding of the root causes of the conflict. The prevalent reading of the Darfur conflict, centred on the Sudanese state's rogueness, has maintained that the necessary steps were to 'protect' the victims and 'punish' the perpetrators, neglecting the search for a solution to the underlying causes of the conflict. The USA was certainly engaged in the Abuja negotiations in 2005–06 but in the end this process was focused more on a 'deadline diplomacy' strategy than on a holistic approach to the conflict dynamics.[65] Despite recently renewed efforts by Qatar to host negotiations, the conflict in Darfur can today be qualified as unresolved at best.

Conclusion

The 'rogue state' discourse has perpetuated the image of a state that is unwilling to collaborate and only understands the language of threats and sanctions. This overlooks not only the internal dynamics in Sudan, but also the actual lines of cooperation between Khartoum and Washington. It also fails to take into account the fact that, over the years, Khartoum has developed a strong resistance to the endless threats of increased sanctions. The USA's Sudan policy has been marked by constant tension between a willingness to cooperate with Sudan and a push for more threats and sanctions to punish it for the crimes committed in Darfur. Sudan still figures on the US list of State Sponsors of Terrorism, even though paradoxically it is in this field that the country has been the most cooperative, serving as an invaluable partner for the USA in its war on terror. A reading of the conflict based solely on the 'fragile state' label would not have revealed all the intertwined dynamics of the conflict either, but a greater emphasis on the Sudanese state's internal weaknesses and instability could have led to a better understanding of the root causes of the conflict.

Notes on Contributor

Maria Gabrielsen Jumbert is Senior Researcher at the Peace Research Institute Oslo, Norway, where she coordinates the research group on Humanitarianism. Her research focuses on norm-production in international relations, the internationalisation of internal conflicts, surveillance of borders and humanitarian crisis, and the conflict dynamics in Sudan and East Africa. Her research has been published in the *Journal of Modern African Studies*, the *Human Security Journal*, and *Espaces, Populations, Sociétés*, among others.

Notes

1. The findings presented here are based on the research carried out for my doctoral thesis, including fieldwork in Sudan in 2007 and 2009 and in countries with intense social and diplomatic mobilisation concerning Darfur (USA, France, Norway), as well as on a total of over 100 interviews with government officials, diplomats and officials from international organisations, activists and civil society representatives in each country. Because of the sensitivity of the topics discussed, many of the interviews with government and UN officials have had to be anonymised. Gabrielsen Jumbert, "The Internationalization of the Sudanese Conflicts."
2. Finnemore and Sikkink, "International Norm Dynamics"; Marullo et al., "Frame Changes and Social Movement Contraction"; and Carpenter, "Governing the Global Agenda."
3. Flint and de Waal, *Darfur*.
4. Ibid.
5. Mans, "Briefing," 291.
6. Kuper, "Sudan Violence"; and Power, "Remember Rwanda."
7. Joint Communiqué between the government of Sudan and the United Nations on the occasion of the visit of the Secretary General to Sudan, 29 June–3 July 2004. Accessed October 1, 2013. http://www.un.org/news/dh/sudan/sudan_communique.pdf.
8. Nathan, "The Making and Unmaking," 431.
9. Interview, Hassan Abdel Atti, independent consultant, Khartoum, 21 November 2007.
10. UNSC, Resolution 1769 (2007), S/RES/1769, 31 July 2007.
11. Report of the International Commission of Inquiry on Darfur, 161.
12. Ibid.
13. UNSC, Resolution 1593 (2005), S/RES/1593, 31 March 2005. See also Gabrielsen Jumbert, "1593 (2005)."
14. Gabrielsen Jumbert and Lanz, "Globalised Rebellion."
15. Interviews, Tom Vraalsen, former Special Envoy of the UN Secretary General for Humanitarian Affairs for the Sudan, 28 February 2006; and Hilde Frafjord Johnson, former Norwegian minister of development, 23 May 2006.
16. OECD, "Fragile States 2013," 15.
17. Ibid.
18. Carment and Samy, "Assessing State Fragility."
19. *Foreign Policy*/Fund for Peace, "2013 Failed State Index." Accessed October 1, 2013. http://www.foreignpolicy.com/articles/2013/06/24/2013_failed_states_interactive_map.
20. See the Introduction by Grimm et al., and Rocha de Siqueira, this issue.
21. OECD, "Fragile States 2013," 35; and Collier and Hoeffler, "Aid, Policy and Growth."
22. Marquis, "US Declares 'Rogue Nations'."
23. US Department of State, "State Sponsors of Terrorism." Being listed here leads to a series of sanctions imposed by the USA, primarily 'restrictions on US foreign assistance; a ban on defense exports and sales; certain controls over exports of dual use items; and miscellaneous financial and other restrictions'.
24. Rose, "Defining the Rogue State."

25. Interviews, Sam Bell, National Advocacy Director at the Genocide Intervention Network, Washington, DC, 14 April 2008; and John Prendergast, co-founder, Enough Project, Washington, DC, 22 May 2008.
26. Straus, "Darfur and the Genocide Debate."
27. Blayton, "Human Rights Reporting on Darfur," posted on Alex de Waal's 'Making Sense of Darfut' blog, 21–24 August 2009. See also Murphy, "Narrating Darfur."
28. Booker and Colgan, "Genocide in Darfur."
29. de Waal, "Counter-insurgency on the Cheap."
30. de Waal, "Genocide by Force of Habit?"
31. Marchal and Osman, "Les ambitions internationales."
32. Petterson, *Inside Sudan*.
33. Marchal and Osman, "Les ambitions internationales."
34. US Department of State, "Chiefs of Mission by Country, 1778-2005, Sudan."
35. George W. Bush, "State of the Union Address", 29 January 2002.
36. Rose, "The Osama Files."
37. Interview, former State Department official, Washington, DC, 23 May 2008.
38. Aba, "George W Bush."
39. Interview, former State Department official, Washington, DC, 23 May 2008.
40. Kansteiner, "The Administration's Commitment to Sudan."
41. Daly, *Darfur's Sorrow*.
42. Roger Winter first mentioned Darfur in testimony before the US Congressional Committee on International Relations in May 2003, describing it as a 'new conflict zone that is not being adequately addressed'. Andrew Natsios visited Darfur a few months later. Flint and de Waal, *Darfur*.
43. Ibid.
44. Ryu, "Sudan Government Rejects Foreign Military Intervention."
45. Aballe, "Globalisation de la justice."
46. International Commission on Intervention and State Sovereignty, "The Responsibility to Protect."
47. Loconte, "The Failure to Protect."
48. Bellamy, *Responsibility to Protect*; Hehir, *The Responsibility to Protect*; and Chandler, "Unravelling the Paradox."
49. Lanz, "Save Darfur," 674. Author's emphasis.
50. Interview, former State Department official.
51. Interview, former UN official, New York, 24 April 2008.
52. Seymour, *No Peace to Keep*.
53. Flint, "Darfur's Outdated Script."
54. Dezalay, "Lawyering War or Talking Peace?" Report of the International Commission of Inquiry on Darfur.
55. Interview, former UN official.
56. Vinjamuri and Snyder, "Advocacy and Scholarship"; and Caney, *Justice Beyond Borders*.
57. Koller, "La Cour Pénale Internationale."
58. Aballe, "Globalisation de la justice."
59. Natsios, "Waltz with Bashir"; de Waal, "Sudan and the International Criminal Court"; and Enough Project, "Enough Project Praises ICC Action."
60. Lanz, "Conflict Management and Opportunity Cost."
61. Johnson, *The Root Causes*; Daly, *Darfur's Sorrow*; and Sørbø, "Local Violence."
62. Rolandsen, 'Sudan."
63. de Waal, *War in Darfur*, 4.
64. George W. Bush, "Address to the United Nations," 21 September 2004.
65. Nathan, "The Failure of the Darfur Mediation."

Bibliography

Aba, Jean Daniel. "George W Bush: Une bonne surprise pour les africains" (George W Bush: A Nice Surprise for Africans). *Géopolitique africaine*, no. 15–16 (2004): 85–94.

Aballe, Vanessa. "Globalisation de la justice: vers une remise en cause de la suprématie des états?' (Globalisation of Justice: Towards a Questioning of the Supremacy of States?) *Revue Politique et parlementaire* 1049, no. 10–12 (2008): 132–154.

Bellamy, Alex J. *Responsibility to Protect*. Cambridge: Polity, 2009.

Booker, Salih, and Ann-Louise Colgan. "Genocide in Darfur." *The Nation*, July 12, 2004. http://www.thenation.com/article/genocide-darfur#.

Caney, Simon. *Justice Beyond Borders: A Global Political Theory*. Oxford: Oxford University Press, 2005.

Carment, David, and Yiagadeesen Samy. "Assessing State Fragility: A Country Indicators for Foreign Policy Report." Canadian International Development Agency, 15 June 2012. http://reliefweb.int/sites/reliefweb.int/files/resources/1402.pdf.

Carpenter, R. Charli. "Governing the Global Agenda: Gate-keeping and Issue Adoption in Transnational Advocacy Networks." In *Who Governs the Globe*, edited by Deborah Avant, Martha Finnemore and Susan Sell, 202–237. Cambridge: Cambridge University Press, 2010.

Chandler, David. "Unravelling the Paradox of 'The Responsibility to Protect'." *Irish Studies in International Affairs* 20 (2009): 27–39.

Collier, Paul, and Anke Hoeffler. "Aid, Policy and Growth in Post-conflict Societies." *European Economic Review* 48, no. 5 (2004): 1125–1145.

Daly, M. W. *Darfur's Sorrow: A History of Destruction and Genocide*. New York: Cambridge University Press, 2007.

de Waal, Alex. "Counter-insurgency on the Cheap." *London Review of Books* 26, no. 15. http://www.lrb.co.uk/v26/n15/alex-de-waal/counter-insurgency-on-the-cheap.

de Waal, Alex. *War in Darfur and the Search for Peace*. Cambridge, MA: Global Equity Initiative, Harvard University, 2007.

de Waal, Alex. "Sudan and the International Criminal Court: A Guide to the Controversy." OpenSecurity, July 14, 2008. http://www.opendemocracy.net/article/sudan-and-the-international-criminal-court-a-guide-to-the-controversy.

de Waal, Alex. "Genocide by Force of Habit?" *African Arguments*, March 23, 2009. http://africanarguments.org/2009/03/23/genocide-by-force-of-habit/.

Dezalay, Sara. "Lawyering War or Talking Peace? On Militant Usages of the Law in the Resolution of Internal Armed Conflicts: A Case Study of International Alert." In *Lawyers and the Construction of Transnational Justice*, edited by Yves Dezalay and Bryant G. Garth, 60–83. London: Routledge, 2011.

Enough Project, "Enough Project Praises ICC Action against Alleged Darfur War Criminal, Cites Evidence of War Crimes at South Sudan Border." December 2, 2011. http://www.enoughproject.org/news/enough-project-praises-icc-action-against-alleged-darfur-war-criminal-cites-evidence-war-crimes.

Finnemore, Martha, and Kathryn Sikkink. "International Norm Dynamics and Political Change." *International Organization* 52, no. 4 (1998): 887–917.

Flint, Julie, and Alex de Waal. *Darfur: A Short History of a Long War*. London: Zed Books, 2005.

Flint, Julie. "Darfur's Outdated Script." *New York Times*, July 9, 2007. http://www.nytimes.com/2007/07/09/opinion/09iht-edflint.1.6567583.html.

Gabrielsen Jumbert, M. "The Internationalization of the Sudanese Conflicts: From South Sudan to Darfur – Agenda Setting, Mobilization and Qualifications." PhD thesis, CERI-Sciences Po Paris, 2010.

Gabrielsen Jumbert, Maria. "1593 (2005): Rapports du Secrétaire Général sur le Soudan" (1593 (2005): Reports of the Secretary-General on the Sudan). In *Les Grandes Résolutions du Conseil de Sécurité des Nations Unies*, edited by Mélanie Albaret, Emmanuel Decaux, Nicolas Lemay-Hébert and Delphine Placidi-Frot, 399–408. Paris: Dalloz, 2012.

Gabrielsen Jumbert, Maria, and David Lanz. "Globalised Rebellion: The Darfur Insurgents and the World." *Journal of Modern African Studies* 51, no. 2 (2013): 193–217.

Hehir, Aidan. *The Responsibility to Protect: Rhetoric, Reality and the Future of Humanitarian Intervention*. New York: Palgrave Macmillan, 2012.

International Commission on Intervention and State Sovereignty. "The Responsibility to Protect." December 2001. http://responsibilitytoprotect.org/ICISS%20Report.pdf.

Johnson, Douglas H. *The Root Causes of Sudan's Civil Wars*. Oxford: James Currey, 2003.

Kansteiner III, Walter H. "The Administration's Commitment to Sudan." Testimony before the Senate Foreign Relations Committee Subcommittee on African Affairs. Washington, DC, 11 July 2002. http://2001-2009.state.gov/p/af/rls/rm/11843.htm.

Koller, Sylvie. "La Cour Pénale Internationale: ses ambitions, ses faiblesses, nos espérances" (The International Criminal Court: Its Ambitions, Its Weaknesses, Our Hopes). *Etudes* 398, no. 1 (2003): 33–42.

Kuper, Jo. "Sudan Violence Approaches Scale of Rwanda Genocide." *OneWorld.net*, April 3, 2004. http://www.commondreams.org/headlines04/0403-01.htm.

Lanz, David. "Conflict Management and Opportunity Cost: The International Response to the Darfur Conflict." September 2008. http://www.fride.org/download/COM_Darfur_cost_ENG_sep08.pdf.

Lanz, David. "Save Darfur: A Movement and its Discontents." *African Affairs* 108, no. 433 (2009): 669–677.

Loconte, Joseph. "The Failure to Protect: Lessons from Darfur." *The American Interest*, Winter (2007): 20–31.

Mans, Ulrich. "Briefing: Sudan – The New War in Darfur." *African Affairs*, no.103 (2004): 291–294.

Marchal, Roland, and Oussama Osman. ""Les ambitions internationales du Soudan islamiste" (The International Ambitions of Islamist Sudan). *Politique Africaine*, no. 66 (1997): 74–87.

Marullo, Sam, Ronald Pagnucco, and Jackie G. Smith. "Frame Changes and Social Movement Contraction: US Peace Movement Framing after the Cold War." *Sociological Inquiry* 66, no. 1 (1996): 1–28.

Marquis, Christopher. "US Declares 'Rogue Nations' Are Now 'States of Concern'." *New York Times*, June 20, 2000. http://www.nytimes.com/2000/06/20/world/us-declares-rogue-nations-are-now-states-of-concern.html.

Murphy, Deborah. "Narrating Darfur: Narrating Darfur in the US Press, March–September 2004." In *War in Darfur and the Search for Peace*, edited by Alex de Waal, 314–336. Cambridge, MA: Global Equity Initiative, Harvard University, 2007.

Nathan, Laurie. "The Failure of the Darfur Mediation." *Ethnopolitics* 6, no. 4 (2007): 495–511.

Nathan, Laurie. "The Making and Unmaking of the Darfur Peace Agreement." In *War in Darfur and the Search for Peace*, edited by Alex de Waal, 245–266. Cambridge, MA: Global Equity Initiative, Harvard University, 2007.

Natsios, Andrew. "Waltz with Bashir: Why the Arrest Warrant against Sudan's President will Serve Neither Peace nor Justice." *Foreign Affairs*, March 23, 2009. http://www.foreignaffairs.com/articles/64904/andrew-natsios/waltz-with-bashir.

OECD. "Fragile States 2013: Resource Flows and Trends in a Shifting World." DAC International Network on Conflict and Fragility. Accessed 1 October 2013. http://www.oecd.org/dac/incaf/FragileStates2013.pdf.

Petterson, Donald. *Inside Sudan: Political Islam, Conflict and Catastrophe*. Boulder, CO: Westview Press, 2003.

Power, Samantha. "Remember Rwanda, but Take Action in Sudan." *New York Times*, April 6, 2004. http://www.nytimes.com/2004/04/06/opinion/remember-rwanda-but-take-action-in-sudan.html.

Rolandsen, Øystein H. "Sudan: The Role of Foreign Involvement in the Shaping and Implementation of the 2005 Comprehensive Peace Agreement." In *Mediation and Liberal Peacebuilding: Peace from the Ashes of War?* edited by Mikael Eriksson and Roland Kostic, 76–91. London: Routledge, 2013.

Rose, David. "The Osama Files." *Vanity Fair*, January 2002. http://www.vanityfair.com/politics/features/2002/01/osama200201.

Rose, Jason. "Defining the Rogue State: A Definitional Comparative Analysis within the Rationalist, Culturalist, and Structuralist Traditions." *Journal of Political Inquiry*, no. 4 (2011): 1–36.

Ryu, Alisha. "Sudan Government Rejects Foreign Military Intervention in Darfur." Voice of America News, MilitaryInfo.com, July 26, 2004. http://www.militaryinfo.com/news_story.cfm?textnewsid=1094.

Seymour, Lee J. M. *No Peace to Keep: Darfur in Perspective*. SWP Comments 10. Berlin: Stiftung Wissenschaft und Politik (SWP), 2007.

Straus, Scott. "Darfur and the Genocide Debate." *Foreign Affairs* 84, no. 1 (2005): 123–133.

Sørbø, Gunnar M. "Local Violence and International Intervention in Sudan." *Review of African Political Economy* 37, no. 124 (2010): 173–186.

US Department of State, "Chiefs of Mission by Country, 1778-2005, Sudan." Accessed October 1, 2013. http://www.state.gov/r/pa/ho/po/com/11280.htm.

US Department of State, "State Sponsors of Terrorism." Accessed October 1, 2013. http://www.state.gov/j/ct/list/c14151.htm.

Vinjamuri, Leslie, and Jack Snyder, "Advocacy and Scholarship in the Study of International War Crime Tribunals and Transitional Justice." *Annual Review of Political Science* 7 (2004): 345–362.

State disintegration and power politics in post-Suharto Indonesia

Felix Heiduk

Department of Political Science and International Studies, University of Birmingham, UK

This article illustrates how discourses on 'state fragility' have been instrumentalised by the Indonesian military in order to consolidate its political and economic power after the fall of Suharto. In the wake of Indonesia's transition to democracy violent conflicts escalated in East Timor, Aceh, Papua, the Moluccas and Sulawesi. Most notably East Timor's successful secession spawned fears over the potential 'balkanisation' of Indonesia. In this context the Indonesian military, which had been shunned for its involvement in Suharto's New Order, managed to re-establish itself as the 'guardian of the nation'. Based on fieldwork in Indonesia, the article describes how post-9/11 discourses over a potential break-up of Indonesia were used by the Indonesian military to reconsolidate its power in the post-Suharto era. The research findings illustrate that, against the looming threat of state disintegration, attempts to revoke the military's prerogatives have either failed or have been aborted during the planning stages.

Introduction

In the context of the Asian financial crisis of 1997 a dictatorship in Indonesia that had lasted more than 30 years finally came to an end. The end of Suharto's New Order, throughout which the Indonesian armed forces (Tentara Nasional Indonesia – TNI) had safeguarded authoritarian rule, marked the start of the country's remarkable transition towards democracy. Indonesia's transition process featured, among other aspects, a general overhaul and liberalisation of the political system, including the establishment of a multiparty system, freedom of the press and the first free and fair elections in the country since 1956. Indonesia's democratisation also involved the decentralisation of a highly centralised political system, in which political power had largely been concentrated in the hands of Suharto, as well as attempts to reform the powerful military, which had backed Suharto's New Order and was the main instrument used to repress any form of opposition in the country.

However, Indonesia's transition process quickly became overshadowed by concerns over the future stability and territorial integrity of the country. East Timor seceded from Indonesia in 1999; in addition, post-Suharto Indonesia was troubled by the outbreak of communal violence between Christians and Muslims in the Moluccas and parts of Sulawesi, as well as by the escalation of secessionist conflicts in Indonesia's outermost provinces of West-Papua and Aceh. Many observers concluded that the inability of the Indonesian state to maintain control over its conflict-ridden provinces put the country at high risk of disintegration, raising the prospect of the balkanisation (*balkanisasi*) of Southeast Asia's largest state.[1]

Without refuting the significance of the rising levels of armed violence and the strengthening of centrifugal forces in regions such as West-Papua and especially Aceh in post-Suharto Indonesia, this article argues that notions of state disintegration and *balkanisasi* were instrumental to the TNI's political comeback. In danger of losing many of the privileges it had enjoyed under Suharto, the military used the threat of Indonesia's impending disintegration to lift the issue of military reform above politics. In successfully linking the debate over state fragility with the debate over military reform by arguing that the planned wide-ranging reforms would weaken the military's ability to safeguard the stability of the nation, the TNI was able to curtail, and at times even to halt, various reforms in the country's security sector.

This article builds on field research conducted in Indonesia's capital, Jakarta, as well as in the province of Aceh. Semi-structured interviews were conducted with an initial set of respondents presumed to be experts on the issue under investigation; snowball sampling was then used to identify, via the pool of initial respondents, other appropriate interview partners (including military officers, government officials, journalists, NGO workers and policy advisers). In addition to expert interviews, public sources such as newspaper reports, newspaper interviews, NGO reports and secondary sources were also included in the analysis. The study seeks to contribute to existing scholarship on the impact of security challenges on military reform in Indonesia by first emphasising that the scope and content of military reform has been inhibited by a dominant perspective on the impending disintegration of the country shared by most actors involved in the policy process, which has severely reduced the policy options considered.[2] Second, the article will emphasise that the notions of state fragility that have dominated Indonesia's security discourse have had implications beyond Indonesia, as they have enabled the connection of post-9/11 narratives viewing failed states as the generators of international terrorism with domestic narratives on *balkanisasi*.

Furthermore, the article aims to contribute to the critical scholarship on state fragility. Much of this literature has either focused on the conceptual and analytical shortcomings of state fragility,[3] revealing its inherently Western-centric bias, or it has regarded state fragility as a label used by Western powers to identify certain states as threats to Western security and economic interests; such a label has enabled these powers to expand the array of suitable policy responses to weak or failed states to include military interventions and 'neo-trusteeships'.[4] By focusing on the domestic power politics behind notions of state fragility in Indonesia, the article attempts to introduce a different perspective that goes beyond the centre–periphery dichotomy found in much of the critical scholarship on state fragility, according to which the term is simply a label stuck on postcolonial states to legitimise Western neo-imperialism.

Theoretically based on the work of the 'Copenhagen School', which has emphasised the importance of the social construction of security threats, this article enquires into how *balkanisasi* has been instrumentalised by the TNI in order to safeguard its privileges in the post-Suharto era. An understanding of security threats as socially constructed, and thus the assumption that a change in policy resulting from a successful threat construction is based on discursive processes,[5] not only lends itself to a specific set of research questions but also provides this analysis with a specific modus operandi. The analysis will first of all seek to determine how Indonesia's looming disintegration came to be perceived as the country's foremost security threat by analysing the rhetorical structures used to securitise the country's territorial integrity. In a second step, in addition to detecting the rhetorical structures employed in constructing the threat of *balkanisasi*, our analysis attempts to investigate the effectuation of securitisation moves via observable changes in government policy. Hence the article assesses how the salience of *balkanisasi* has affected the pace and scope of security sector reform. Finally, in the context of the debates over the looming disintegration of Indonesia and the army's continued dominance in internal security, the article shows how the TNI was able to improve its international image and re-establish itself as a key partner of international actors, despite its tarnished human rights record. The article begins with a review of the main claims of securitisation theory on the relationship between language and security policy. It then turns to the case of Indonesia, first discussing the historical role of the armed forces in Indonesian politics and the military reforms initiated after 1998. Subsequently the article examines how fears over the potential balkanisation of Indonesia became instrumental in obstructing many of the reformist policies launched after the fall of Suharto; in addition, it describes how the discourses over Indonesia's potential disintegration resonated outside the country. The article concludes with the observation that security sector reform in Indonesia has largely come to a standstill over the past decade, resulting in little change in the rhetoric and practices of the armed forces.

Constructing (in)security: some theoretical considerations

Arguing that any understanding of (in)security essentially rests on a discursive construction of various issues as threats and security problems, the proponents of the constructivist turn in Security Studies have established the theoretical concept of 'securitisation'. For the Copenhagen School the main focus of securitisation theory is the political use of language, with a concentration on the construction of (in)security and the 'power politics' of threat construction.[6] The proponents of this view therefore contest any objective conceptualisation of (in) security. Their definition of security as a 'speech act' suggests that it is the act of designating an issue as a threat or security problem that makes it performative. The work of the Copenhagen School has become one of the starting points for many researchers interested in the social construction of security.[7]

As a theoretical framework securitisation theory's focus on how security threats are socially constructed directs the attention of the analyst away from abstract considerations over what security and insecurity 'really' are and towards the socio-political practices that render something a threat to security. From that perspective the theory seeks to provide an understanding of how security threats emerge and why some phenomena are constructed as threats while others are not. Securitisation theory holds that it is the articulation of (in)security that 'makes' (in)security;[8] thus, by successfully arguing the urgency and priority of an issue deemed to be a security threat, an actor effectuates an extreme form of 'politicisation' of the alleged security threat. The constructed security threat thereby introduced into the realm of public policy, by virtue of its designation as an existential threat, enables policy makers to take to 'emergency measures'. Because of their perceived urgency and priority these measures often take place outside 'normal' political procedures and rules.[9]

Therefore securitisation basically involves a two-stage process. The first stage consists of the enunciation of (in)security via a specific speech act, which is based upon a certain 'rhetorical structure' that makes a case for the urgency of a threat by signifying that survival will be threatened if priority of action is denied. The second stage of the process consists of the acceptance of this 'securitisation move' by the audience (the referent object in need of protection). Audience acceptance in turn allows the elevation of the constructed threat beyond the realm of 'normal' politics. This elevation of the issue is to be understood primarily as its transfer 'beyond the democratic process of government' by means of its successful securitisation.[10]

Building on the work of the Copenhagen school, later scholarship has tried to refine the concept of securitisation. For the most part scholars have taken issue with the School's assumption that simply by 'uttering the term security the previous state of affairs changes'.[11] For example, in line with this reasoning, Floyd argues that securitisation as a practice is only successful or complete when 'the warning/promise made in the speech act is followed by a change in relevant behaviour by a relevant agent [...] that is justified by this agent with reference to the declared threat'.[12] Such a behavioural change may consist of anything from an increase in funding for security agents to the creation of new offices or programmes, to the establishment of international agreements or regimes to address security threats.

The TNI and politics in Indonesia

The political influence of the TNI – past and present – is closely linked to the founding myth of the Indonesian military. Through the 'militarisation of Indonesia's history',[13] part of the general enhancement of the military's political role beginning in the 1960s, the TNI was presented as the key national actor responsible for freeing Indonesia from colonial oppression and thus enabling the formation of the Republic of Indonesia.[14] As Rizal Sukma asserts, this 'led to the claim that the military was not only identified with the birth of Indonesia, but also in creating the Republic'.[15] In line with these claims the military's *dwifungsi* (dual function) doctrine stipulated that its main function was not simply the territorial defence of the country, but also safeguarding the integrity of the Indonesian Republic. This second duty has been interpreted by large parts of the military establishment as encompassing a wide range of socio-political roles through which the military should actively contribute to the stability of the country. During Suharto's New Order military officers held leading positions in Suharto's main political party, 'Golkar' (Partai Golongan Karya – Party of the Functional Groups), as well as in the government, the administration and the economy. The military were also allotted their own parliamentary fractions in the national and regional parliaments.[16] The military's influence was further enhanced through the structural counterpart to the *dwifungsi* doctrine, the territorial command structure, which established military structures parallel to the civilian administration across the country. In effect, this meant that, from the national level down to the village level, every civilian administrative unit was shadowed by a military unit.[17] This territorial command structure enabled soldiers to carry out the socio-political aspects of the *dwifungsi* doctrine.

With the fall of Suharto's New Order the military's involvement in Indonesian politics came under close scrutiny. Under pressure to reform it embarked on a series of widespread reforms aimed at the extraction of the military from the political arena. In 1998 an electoral bill called for the abolition of military factions in the national and regional legislatures by 2004 and the elimination of the military's offices for political and social affairs. In the same year the TNI severed its ties with Golkar. Reforms continued in 1999, when a bill was introduced that forbade active military officers from holding civilian positions in the government or the bureaucracy. In 2000 the military's *dwifungsi* was officially terminated; in addition, two decrees were issued that separated the police from the military and reduced the latter's official role to that of external defence. Moreover, beginning in late 1999, discussions over the future of the territorial command structure, which was at the core of the TNI's institutional interests and until that point had been excluded from the reform agenda, gained momentum. One of the leading reformists within the TNI, Major-General Agus Wirahadikusumah, described the territorial command structure as 'precisely what is obstructing democratisation, and it also conflicts with the armed forces' own efforts to carry out internal reforms'.[18] A proposal to disband the territorial command structure, drafted by reformers within the military with input from civil society organisations, was seen as an indicator of the 'seriousness' of the military reform.[19]

The end of the New Order brought about not only the implementation of institutional reforms of the military, but also changes at the policy level. During the Suharto era the government had exclusively dealt with internal security threats through a 'military-dominated security approach'.[20] By means of its grip on internal security policies and its self-proclaimed role as the guardian of the state, the military had been able to validate its position at the centre of Indonesian politics. With the fall of Suharto in 1998, however, the debates over Indonesia's security policies became increasingly pluralised. New reformist ideas were proposed by small but (at least briefly) influential circles of reform-minded military officers, politicians and academics, openly challenging the established beliefs concerning the military's central role in internal security and its function as the guardian of the state.[21] The exposure of the vast human rights abuses committed by the TNI during its counter-insurgency campaigns in East Timor, West-Papua and Aceh during the Suharto era increased demands for an end to its internal security function. Under pressure from the public outcry the

TNI's then Commander-in-chief, General Wiranto, publicly apologised to the people of Aceh for the atrocities committed by the Indonesia military in the province during the Suharto era.[22] Suharto's successor, President Nacharuddin Jusuf Habibie, also apologised for the past actions of the Indonesian security forces.

Pressure for further military reform also led to more general changes in the policies enacted by Jakarta *vis-à-vis* trouble spots such as Aceh and Papua. Habibie launched a far-reaching decentralisation process that offered Special Autonomy status to Aceh and West-Papua, pledging to find political solutions to both conflicts. The parliamentary speaker at the time, Akbar Tanjung, told reporters that 'we reject the security approach and military action to resolve the problems in Aceh', adding that 'we want a real dialogue set up to reconcile the Acehnese people with the rest of the nation' (*New York Times*, November 26, 1999). When a resurgence in clashes between the TNI and Acehnese Gerakan Aceh Merdeka (Free Aceh Movement – GAM) guerrillas beginning in late 1999 prompted the TNI to call for the re-imposition of martial law in Aceh, President Abdurrahman Wahid (Habibie's successor) rejected the request, to the dismay of many military officers. He instead promised to put an end to the military-driven 'security approach' by entering into peace talks with GAM in 2000. As part of this overall change in policy President Wahid even went so far as to declare threats against the territorial integrity of Indonesia to be a thing of the past, telling reporters: 'We have been able to maintain the territorial integrity of Indonesia', and 'We can say that the danger of disintegration is already passed'.[23] Thus, in 1999 and 2000, the New Order's 'security approach', featuring the army at the centre of internal security, was increasingly being challenged by reformers who called for the government to '"normalize" politics and the "emergency conditions" that had characterized politics since the army's rise to power in 1965'.[24]

Balkanisasi: constructing state fragility in post-Suharto Indonesia

However, the aforementioned institutional reforms and the changes undertaken with regard to the country's internal security policies were only supported by a small faction within the military establishment, as Marcus Mietzner describes: 'There is no doubt that the mainstream of the armed forces opposed the radical reform measures [...] and that it used every opportunity to halt and overturn them'.[25] In particular, the attempts to loosen the military's grip on internal security were met with resistance from many in the TNI. As a consequence, there was widespread hostility among military officials to any political solution to the Aceh conflict, as this was regarded as a first step towards Aceh's secession from Indonesia.[26] Indeed, from 1999 onwards, leading military figures repeatedly declared the disintegration of the Negara Kesatuan Republik Indonesia (Unitary State of the Indonesian Republic – NKRI) to be the main security threat to the country.[27] In January 2000 Chief of Staff General Tyasno Sutarto warned that the threat of national disintegration was an extremely serious issue requiring immediate attention. He also called for a more determined effort to curb separatism, asserting that the Indonesian people's vigilance against the threat of national disintegration had wavered. Addressing 'all TNI personnel, and especially army, and the general public', he 'appeal[ed] to all sides to cooperate in efforts to increase our national vigilance'.[28] His successor, Ryamizard Ryacudu, used even more alarmist language, stating that 'if I withdraw the troops from Papua on Saturday, there is no doubt that on Sunday they [the separatists] would declare independence'. He further added: 'Separatists in Aceh and Papua, if left alone, could become seeds of disintegration'. In order to metaphorically illustrate the imminent danger of Indonesia's disintegration, Ryacudu compared areas of separatist and communal conflicts to sparks in a haystack: 'You only need to blow on it a little and it will ignite'.[29] In addition, leading military figures, in the context of *balkanisasi* threat, reasserted the key role of the military as the main actor in charge of preserving the integrity of the Indonesian state. As Ryacudu claimed, 'the entire responsibility of defending Indonesia's unity lies in the hands of the army'.[30] In other words, these leaders were emphasising that the survival of the country largely depended on the military's ability to deal with *balkanisasi*.[31]

The TNI was quick to tie the threat of *balkanisasi* to the debates over military reform. Directly addressing the proponents of military reform, the army's Chief of Staff, General Ryacudu, argued that all plans to reduce the military's territorial command structure should be aborted. In response to demands for a reduction in or even the dissolution of the territorial command structure, Ryacudu declared that the 12 existing Military Area Commands (Kodams) were insufficient to enable the TNI to prevent the Indonesian state from disintegrating.[32] The TNI not only emphasised the importance of maintaining its territorial structure for the defeat of centrifugal forces, but also called for its expansion through the establishment of a new Aceh Kodam. These demands were echoed by politicians with close military ties. Muhammad Nasir Jamil, a member of the provincial parliament in Aceh, blamed the lack of a special military command for the upsurge of violence in Aceh: 'If Aceh had its own military command, like it did in the past, it would be easier for the military to coordinate in the field and curb the clashes' (*Jakarta Post*, December 29, 2001). By depicting the disintegration of Indonesia as the country's prime security threat in the post-Suharto era, the TNI effectively elevated the issue beyond the sphere of 'normal politics' by constructing it as an existential threat: the survival of the entire country was at stake, not just that of the administration in power. By effectively linking the threat of an Indonesian break-up to military reform, insinuating that any further reforms would severely weaken the TNI's ability to preserve the unitary state, the TNI created a narrative that characterised military reform as a problem for Indonesia's stability, rather than a solution to it.

Indeed, under Wahid's successor, President Megawati Sukarnoputri, *balkanisasi* became a key priority from 2001 onwards. The six-point working programme presented by Megawati upon coming to power included the defence of national unity. At the start of her presidency in 2001 Megawati seemed to reject the hardline military approach to the secessionist conflicts in Aceh and West-Papua, publicly apologising to the Acehnese and Papuans and promising greater regional autonomy. However, at the same time, she emphasised unity: 'One thing remains clear: that all this must be in the context of maintaining the territorial integrity of the unitary state of the Republic of Indonesia' (*Kyodo News*, August 20, 2001). During her annual state-of-the-nation address in 2002 Megawati told the parliament that the top priority of her government would be to defeat the separatist movement in Aceh, labelling GAM a 'terrorist' organisation that needed to be crushed (*The Australian*, August 2, 2002). She also referred to the 'threat of disintegration that has been afflicting the nation and country in recent years', claiming that her government would give priority to ending the armed conflicts in Aceh, Papua and other provinces.[33]

Taking the traditional view of the military establishment regarding the central role of the military in internal security, both Megawati and her Defence Minister, Sudarsono, were quick to point out that the TNI was holding Indonesia together in the face of the country's looming disintegration.[34] Megawati's perception of the role of the armed forces in post-Suharto Indonesia led her to dismiss the demands of democratic reformers that the impunity of the armed forces be ended: 'Suddenly we are aware of the need for a force to protect our beloved nation and motherland from breaking up. Guided by the soldier's oath and existing laws, carry out your duties and responsibilities in the best possible manner without worrying about being involved in human rights abuses. Do your job without hesitation.'[35] Furthermore, Megawati also linked the threat of the disintegration of Indonesia to regional and international security, stating: 'Territorial integrity is not only one of the attributes of the existence of the state, but is also a part of a more stable global order in which borders are not to be changed for any reason' (*Kyodo News*, August 2, 2001).

The perception of the Aceh conflict as the main threat to Indonesia's stability also had repercussions beyond Indonesia's borders. International concerns over the stability of the country steadily increased from 2000 onwards. In testimony to the US Senate in 2000 the then Director of the CIA, George Tenet, stated that 'several leaders in the region remain concerned that Jakarta's loss of East Timor – coupled with growing separatist tensions and communal violence across the archipelago – could result in the Balkanization of the country over the next several years'.[36] In a report to the US Congress the Congressional Research Service similarly found that 'The primary security threats to Indonesia are generally thought to come from within [...] This manifested itself in the former Indonesian province of East Timor, which is now an independent state, as well as in the far west of Indonesia, in Aceh, and in the far eastern part of the nation, in West Papua.'[37] A study published by the Rand Corporation in 2001 describes the question of 'whether Indonesia will survive in its present configuration or whether it will splinter into its component parts' as the most important issue affecting Indonesia's future. According to the study, 'The growing sectarian violence and the demands of the outlying islands for independence or greater autonomy are generating stresses that the Indonesian political system may not be able to withstand'.[38]

Furthermore, some international observers went on to reiterate the central role of the TNI in Indonesia's stability by tying the threat of *balkanisasi* to the ability of the Indonesian military to preserve the territorial integrity of the state. It was hereby argued that 'if the democratic experiment falters and Indonesia becomes more unstable or fragments, it could become a haven for extremists of all stripes. The role of the military, one of the few institutions that cuts across the many divides of Indonesian society, will be critical.'[39] According to this perspective, not only was the future of successive governments in Jakarta threatened by centrifugal forces, but also the security and stability of Indonesia and potentially the entire region.

The impact of *balkanisasi*

In the context of the increasing salience of the threat of *balkanisasi* and the successful self-portrayal of the TNI as the main actor responsible for preserving the integrity and stability of the Indonesian state, many of the policies directed at reforming Indonesia's military proved to be short-lived and limited in scope. These thwarted reforms included efforts to limit the TNI's influence in security affairs in general and its dominant role in internal security affairs (especially in Aceh), changes in the territorial command structure and doctrinal reforms. In Aceh the peace talks between GAM and the Indonesian government, which had produced an armistice in June 2000 (the 'Humanitarian Pause') and the Cessation of Hostilities in Aceh agreement in December 2002, collapsed in March 2003. This failure to achieve a political solution to the Aceh conflict was not simply a result of the GAM's reluctance to agree to a compromise with the government: according to observers, it was equally the result of deliberate attempts by the TNI to undermine the peace talks. Various incidents, notably attacks on international observers by pro-Indonesian protesters who were (according to media reports) transported in military trucks driven by military personnel,[40] illustrated the general unwillingness of the TNI to accept a political solution to the conflict that might have weakened its central role in internal security policies.[41] All this took place in a general political climate dominated by fears about Aceh following the 'East Timor blueprint', resulting in the further disintegration of Indonesia.[42]

The collapse of the peace talks marked the end of the 'soft' approaches towards the Aceh conflict that had been adopted between 2000 and 2002. This policy reversal was indicated by the decision to impose martial law in Aceh in 2003, a move that received almost unanimous support from the parliament and the media.[43] After years of constant warnings about the threat of *balkanisasi*, the decision was also supported by the Indonesian public. A survey conducted by the Asia Foundation in 2003 found that respondents thought that the Aceh conflict was Indonesia's third biggest problem (after 'economic performance' and 'violence'). In a previous survey in 1999 Aceh had not been mentioned at all.[44] At the same time the survey results indicated a general shift in public opinion in favour of the military. Whereas surveys conducted in 1999 and 2000 had shown strong mistrust of the TNI, an Asia Barometer survey in 2004 found that, when respondents were asked to indicate the extent to which they would trust the army to operate in the best interests of society, 85.3% said they trusted the army either 'a lot' (32.2%) or 'to some degree' (53.1%).[45] The army's trustworthiness compared favourably to that of other national institutions, including the parliament, political parties, the legal system and the police.

This positive shift in public opinion in the context of fears over *balkanisasi* was accompanied by a decrease in pressure for military reforms.[46] Because (according to military proponents) any reform of the territorial command structure would weaken the military and endanger the integrity of the nation-state, the territorial command structure was expanded rather than downsized or abolished. In 1999 and 2000 separate Kodams for West-Papua, Ambon and the Moluccas were established. As the influence of the TNI grew, plans for the re-establishment of the Aceh Kodam, a base that had been disbanded in the 1980s, regained momentum. Despite strong opposition from much of the Acehnese population, the military's demands were met in February 2002, when a new Kodam for Aceh was established.[47] The expansion of the territorial command structure led to a stronger permanent presence and enhanced the influence of the TNI in Aceh; this was regarded by observers as a sign of growing military influence and assertiveness at the national level.[48]

In addition to the reform of the territorial command structure, another key reform intended to loosen the TNI's grip on internal security affairs had been the institutional and operational separation of the military and the police. In Aceh these national reforms were mirrored by the transfer of the operational command over all security operations in the province from the military to the police in 2000. This led to a gradual reduction in the number of military personnel stationed in Aceh, whereas the number of police grew between 2000 and 2001 to an estimated 20,000.[49] These new policies were openly challenged by leading military figures, who called on the TNI to reaffirm its leading role in internal security matters. As General Sudrajat explained:

> The issue of national security can no longer be classified as internal and external threats. The issue of national security must be handled jointly by the TNI and the police. So, the dichotomy of the TNI having the duty of confronting external enemies and the police having the duty of safeguarding internal security is wrong. The issue of national security over the next 10 years will weigh heavily on the side of domestic security.[50]

Against the rising threat of *balkanisasi* in the context of the deteriorating security situation in Aceh, the province was remilitarised; the situation in Aceh was described as 'a counterinsurgency operation dominated by the military'.[51] The military's grip on internal security affairs was further tightened with the imposition of martial law in Aceh in 2003. By that time the military had, *de jure* and *de facto*, regained its dominance in internal security affairs;[52] the attempts made between 2000 and 2002 to limit the TNI's functions to external defence had proven to be unsuccessful. In line with the *de facto* re-establishment of the military as the central state actor in internal security, and in a strategic context in which the main security threats to Indonesia were viewed as stemming from separatists and terrorists, Indonesia's Defence White Book, published in 2003, ascribes a key role to the TNI in what is termed 'Operations Other Than War'.[53]

The continued involvement of the military in internal security has also limited the effects of doctrinal reforms. For the time being the general identity of the TNI is still largely one of praetorianism. The idea of the TNI as the guardian of the state is enshrined in the *Sapta Marga*, the oath taken by all soldiers, which describes one of the military's main functions as preserving the integrity of the 'Unitary State'.[54] Likewise, based on the assessment that 'armed separatist actions' constitute one of the country's main security problems, Indonesia's Defence White Book holds that the TNI's prime obligation is to protect the territorial integrity of the state.[55] Against this background, as analysts have pointed out, 'There remains a deep contempt for civilian rule and a belief that only the TNI is capable to rise above the petty rivalries and self-interested behaviour of post-Suharto civilian politicians'.[56] Hence, despite the new paradigm of political neutrality and non-involvement in everyday politics, the self-conception of the TNI as a political army still continues to influence the mindset and the strategies of the military.[57]

The salience of *balkanisasi* has also had repercussions outside Indonesia. The broadcasting of footage showing the massacres that the TNI committed in East Timor in 1991 sparked public outrage in the USA, causing the US Congress to restrict military aid to Indonesia. The suspension of all International Military Education and Training programmes in Indonesia was followed by a ban on the sale of fighter planes to it in 1993 and a ban on the sale of small arms and riot control equipment in 1994. The TNI's international reputation was further tarnished in 1999 as a result of the human rights violations committed by the army and the army-backed pro-Indonesian militias following East Timor's vote on independence. President Clinton was forced to ban all military training programmes and impose an arms embargo such that, by late 1999, US–Indonesia military relations had effectively been severed. A law passed by the US Congress (the Foreign Operations Appropriations Act) imposed various conditions that Jakarta would have to meet before military ties could be re-established and the arms embargo lifted. These conditions included (among others) accountability for military personnel involved in human rights atrocities and the establishment of civilian control over the armed forces.

However, the aftermath of 9/11 created new motivations for the renewal of US–Indonesian relations. Fears that fragile states in Southeast Asia, notably the Philippines and Indonesia, could become safe havens for transnational terror networks led to a gradual US rapprochement with Indonesia's security forces. Thus, after 9/11, fears over Indonesia's instability were linked to fears about Indonesia becoming a 'hospitable environment for international terrorism'. This latter concern was directly connected with Indonesia's 'porous borders', 'weak government and law enforcement', 'economic distress' and 'communal strife'.[58] Growing concern over fragile states as potential refuges for transnational terror networks led the Pentagon to propose a policy shift. For example, in late 2001 the then Deputy Secretary of Defence, Paul Wolfowitz, referred to 'a significant al Qaeda presence in Indonesia' as the main reason behind his proposal to revive US military ties with the country.[59] In 2002 the then Secretary of Defence, Donald Rumsfeld, argued that the suspension of military aid to Indonesia should be reconsidered in the light of concerns over the presence of terror networks on the archipelago.[60] At the same time proponents of closer military ties within the US defence and intelligence establishment were quick to identify the TNI as one of the key actors in any counter-terrorism cooperation with Indonesia.[61] Although the US Congress was initially sceptical regarding calls for closer ties with the TNI, a revision of the Foreign Operations Appropriations Act in 2005 allowed the US administration to bypass the conditions imposed by the act by claiming a national security waiver. Shortly thereafter the Bush administration sidestepped the restrictions on military ties with Indonesia, claiming mutual security concerns in the context of the 'Global War on Terror' (GWOT) as its main reason for lifting the arms embargo and re-establishing military relations.

Clearly, the US decision to re-establish military ties with Indonesia was not simply the direct result of the Indonesian military's securitising moves; the USA certainly followed its own agenda in the context of its GWOT. However, the notion of fragile states as safe havens for terrorists did produce an opportunity for the US defence establishment to actively push for the re-establishment of military ties with Indonesia. In addition, it enabled Indonesian elites to link their notions of *balkanisasi* to the global discourse on failed states and terrorism by labelling separatist organisations such as the GAM 'terrorists' and by repeatedly referring to the danger the disintegration of Indonesia would pose for international security. The interpenetrative correspondence between these discourses proved to be instrumental in facilitating the TNI's rehabilitation of its tarnished international image, allowing it to transform from pariah to partner within the period of a few years – despite the fact that it had failed to fully comply with the Foreign Operations Appropriations Act.

Conclusion

The above analysis has shown how the construction of the threat of *balkanisasi* has enabled the TNI to limit, and at times abort, various important aspects of military reform, allowing it to retain many of its privileges. The acceptance by key domestic players, first and foremost the Megawati government, of the idea that Indonesia was under imminent threat of disintegration during its transition to democracy further enabled the military *de facto* to autonomously run all counterinsurgency operations in Aceh and West-Papua and to retain its tight control over internal security affairs in the country, despite the demands of reformers. Although the TNI was forced to give up its direct role in Indonesian politics after the fall of Suharto, by preserving many of its structural powers the military continues to play an important 'behind-the-scenes' role in the political arena. In addition, the positive reception of the notion of impending *balkanisasi* and the acceptance of the key role of the military in preserving Indonesia's stability against centrifugal forces by the USA and others have provided new opportunities for the TNI to rehabilitate its tarnished image in the international community. The securitisation of fears about the potential disintegration of Indonesia has also enabled the issue of separatist conflicts between Jakarta and outer provinces such as Aceh and West-Papua to be framed solely as threats to the nation-state – thereby ignoring the legitimate grievances of the population in Aceh and in other zones of civil strife in Indonesia. This has paved the way for overtly militaristic, coercive responses to the conflicts in Aceh and other parts of the archipelago, which in turn have led to human rights violations by security forces that have often exacerbated these conflicts. The situation in Aceh changed only after the Boxing Day 2004 tsunami devastated large parts of the province, which facilitated the brokering of a peace deal between the GAM and Jakarta under heavy domestic and international pressure. However, this partial de-securitisation has been limited to Aceh only. For Indonesia's other conflict zones, especially Papua, the securitising rhetoric and the coercive, militaristic approach have remained in place.[62]

With regard to the general debate on state fragility, this study shows how notions of state fragility can be used by state actors, such as security forces, in so-called 'weak' states to advance their own particular interests through the use of certain referential frames accepted by domestic and international audiences. Thus, in contrast to much of the literature, this case study demonstrates that 'weak' states are not merely recipients of the discursive formations developed by Western powers. On the contrary, notions of state fragility and the commonly associated security threats have been carried by and have served to advance the specific interests of the Indonesian military, domestically and internationally. At the domestic level fears over the imminent disintegration of the country have severely restricted reforms of the security sector in the post-Suharto era; these fears have also resonated internationally, especially after 9/11, in conjunction with a more general shift in the global threat perception of the USA and its allies. The increasingly influential idea that the absence of internal stability is the root of the state fragility perceived as threatening the security of the West, and the resulting discursive shift, have affected Western views of the TNI, promoting it from *persona non grata* to an ally in the GWOT.

To be sure, this is not to suggest that the Indonesian military has been able to manipulate the minds of policy makers in the USA and elsewhere directly, nor that the USA had no agenda of its own in re-establishing full military ties with Indonesia. However, what this study illustrates is that, contrary to much of the critical scholarship on state fragility, the concept is not exclusively rooted in Western discourses. In addition, there seem to be many more reciprocal effects between Western and non-Western ideas of state fragility than has previously been assumed.

Notes on Contributor

Felix Heiduk is Lecturer in the Department of Political Science and International Studies, University of Birmingham. He has published on security sector reform, civil–military relations and Southeast Asian security in journals such as the *Pacific Review*, *European Security* and *Cooperation and Conflict*. He recently edited a book, *Security Sector Reform in Southeast Asia – From Policy to Practice*, which will be published by Palgrave in early 2014.

Notes

1. Wanandi, "Indonesia"; Malley, "Indonesia"; Huxley, *Disintegrating Indonesia?* and Weatherbee, "Indonesia." Describing the fragmentation, disintegration or break-up of a state into smaller, often hostile states, the term 'balkanisation' has traditionally been used in reference to the political situation in the Balkans during the late 19th and early 20th centuries, when the Balkan region of the Ottoman Empire split up into smaller warring states. With regard to post-Suharto Indonesia, the term *balkanisasi* has been used to refer to the break-up of Yugoslavia in the early 1990s, which was accompanied by the so-called Yugoslav wars, as well as internal strife in Bosnia and Kosovo. The use of the term is generally pejorative.
2. Moore, "The Indonesian Military's Last Years in East Timor"; Roosa, "Finalising the Nation"; Honna, "Security Challenges and Military Reform"; and Beeson and Bellamy, *Securing Southeast Asia.*
3. Call, "The Fallacy of the 'Failed State'"; Gruffydd Jones, "The Global Political Economy of Social Crisis"; and Wai, "Neo-patrimonialism."
4. Bøås and Jennings, "Failed States"; Duffield, "Liberal Interventionism," 116–129; and Manjikian, "Diagnosis, Intervention, and Cure."
5. Buzan et al., *Security.*
6. Ibid., 32.
7. Sjöstedt, "Ideas, Identities and Internalization"; Floyd, "Can Securitization Theory be Used in Normative Analysis?" Croft, *Securitizing Islam*; Salter, "Securitization and Desecuritization"; McDonald, "Securitization"; and Vuori, "Illocutionary Logic and Strands of Securitization."

8. Buzan et al., *Security*, 31.
9. Ibid., 26.
10. Vuori, "Illocutionary Logic and Strands of Securitization," 66.
11. Balzacq, "The Three Faces of Securitization," 180.
12. Floyd, "Can Securitization Theory be Used in Normative Analysis?" 429.
13. McGregor, *History in Uniform*, 26.
14. In fact, the military was far from being a unitary actor. The first separatist rebellion after independence was led by religious leaders and disgruntled army officers from the outer islands. See McVey, "The Post-revolutionary Transformation." Thanks to the second reviewer for bringing this to my attention.
15. Sukma, "Civil–Military Relations," 151.
16. Vatikiotis, *Indonesian Politics under Suharto*, 70.
17. At the national level the territorial command structure rested on the army's 12 Kodam (regional commands). The Kodam formed the basis for the administration, logistics, personnel, training and general welfare of all assigned and attached army units in the region. Each Kodam was then divided into smaller administrative units: the Military Resort (Garrison) Commands (Korem), Military District Commands (Kodim) and Military Subdistrict Commands (Koramil). At the lowest level non-commissioned officers were stationed in every village in the country.
18. Bourchier and Hadiz, *Indonesian Politics and Society*, 306.
19. Mietzner, *The Politics of Military Reform*, 21.
20. Chauvel and Aspinall, "Constructing Separatist Threats."
21. Honna, *Military Politics and Democratization in Indonesia.*
22. Honna, "Military Ideology," 86.
23. "Indonesia's Wahid: 'We Are Beginning the Rule of Law'." *Businessweek*, May 28, 2000. http://www.businessweek.com/stories/2000-05-28/indonesias-wahid-we-are-beginning-the-rule-of-law-intl-edition.
24. Chauvel and Aspinall, "Constructing Separatist Threats," 70.
25. Mietzner, *The Politics of Military Reform*, 27.
26. Schulze, "Insurgency and Counter-insurgency," 236.
27. This is not to suggest that concerns over the integrity of the Indonesian state only emerged after the fall of Suharto. On the contrary, such concerns worried Indonesia's elite even before the country's independence. See Aspinall and Berger, "The Break-up of Indonesia?"
28. "Army Chief says Threat of National Disintegration 'Extremely Serious'." BBC Summary of World Broadcasts, 28 January 2000.
29. "Indonesian Army Chief says Troops must Stay in Papua, Aceh." BBC Summary of World Broadcasts, 14 October 2004.
30. Ibid.
31. Interviews with Ikrar Nusa Bhakti, Research Fellow at LIPI, Jakarta, 25 January 2005; and General (ret) Kiki Syahnakri, Jakarta, 26 January 2005.
32. "Indonesian Army Chief to Increase Military Area Commands." BBC Summary of World Broadcasts, 17 October 2002.
33. Interview with Wirjono Sastrohandojo, negotiator for the Indonesian government during the Aceh peace talks, Jakarta, 9 February 2005. See also "Megawati promises tougher action on Aceh separatists." *Jakarta Post*, August 2, 2002.
34. Sudarsono, Juwono, Indonesia's Minister of Defence, Luncheon Speech, United States Indonesia Society, 5 April 2005. http://www.usindo.org/resources/luncheon-speech-by-the-minister-of-defense-of-indonesia-h-e-juwono-sudarsono.
35. Bourchier, "Combat zone."
36. George J Tenet, Director, CIA, Testimony on "The Worldwide Threat in 2000: Global Realities of our National Security." US Senate, Committee on Intelligence, 2 February 2000, https://www.cia.gov/news-information/speeches-testimony/2000/dci_speech_020200.html.
37. Vaughn, *Indonesia*, 8.
38. Rabasa and Chalk, *Indonesia's Transformation*, 27.
39. Rabasa, "Stop Snubbing Indonesia's Military."
40. Schulze, "Forcing the Issue," 24.
41. ICG, *Aceh: How Not to Win Hearts and Minds.*
42. Crouch and Aspinall, *The Aceh Peace Process*, 15. See also HD Centre, "Aceh Initiative."
43. Interviews with Adi Warsidi, journalist for *Koran Tempo* newspaper, Banda Aceh, 17 March 2005; and Radzie, journalist for *Aceh Kita* newspaper, Banda Aceh, 17 March 2005.
44. Asia Foundation, *Democracy in Indonesia*, 43.
45. https://www.asiabarometer.org/en/surveys/2004.
46. Interview with General (ret) Agus Widjojo, Adviser for Security Sector Reform at the United Nations Support Facility for Indonesian Recovery, Jakarta, 14 March 2005.
47. ICG, *Aceh: Slim Chance for Peace*, 9.
48. Sukma, *Security Operations in Aceh*, 16.
49. Amnesty International, "Indonesia."

50. "Army will step in if elections turn bloody." *Kompas* (Jakarta), December 23, 2003. http://www.asia-pacific-solidarity.net/southeastasia/indonesia/indoleft/2003/kompas_ tni-ad_231203.htm.
51. Sukma, *Security Operations in Aceh*, 13.
52. Interview with Hari Prihatono, researcher at the Propatria Institute, Jakarta, 20 January 2005.
53. Ministry of Defence of the Republic of Indonesia, *Defending the Country*, 45.
54. Mulyono and Radityawara Hidayat, "'Sapta Marga'," 235–260.
55. Ministry of Defence of the Republic of Indonesia, *Defending the Country*, 53.
56. Sebastian and Iisgindarsah, "Taking Stock of Military Reform," 30.
57. Sukma, "Civil–Military Relations."
58. Rabasa, "Stop Snubbing Indonesia's Military."
59. Wolfowitz, "Of Missiles and Terrorism."
60. Donald Rumsfeld, "Media Availability with Indonesian Minister of Defense Matori Abdul Dajalil," 13 May 2002. http://www.defense.gov/transcripts/transcript.aspx? transcriptid=3443.
61. Murphy, "US Rapprochement with Indonesia."
62. Supriatma, "TNI/Polri in West Papua"; and Heiduk, "Two Sides of the Same Coin?" 295–314.

Bibliography

Amnesty International. "Indonesia: Amnesty International Briefing on the Deteriorating Human Rights Situation in Aceh for Participants in the asean Regional Forum (AFR), July 2001." London, 2001.

Asia, Foundation. *Democracy in Indonesia: A Survey of the Indonesian Electorate 2003*. Jakarta: Asia Foundation, 2003.

Aspinall, Edward, and Mark T. Berger. "The Break-up of Indonesia? Nationalisms after Decolonisation and the Limits of the Nation-state in Post-Cold War Southeast Asia." *Third World Quarterly* 22, no. 6 (2001): 1003–1024.

Balzacq, Thierry. "The Three Faces of Securitization: Political Agency, Audience and Context." *European Journal of International Relations* 11, no. 2 (2005): 171–201.

Beeson, Mark, and Alex J. Bellamy. *Securing Southeast Asia: The Politics of Security Sector Reform*. London: Routledge, 2007.

Bøås, Morten, and Kathleen M. Jennings. "'Failed States' and 'State Failure': Threats or Opportunities?" *Globalizations* 4, no. 4 (2007): 475–485.

Bourchier David. "Combat zone." *Inside Indonesia* 71 (Jul.–Sep. 2002) http://www.insideindonesia.org/feature-editions/combat-zone.

Bourchier, David, and Vedi R. Hadiz. *Indonesian Politics and Society: A Reader*. London: Routledge, 2003.

Buzan, Barry, Ole Wæver, and Jaap de Wilde. *Security: A New Framework for Analysis*. Boulder, CO: Lynne Rienner, 1998.

Call, Charles T. "The Fallacy of the 'Failed State'." *Third World Quarterly* 29, no. 8 (2008): 1491–1507.

Chauvel, Richard, and Edward Aspinall. "Constructing Separatist Threats: Security and Insecurity in Indonesian Aceh and Papua." In *Critical Security in the Asia-Pacific*, edited by. Anthony Burke, and Matt McDonald, 89–104. Manchester: Manchester University Press, 2007.

Croft, Stuart. *Securitizing Islam*. Cambridge: Cambridge University Press, 2012.

Crouch, Harold A., and Edward Aspinall. *The Aceh Peace Process: Why It Failed*. Washington, DC: East-West Center, 2003.

Duffield, Mark. "Liberal Interventionism & the Fragile State: Linked by Design." In *Empire, Development and Colonialism: The Past in the Present*, edited by. Vernon Hewitt, and Mark Duffield, 116–129. Woodbridge: James Currey, 2009.

Floyd, Rita. "Can Securitization Theory be Used in Normative Analysis? Towards a Just Securitization Theory." *Security Dialogue* 42, no. 4–5 (2011): 427–439.

Gruffydd Jones, Branwen. "The Global Political Economy of Social Crisis: Towards a Critique of the 'Failed State' Ideology." *Review of International Political Economy* 15, no. 2 (2008): 180–205.

HD Centre. "Aceh Initiative – Internal Review." Henri Dunant Centre for Humanitarian Dialogue, Geneva, 2003.

Heiduk, Felix. "Two Sides of the Same Coin? Separatism and Democratization in Post-Suharto Indonesia." In *Democratization in Post-Suharto Indonesia*, edited by. Marco Bünte and Andreas Ufen, 295–314. London: Routledge, 2009.

Honna, Jun. "Military Ideology in Response to Democratic Pressure during the Late Suharto Era: Political and Institutional Contexts." In *Violence and the State in Suhartos Indonesia*, edited by Benedict Richard O'Gorman Anderson, 54–89. Ithaca, NY: Cornell University Press, 2001.

Honna, Jun. *Military Politics and Democratization in Indonesia*. London: Routledge, 2003.

Honna, Jun. "Security Challenges and Military Reform in Post-authoritarian Indonesia: The Impact of Separatism, Terrorism, and Communal Violence." In *The Politics of Military Reform: Experiences from Indonesia and Nigeria*, edited by. Jürgen Rüland, Maria-Gabriela Manea, and Hans Born, 185–201. Heidelberg: Springer, 2012.

Huxley, Tim. *Disintegrating Indonesia? Implications for Regional Security*. London: International Institute for Strategic Studies, 2002.

ICG. *Aceh: How Not to Win Hearts and Minds*. Brussels: International Crisis Group, 2003.

ICG. *Aceh: Slim Chance for Peace*. Brussels: International Crisis Group, 2002.

Malley, Michael. "Indonesia: The Erosion of State Capacity." In *State Failure and State Weakness in a Time of Terror*, edited by. Robert I. Rotberg, 183–218. Washington, DC: Brookings Institution Press, 2003.

Manjikian, Mary. "Diagnosis, Intervention, and Cure: The Illness Narrative in the Discourse of the Failed State." *Alternatives: Global, Local, Political* 33, no. 3 (2008): 335–357.

McDonald, Matt. "Securitization and the Construction of Security." *European Journal of International Relations* 14, no. 4 (2008): 563–587.

McGregor, Katharine, E. *History in Uniform: Military Ideology and the Construction of Indonesia's Past*. Singapore: nus Press, 2007.

McVey, Ruth. "The Post-revolutionary Transformation of the Indonesian Army." *Indonesia*, no. 11 (1971): 131–176.

Mietzner, Marcus. *The Politics of Military Reform in Post-Suharto Indonesia: Elite Conflict, Nationalism, and Institutional Resistance*. Washington, DC: East-West Center, 2006.

Ministry of Defence of the Republic of Indonesia. *Defending the Country: Entering the 21st Century*. Jakarta, 2003.

Moore, Samuel. "The Indonesian Military's Last Years in East Timor: An Analysis of Its Secret Documents." *Indonesia* 72 (2001): 9–44.

Mulyono, Edy, and Eri Radityawara Hidayat. "'Sapta Marga': The Indonesian Armed Forces' Code of Conduct and its Implementation in the Post-New Order Era." In *Military Ethics: International Perspectives,* edited by Stefan Seilerand Jeff Stoufer 235–260. Kingston: Canadian Defence Academy Press, 2010.

Murphy Ann Marie. "US Rapprochement with Indonesia: From Problem State to Partner." *Contemporary Southeast Asia: A Journal of International and Strategic Affairs* 32, no. 3 (2010): 362–387.

Rabasa Angel. 2002. "Stop snubbing Indonesia's military." *International Herald Tribune,* August 2. http://www.rand.org/commentary/2002/08/02/IHT.html.

Rabasa, Angel, and Peter Chalk. *Indonesia's Transformation and the Stability of Southeast Asia*. Santa Monica, CA: Rand Corporation, 2001.

Roosa, John. "Finalising the Nation: The Indonesian Military as the Guarantor of National Unity." *Asia Pacific Viewpoint* 48, no. 1 (2007): 99–111.

Salter, Mark B. "Securitization and Desecuritization: A Dramaturgical Analysis of the Canadian Air Transport Security Authority." *Journal of International Relations and Development* 11, no. 4 (2008): 321–349.

Schulze, Kirsten E. "Forcing the Issue." *The World Today* 59, no. 6 (2003): 24–25.

Schulze Kirsten E. "Insurgency and Counter-insurgency: Strategy and the Aceh Conflict, October 1976–May 2004." In *Verandah of Violence: The Background to the Aceh Problem*, edited by Anthony Reid, 225–271. Singapore: NUS Press, 2006.

Sebastian Leonard, C. and Iisgindarsah. "Taking Stock of Military Reform in Indonesia." In *The Politics of Military Reform: Experiences from Indonesia and Nigeria*, edited by Jürgen Rüland, Maria-Gabriela Manea and Hans Born, Heidelberg: Springer, 2012.

Sjöstedt, Roxanna. "Ideas, Identities and Internalization: Explaining Securitizing Moves." *Cooperation and Conflict* 48, no. 1 (2013): 143–164.

Sukma Rizal. "Civil–Military Relations in Post-authoritarian Indonesia." In *Democracy under Stress: Civil–Military Relations in South and Southeast Asia*, edited by Paul Chambersand Aurel Croissant, 29–56. Bangkok: Institute of Security & International Studies, Chulalongkorn University, 2010.

Sukma, Rizal. *Security Operations in Aceh: Goals, Consequences, and Lessons*. Washington, DC: East-West Center, 2004.

Supriatma, Antonius Made Tony . "TNI/Polri in West Papua: How Security Reforms Work in the Conflict Region." *Indonesia*, no 95 (2013): 93–124.

Vatikiotis Michael, R. J. *Indonesian Politics under Suharto: The Rise and Fall of the New Order*. London: Routledge, 2004.

Vaughn, Bruce. *Indonesia: Domestic Politics, Strategic Dynamics, and American Interests: crs Report for Congress RL32394*, Washington DC: Congressional Research Service, 2005.

Vuori, Juha A. "Illocutionary Logic and Strands of Securitization: Applying the Theory of Securitization to the Study of Non-democratic Political Orders." *European Journal of International Relations* 14, no. 1 (2008): 65–99.

Wai, Zubairu. "Neo-patrimonialism and the Discourse of State Failure in Africa." *Review of African Political Economy* 39, no. 131 (2012): 27–43.

Wanandi, Jusuf. "Indonesia: A Failed State?" *Washington Quarterly* 25, no. 3 (2002): 135–146.

Weatherbee, Donald E. "Indonesia: Political Drift and State Decay." *Brown Journal of World Affairs* 9, no. 1 (2002): 23–33.

Wolfowitz Paul. 2001. "Of Missiles and Terrorism." *Far Eastern Economic Review,* November 8. http://www.defense.gov/transcripts/transcript.aspx?transcriptid= 2245.

When it pays to be a 'fragile state': Uganda's use and abuse of a dubious concept

Jonathan Fisher

International Development Department, University of Birmingham, UK

The labelling of certain states as 'fragile states' has often been portrayed as an act of domination by Western donors over the developing world. Nonetheless, this type of categorisation also presents opportunities to non-Western governments. This article suggests that the aid-dependent government of Uganda has increased its room for manoeuvre with donors by emphasising the degree of instability in the north of the country. By using this notion of state fragility, the Ugandan regime has successfully persuaded donors to continue their support, despite its domestic transgressions. The article will also attempt to explain the regime's use of a contradictory, but equally persuasive, international discourse that presents Uganda as stable, strong and secure. In exploring how Kampala has successfully employed both narratives to carve out greater agency with donors, the article will emphasise the significance of donors' physical detachment from the Ugandan 'periphery' in this dynamic.

Introduction

Though increasingly criticised by scholars, the notion of the 'fragile state' has become a central and influential one for Western policy makers. Since the mid-2000s major Western donor institutions have steadily realigned their development and security programmes to focus on entities they categorise as 'fragile', to the extent that UK Department for International Development (DFID) officials have been known to refer to their department as a 'fragile states donor'.[1] This growing donor emphasis on prioritising relations with 'fragile states' as members of a separate, identifiable category has had important ramifications for the overall nature of donor–recipient engagement: for donors 'fragile states' merit a distinctive type and level of international support. Moreover, many donors consider sustained international intervention in 'fragile states' to be more justifiable – and more altruistic – than support given to 'stronger' states.[2]

These and other issues related to the state fragility label have been subjected to increasing scholarly scrutiny in recent years. However, in focusing on how Western actors have used the concept and how this has affected developing states, the literature has largely overlooked the agency of these states or their governments in this dynamic. Although the term has clearly been created and applied by Western actors, their 'fragile states' agenda has nevertheless provided important opportunities for 'weak state' governments to secure agency in the international system. This aspect of the 'fragile states' label requires further attention.

This article will advance the critique of the 'fragile states' concept by focusing on how its manipulation, instrumentalisation and reconstruction by one such state has allowed that country to carve out agency in an international system whose structures would otherwise render it weak and subordinate. In order to support this contention with solid and in-depth empirical evidence, a single case study will be explored: the regime in Uganda, which has been led by Yoweri Museveni since 1986. The findings of the study, however, have relevance far beyond this one state, as will be highlighted in the final part of the article.

The selection of Uganda is based on four main considerations. First, over half the states typically characterised as 'fragile' by organisations such as the OECD are located in Africa.[3] Second, Uganda has been heralded as a successful model of post-conflict reconstruction by donors, practitioners and some academics since the 1990s (see below), but nevertheless continues to appear on lists of 'fragile' and 'failed' states.[4] It therefore provides an interesting puzzle for any exploration of the 'fragile state' concept. Third, the Museveni regime has been heavily dependent upon Western donor aid over the past two decades, and has arguably been in a structurally weak position in the global system as a result. Finally, despite this position, the regime has nevertheless proven itself to be strongly committed to securing agency in its relations with donors; it therefore provides a valuable case study for exploring the dynamics of African states engaging with Western discourses.

The article will investigate how the Museveni regime, using a variety of 'image management' strategies, has successfully employed the discourse of state fragility – particularly in relation to various domestic insurgencies – in order to secure sustained international support and avoid censure for governance transgressions during the 1990s and 2000s. This strategy has bolstered existing donor rationales for extending support, notably those linked to counter-terrorism. In the process, the article will suggest, the regime has been able to establish a significant degree of agency in its relationship with donors.

It will also be made clear, however, that the Museveni government has simultaneously challenged the 'fragile state' label for Uganda by promoting a parallel discourse focused on the rebuilding of the country under the present regime. This narrative has centred on the 'strong' Ugandan state and has also been effectively deployed by Kampala in encounters with donors as a means of securing international assistance. This perception of Uganda has been internalised by donor officials dealing with the east African country alongside that of the 'fragile' Ugandan state, demonstrating the potential for African agency in reshaping donor-'authored' concepts. The regime's success in portraying Uganda to donors as a simultaneously 'strong' and 'fragile' state also provides further evidence of the conceptual weakness of the 'fragile states' terminology and highlights crucial conceptual and practical challenges for the donors designing interventions in these states.

As part of this analysis it is crucial to explain why donor officials have largely been willing to accept both these narratives on Uganda. By way of conclusion, therefore, the contrast between donors' personal, daily experience of the secure Ugandan capital (the 'centre') and their rare, usually fleeting, stage-managed and highly securitised encounters with the distant rebel-ridden periphery, at least until the later 2000s, will be emphasised. These divergent security environments, it will be concluded, have provided the regime with an ideal opportunity to present multiple, equally persuasive narratives on Ugandan state fragility to donors.

In making these arguments the article will be divided into four sections. The first will describe how the fragile state concept has been criticised by scholars in recent years and will examine the extent to which the agency of fragile states is (and could be) considered part of this debate. Sections two and three will explore the two contrasting images of state fragility presented to donors by the Ugandan government since the 1990s. With a particular focus on the regime's characterisations of the war in northern Uganda and the pre-Museveni 'chaotic' era of Idi Amin and Milton Obote and on how these images have complemented existing donor rationales for continued support, these sections will show how the government has secured agency in its relations with international 'partners'. The article will then conclude by investigating how centre–periphery dynamics and information asymmetry have made it easier for donors to simultaneously accept two opposing narratives, and what the wider implications of this dispensation might be.

'Donors', 'donor officials' and policy making on Africa: a conceptual and methodological note

In exploring these two narratives the article adopts a constructivist methodology that understands donor perceptions of the stability of foreign states as changeable, dynamic and ultimately formed through direct and indirect interactions with a variety of information sources on the topic, both directly and indirectly. Focusing on the role of the Ugandan government as an 'information source', the article will draw upon semi-structured interviews conducted between 2008 and 2013 with current and former Western donor officials and current and former Ugandan government and military officials. Because of the sensitivity of much of this information, the identities of most of the interviewees have been anonymised by mutual consent.

The interview data will be complemented by a discourse analysis of the statements and speeches of Ugandan officials, both in Uganda and abroad, on a variety of topics, as well as by the transcripts of interviews and roundtables involving such officials available through the media and policy institutes. By evaluating the lobbyist disclosure forms submitted to the US Department of Justice since the 1990s, Uganda's use of US lobbyists to influence the views of donors will also be considered. Accounts of donor visits to and around Uganda, available through Ugandan and international media sources, and donor and international NGO (INGO) reports will also be examined and, where possible, triangulated with existing interview data. Finally, the study will draw upon insights garnered by the author during a Research Fellowship in the UK Foreign and Commonwealth Office (FCO) that began in January 2013. This fellowship was on a 'background' basis only, and therefore no specific information or data from it will be cited in the article. The experience has nevertheless informed the author's judgment throughout the study.

Any discussion of the 'donor community' runs the risk of making generalisations about a group of actors and institutions who in reality are often markedly different from one another along organisational and national lines. In the case of Uganda, however, broadly similar perspectives on the country's fragility and integrity have been shared by Western donor governments – in particular, by the two largest bilateral donors, whose policies and approaches are explored in greatest depth in this study: the USA and the UK. Although this permits an analysis of donors as a collective entity, it must be acknowledged that, even among Uganda's donors, different priorities and agendas have existed and occasionally collided.[5]

The differences of perspective between donor officials in Western capitals and 'in-country' embassies or aid agencies, however, are more pertinent for this enquiry. The present study focuses primarily on how the Ugandan government has engaged with – and attempted to directly manage the perceptions of – donor officials within Uganda itself, rather than donor headquarters staff *per se* (although many such staff members have, of course, visited the country). It is argued that, although donor policy towards states like Uganda is driven by officials in headquarters with national strategies and interests in mind,[6] the views of 'in-country' staff considerably influence these strategies through written dispatches and personal exchanges during trips back to headquarters and while hosting visiting staff.

This is not to say that outspoken ambassadors, for example, can often force through rapid changes in their government's entire approach to a state when their colleagues at home disagree with their stance. It is nevertheless clear that changes in perceptions at the local donor level often lead to similar changes at the headquarters level over a period of time – as with the changing US views of Kenya's Moi regime in the early 1990s, for example. This subject has been under-explored and under-theorised in the academic literature, an assertion based on the author's interviews with a range of current and former donor officials who have worked at national headquarters, as well as on his observations of the policy-making process within the FCO, consultations of FCO archival material and information available from *Wikileaks*.

Fragile states and agency

Since the 1980s, the concept of the 'fragile state' has been utilised by scholars according to various labels,[7] to describe, at the most basic level, a state that cannot exercise those functions expected of it in the post-Westphalian era.[8] Since 9/11 the notion has also become popular with policy makers.[9] The term has, nevertheless, attracted substantial criticism from academic commentators. Much of this critical analysis has concentrated on exposing the category's weak conceptual underpinnings.[10] Another major strand of this literature condemns the concept as rooted in objectionable notions of imperialism and the 'otherness' of non-Western states,[11] which insidiously provide legitimacy for Western governments that propose and attempt to carry out interventions in states they categorise as 'fragile'.[12]

The focus of much of this commentary has been on the Western policy-making community, examining how Western actors have used the concept for their own ends and the consequences of the resulting interventions. The 'fragile states' in question (along with their governments) have largely been considered to be the passive objects of Western political and discursive domination. Indeed, with some limited exceptions, the academic critics of the 'fragile states' agenda have devoted little attention to the agency (potential or otherwise) of these states in the international system.[13] This omission is problematic, as it implies that there is little of interest to say about how fragile states have used or responded to the concept as independent actors exercising agency in the global arena.

Drawing such a conclusion would clearly be rash: political scientists have demonstrated in recent years that even the weakest of states can carve out agency in its relationships with the international system by strategically engaging with key donor discourses.[14] In his exposition of 'extraversion', for example, Bayart has convincingly argued that a variety of African states have used 'the discourse of democracy' in their interactions with donors as a means of extracting resources, describing how leaders have used 'duplicity' and 'make-believe' to manipulate their Western patrons.[15] Similarly, in their exploration of African 'ownership', Whitfield and Fraser have pointed to the political and diplomatic space secured with donors by regimes in contemporary Rwanda and Ethiopia. The authors assert that these countries have been 'playing the card of the "donor darling" and "good reformer"' in their dialogues and engagement with the donor community.[16] Beswick and Fisher have further developed this argument, showing how the Rwandan and Ugandan governments have each secured substantial room for manoeuvre in otherwise aid-dependent relationships with Western donors by promoting themselves in line with well established donor discourses on security, regional peacekeeping and counter-terrorism.[17]

A slight ambiguity arises in this literature, however, as to the relationship between these 'Western' discourses and African agency. In the analyses cited above the relationship between African states and governments and those in the West appears to be somewhat transactional: African self-promotion (and actions) in line with Western narratives is 'exchanged' for increased aid and decreased donor scrutiny of domestic governance trends. More broadly African actors are considered, albeit implicitly, in terms of their 'accessing' discourses, which have been 'authored' and continue to be regulated by those in the West. Clearly, aid disbursements reflect the agendas and priorities of donor bureaucracies, whether they align with 'recipient need' or (as is more common) 'donor interests'. The question of whether the authorship of these discourses can change over time, as they interact with and are to some degree 'managed' by recipient governments, however, remains less clear.

In exploring how the Ugandan regime has engaged with and attempted to reframe donor perceptions of the country's fragility and integrity, therefore, this study understands the securing of agency at two levels. First, agency can be carved out through a regime's alignment with donor discourses that encourage the more direct disbursement of greater amounts of aid and discourage political conditionalities and other donor censuring of domestic activities. At a broader level, however, agency can also be secured through the regime's reshaping of the discourse itself, in this case the discourse on state fragility. In exploring how Kampala has succeeded in persuading donors to see Uganda as both 'fragile' and 'strong', it is argued that the regime has in fact challenged the monolithic, Western-authored notion of state fragility held by these officials, constructing an alternative version of the concept to which donors have largely subscribed. The remainder of this article will therefore delineate how the Ugandan regime has reframed and incorporated the fragile states narrative into its own image management strategies as a means of securing greater agency in its relations with donors.

At the mercy of 'criminals' and 'bandits': Uganda as a 'fragile state'

The current Ugandan government is headed by President Yoweri Museveni and his National Resistance Army/Movement (NRA/NRM), who seized power in January 1986 after waging a lengthy guerrilla war against the two previous regimes: those of Idi Amin (1971–79) and Milton Obote (1980–85). Explicitly focused on ending the years of ethnic and religious 'sectarianism' that had characterised Uganda's political economy since independence, Museveni's government rapidly initiated a number of schemes to rebuild the country. Beginning in 1987 the regime's efforts received the enthusiastic support of the Western donor community; between c 1992 and 2005, these donors financed 50%–60% of Uganda's national budget.[18] Since coming to power the regime has successfully maintained stability throughout the central regions of the Ugandan state (South/Central Uganda, including the cities of Kampala and Entebbe); periodic riots and terrorist attacks in these areas have been dealt with harshly and decisively by security forces.

The same cannot be said, however, for the more peripheral regions of Uganda, which have, to varying degrees, experienced ongoing insecurity at the hands of a number of rebel groups since the mid-1980s.[19] Between the mid-1990s and the early 2000s Western Uganda became the sometime base of the Allied Democratic Forces (ADF), a primarily Islamic anti-Museveni coalition that carried out child abductions and 'hit-and-run' attacks on civilians.[20] Likewise eastern Ugandans have faced intermittent violence from armed cattle rustlers in Karamoja throughout the Museveni era; the regime evinced little interest in their plight until the late 2000s.[21] It is the north of Uganda, however, that has seen the most consistent and widespread instability, primarily at the hands of the Lord's Resistance Army (LRA), a millenarian Christian movement with unclear ideological underpinnings that mercilessly terrorised the region and its citizens between 1987 and 2006. The Museveni government's ambiguous approach to neutralising the rebellion, together with its well known antipathy towards the region's Acholi population, has, however, been highlighted by commentators and diplomats alike as a key reason for the LRA's continued success throughout this period.[22]

Beginning with its earliest engagements with the international donor community, the Museveni regime has made extensive use of this continuing insecurity across Uganda's periphery to promote a narrative of state fragility to its Western partners, with a view to legitimising increased military and development cooperation. For example, one former senior US official notes how the Ugandan leader frequently lobbied Washington officials for 'arms, including helicopters' to help deal with the continued 'instability' in the north.[23] Similarly a 2003 letter from Rosa Whitaker, the head of a Washington public relations firm retained by the Museveni government, asked US chief Africa diplomat Walter Kansteiner to support a 'modest request' from Uganda for greater US military aid, specifically to help slow the marauding LRA's trail of destruction.[24]

In addition, during extended negotiations with donors over Uganda's 'ballooning' military budget between c 1995 and 2003, Museveni continuously justified his regime's extensive spending in this area by referring to the ongoing fragility in the north.[25] During a 1996 meeting with donor representatives in Kampala, the Ugandan leader also consistently justified his government's defence spending levels by arguing that the country might become like 'Cambodia [following the Khmer Rouge regime] or Somalia [post-1991]' if less money were allocated to the military budget, and that the 'security situation [in the north] might get out of hand'.[26] This tactic appears to have reaped substantial rewards for the regime: donors ultimately abandoned attempts to impose a military spending 'cap' on Kampala and have continued to provide military training and support to the Museveni regime ever since,[27] despite growing evidence that such support has in fact been used by the regime to satisfy its own regime maintenance demands.[28]

More generally regime officials have sought to maintain the salience of peripheral Ugandan state fragility in their dialogue with donors by consistently characterising provincial regions as war-torn and under constant threat from rebels. During the 1990s Museveni frequently portrayed northern Uganda as an unstable territory plagued by 'criminals', 'lawbreakers' and 'bandits' in private bilateral meetings with donors and in public speeches attended by international actors (*Daily Monitor*, September 8, 2003).[29] Similarly the Ugandan leader, along with senior army spokespersons, consistently depicted Karamoja as a region of 'lawlessness', 'insecurity' and criminal 'rampages' in public addresses until the mid-2000s (*New Vision*, November 30, December 17, 2001). However, since 9/11, this language, used primarily to refer to the LRA, has largely been replaced by a new discourse that presents the LRA as 'terrorists'.[30] This has served to complement and bolster the regime's reputation among donor nations as a key 'frontline state' against Islamist fundamentalism and terrorism on the African continent, which has been a central rationale for continued donor support over the past 15 years.[31]

Regime officials have also acted to periodically reinforce these narratives of local Ugandan fragilities by managing (to the extent possible) donor perceptions of the security dynamics of these regions. The Ugandan Foreign Ministry arranged a number of stage-managed 'briefing trips' to northern Uganda for Western donor officials in the 1990s and early 2000s, usually in the aftermath of LRA attacks, in order to present a particularly chaotic vision of the area to these individuals (*New Vision*, November 11, 2002).[32] One such trip to Moyo in

September 1996 was hastily organised immediately following an assault. In this instance Western diplomatic and defence officials, given less than an hour's notice, were flown to the site in Ugandan military helicopters, where they were met by rather surprised local military officers.[33] Another visit, this time to Pader District following an LRA massacre in November 2002, coincided with a donor 'briefing' on northern Uganda from Museveni himself; Western diplomats were left shaken by the sight of the 'frightening' situation in the region.[34] Throughout the 1990s and early 2000s the Ugandan leader invited donor officials to a number of meetings on Karamoja, including one in late 2001 in which he 'briefed' representatives from Japan, the EU and the USA on 'the genesis of the insecurity in Karamoja' (*New Vision*, December 17, 2001).

Until the late 2000s when donors established semi-permanent missions in Gulu, donor requests for clearance to visit northern Uganda outside these regime-managed expeditions were frequently met with resistance or disinterest from foreign ministry staff.[35] A number of unaccompanied excursions by US officials to the region during this period had to be abandoned because their travel permits were revoked by regime officials, even as the expedition party was *en route* to its destination.[36] Thus, even the comparatively large size of Washington's contingent of 'in-country' military and security staff has not always enabled the US embassy to collect more in-depth independent data on the northern situation than its European counterparts.

Since coming to power the Museveni regime has evidently used a variety of strategies to depict Uganda as a fragile state to international donors. Although it has rarely employed the phrase 'fragile state' itself, the regime has nevertheless ensured that donors see Uganda through this lens by means of its portrayal of regional lawlessness in the country's northern, western and eastern peripheries. Kampala's motivation for this image management is primarily based on concerns of regime maintenance – seeking to justify Museveni's extensive and increasingly authoritarian tenure in office and to encourage greater international provision of military training and weaponry to the regime's security forces, while also reinforcing and augmenting its image as a central 'frontline state' in the fight against global disorder and international terrorism.

'We cured all that': Uganda as a 'strong state'

Significantly, however, during the same period the Museveni government has also advanced a separate narrative on Ugandan state integrity in its interactions with donors, a narrative that seemingly undermines its promotion of the images of state fragility described above and also challenges the very concept of fragility as applied by donors. Once again, Kampala's use of this strategy has formed part of a broader regime maintenance plan and strategy to secure agency: by depicting itself as the successful architect of a rebuilt, post-conflict Ugandan state, the regime has attracted substantial international assistance from donors who have lauded it as an 'economic success story'. The fact that the regime has simultaneously used and eschewed the discourse of state fragility in its interactions with donors demonstrates quite clearly the questionable conceptual integrity of the term. That it has also successfully convinced many donors to internalise the two contradictory narratives on the Ugandan state also reveals the extent to which the concept has been redefined by Kampala for its own ends. Both of these issues will be revisited in the final section of this article.

Even while depicting Uganda as a 'fragile state', as they have done since the 1990s, Ugandan officials have also advanced a divergent image of the country to the same donors. This second image portrays Uganda as a robust, rebuilt, post-conflict state, presenting a stark contrast to its fragile predecessors. In his private conversations with donors, interviews with Western journalists and speeches at US policy institutes during the 1990s and 2000s, Museveni consistently reminded his audiences of the 'vicious' regimes of Milton Obote and Idi Amin in the context of subjects as diverse as the Global War on Terror, the New Partnership for Africa's Development and the size of Uganda's GDP.[37] Frequently emphasising the NRA's role in ending these two dictatorships, Museveni and his advisers have often explicitly drawn a contrast between the unstable Uganda of Amin and Obote and the secure, strong Uganda of Museveni[38] – a technique that has also been employed domestically to strengthen the regime's legitimacy, particularly during election campaigns.[39] In a September 2005 speech at a major US think-tank, the Ugandan leader clearly expressed this point:

> Now when we came into the government, we had to introduce democracy in such a way that those forms of force polarization [*sic*] [seen under Obote/Amin] did not resurface again...this was a deliberate technique to kill the sectarianism... [Under Obote and Amin] the economy had been informalized...we cured all that...[Under Obote and Amin] state agents were the ones killing people, murders...extrajudicial killings...there was a danger to property...We have ensured that the security of person and property is guaranteed...[we have also achieved] the expansion of infrastructure, the roads, some power and so on.[40]

Kampala's US supporters have also promoted this narrative in their lobbying of US officials in Washington. Congressman Edolphus Towns, for example, who received campaign donations from Scribe Strategies (a public relations firm retained by Uganda's Ministry of Defence between 2005 and 2007) emphasised in a 2005 speech to the US House of Representatives that 'Americans must remember the terror and oppression of the Idi Amin regime...Yoweri Museveni came into office with promises to stabilize the country...he has largely lived up to those promises'.[41]

Likewise, Senator Mary Landrieu, whose May 2004 visit to Uganda was facilitated and later publicised by the Whitaker Group, suggested in a June 2004 speech to her fellow legislators that 'When Idi Amin staged his coup in 1971, now-President Museveni went into exile and began a history of resistance to dictatorship and misrule...Since [his regime] took power in 1986, Uganda has enjoyed the first sustained period of growth and stability that it has known since independence.'[42]

More generally regime officials have frequently sought to advance an image of Uganda under the current government as a successful example of post-conflict reconstruction for other states to emulate. For example, Museveni has drawn attention to Uganda's impressive economic growth rates (around 6.5%–7% per annum) in speeches at the University of Oxford (1998), to the Council on Foreign Relations (2005) and before the UN General Assembly (2009).[43] In a similar vein, in 2009, Oxford University Press published an edited volume entitled *Uganda's Economic Reforms*, which includes contributions from over a dozen Ugandan finance officials; as might be expected, the book advances an image of Uganda as a successful model of post-conflict economic reconstruction to be imitated elsewhere.[44] Kampala's lobbyists have also emphasised the growth issue in their communications with US officials. In a 2007 letter to US Treasury Secretary Henry Paulson Rosa Whitaker stated that 'Uganda is East Africa's leader in attracting foreign direct investment, much of it from the United States...[and]...the economy has grown at an average rate of 5.5% since 2005'.[45]

Indeed, the regime's enthusiasm for promoting Uganda as a successful model of economic and political stability in the aftermath of conflict has led Museveni to adopt an increasingly pedagogic style of engagement with Western actors on this issue. This has even included the president's endowment of a 'Museveni Scholarship' at the University of Oxford – an award that sponsors African doctoral students 'working on issues relating to African economies'.[46] Museveni has also taken on a persona that might best be characterised as professorial in his frequent elucidations in Western capitals of how Uganda has successfully recovered from political instability and economic collapse. In a March 2009 speech at London's Royal Commonwealth Society, for example, the Ugandan leader devoted considerable time to expounding his detailed philosophy on how Africa could develop economically by building infrastructure and increasing industrialisation, as Uganda has.[47]

The regime has also vigorously defended Uganda against direct claims that it is a 'failed state', despite its apparent encouragement of such a classification at other times. Following Uganda's demotion from 21st most failed state to 20th in the 2012 'Failed States Index' published by the US think-tank Fund for Peace, former Ugandan minister James Nsaba Buturo attacked the Fund in Uganda's state-run *New Vision* newspaper as 'dishonest' and 'tendentious', and called its categorisation of Uganda as a failed state as 'outlandish'. In so doing, he drew on the regime narratives described above that contrast the 'secure' NRM state with the 'chaotic' era of Amin and Obote, arguing that 'Uganda's rise from a failed state in the 1970s...to a functioning state now is a [positive!] fairy tale story' (*New Vision*, July 4, 2012). Moses Byaruhanga, one of Museveni's key political advisers, similarly rejected the Fund's findings in an interview with the *Independent* (October 7, 2012), a Ugandan public affairs journal that is widely read by in-country donor missions. Byaruhanga emphatically stated that the Museveni regime '[has] managed to control all our borders...that alone means we are not a failed state'.

It is evident that donor officials have internalised this narrative on Ugandan state integrity in addition to the perspective focusing on Ugandan state fragility. The successful rebuilding of Uganda's state and economy over the past three decades has become a cornerstone of donor discourse on the east African nation. A wide variety of scholars has argued that ever-increasing donor support for Kampala since the early 1990s has been directly premised on this community's delight over the Ugandan 'success story' and its apparent reification of their own reconstruction prescriptions (which are widely held to have failed in most other African states).[48] Furthermore, in the author's private interviews with past and present donor officials who have dealt with Uganda, interviewees have frequently cited the 'strong and stable' state built by Museveni upon the 'ruins' of the pre-1986 Obote and Amin states to explain their long-standing support for his regime, praising the president's 'transformational' effects on Ugandan state integrity.[49]

The same donors, however, have simultaneously justified their support by referring to the threat posed by rebel groups and the perennial insecurity in the more peripheral regions of the country. Since the mid-1990s substantial development and security assistance has been provided to the regime (by the USA and the UK in particular) to help arm and train the 'pitifully underequipped' Ugandan People's Defence Forces (UPDF) in their campaign against the LRA 'menace', and more recently to promote disarmament and reconstruction efforts in these conflict-ridden regions. This support has increasingly been discussed, at Kampala's urging, in the context of global counter-terrorism policy – for example, a US legislator pushed for increased US aid to the Museveni regime in 2005 to help it combat 'its own home-grown terrorism' – but it remains linked to the notion that the Ugandan government is still incapable of protecting its citizens from marauding rebels or providing even basic infrastructure in these regions of the country without international assistance.

The Ugandan government has thus successfully convinced its donors that Uganda represents a 'strong state', while simultaneously persuading them that the opposite is true. This is not to say that every donor official holds, or has held, these apparently contradictory opinions or that some of these discourses – particularly those addressing Uganda's economic success – are not being increasingly challenged by donors.[50] It is clear, however, that many have held contradictory opinions, both at the local and headquarters level, and that the Ugandan government has played a central role in bringing about this state of affairs. In so doing, it has arguably secured a degree of agency that goes beyond the transactional dynamic described at the start of this article. In promoting itself as both fragile and strong, the regime has challenged monolithic donor understandings of state fragility. By successfully persuading many donors to see the country through both of these lenses, it has also redefined how these officials view the state and its integrity from an African perspective.

Donor centre–periphery dynamics and the place of Ugandan agency in the 'fragile states' narrative

In many respects the Museveni regime's parallel presentation of Uganda as both conforming with the existing 'fragile states' narrative in contemporary development thinking and denying it demonstrates the conceptual vagueness of the term. The fact that a category used by policy makers and practitioners can be convincingly manipulated in this manner calls into question its integrity and usefulness; this article thus provides further support for those who have criticised the 'imprecise' and 'incoherent' nature of the fragile states label (see above). This also raises important questions regarding the forms of intervention that donors themselves should pursue within the states they categorise as 'fragile'. If a state can be accepted as being both strong and fragile in different respects, donor promotion of, for example, conflict mitigation and other stabilising interventions over longer-term governance and service-delivery programmes may be far more difficult to justify.

This article clearly shows that the governments of aid-dependent states such as Uganda can access vital donor resources for regime maintenance purposes by positioning themselves within (or outside) internationally devised narratives on issues such as state fragility, and by challenging and reshaping these narratives. In this way states such as Uganda seem to have secured agency at several levels in their relationship with donors, a relationship otherwise characterised by disparity and asymmetry. This conclusion is not, however, wholly satisfactory in its current form, as it does not explain *why* donor officials might comfortably accept the coexistence of two contradictory images of a state like Uganda in their conceptual world-view. Nor, indeed, does it clarify how representatives of governments with access to vast quantities of information might come to rely so heavily – consciously or otherwise – on the pronouncements of an African regime in building their perceptions about a country. The remainder of this article will therefore attempt to develop an understanding of why donor officials in Uganda or elsewhere might become dependent on a 'host government' for information on that state's integrity.

In this regard, it is important to consider the political economy of information gathering for donor officials dealing with a state like Uganda. Western embassies and aid offices in Uganda, as elsewhere across the globe, are located in the country's capital, Kampala. Kampala is also the heart of Uganda's government, home to the country's parliament, all ministries of state, the supreme court, the executive mansion and key elements of the country's economy and infrastructure; Uganda's only international airport (along with a UN Regional Service Centre) is also only a 30-minute drive from the city. Although it was hit hard by the conflict that brought Museveni to power, the city was rapidly rebuilt and developed by the NRM government during the late 1980s and early 1990s, and it has steadily grown into a safe, bustling, modern metropolis populated by skyscrapers, shopping malls, international hotels and restaurants.

Donor officials live and work within this secure and familiar environment and their time spent in the northern and eastern parts of the country has generally been quite limited, although this situation has gradually changed since the LRA's departure from Ugandan territory in 2006.[51] A 2007 UK government report noted that DFID officials in Uganda spent fewer than five days per year in rural areas; donor interviewees have observed that, particularly during the years of LRA insurgency in the north, few donor personnel expressed much 'interest' in leaving Kampala during their tours of duty.[52] Even the US mission in Uganda, the largest donor representation in the country, did not establish an office in Gulu until 2006. Indeed, before 2006 many donor missions only operated in northern Uganda indirectly through local NGOs, further reducing the amount of physical time the organisations' officials spent in the region.[53] Visiting senior donor delegations to Uganda have often stayed overnight in hotels or embassy accommodation in Kampala or Entebbe, while those visiting areas outside the capital have invariably been flown out and back again within a matter of hours.[54]

Although much of this behaviour stems from legitimate security concerns, a major consequence has been that donors' personal experiences of 'Uganda' have generally been confined to urban Kampala. It is easy to see how such officials could have come to internalise different narratives on the same state: donors have become personally familiar with the 'strong' Ugandan state, while their encounters with Uganda's 'fragile' periphery have been largely indirect, mediated and impersonal. This permits an 'othering' of the periphery in donor minds, which allows it to sit more comfortably alongside their own contrasting view of the stable 'centre' in forming overall perceptions of the Ugandan state. Aspects of this dispensation can be found in Duffield's description of the 'bunkerisation' of the aid industry, whereby donors form perceptions of the countries they are based in from behind the 'razor-wire' fences of 'militarized [...] fortified compounds', 'intimidating structures designed to keep the public out'.[55]

It is crucial to acknowledge, however, that the Ugandan government has also consistently and proactively attempted to manage donor access to the periphery (as discussed above) and to third-party information on the region in order to position itself as the key 'intelligence source' for donors in this regard. This has involved a concerted effort on the part of regime officials to manage research activity and information dissemination in and related to Uganda's periphery that has been undertaken or funded by Western actors. An increasingly restrictive and stringent NGO registration and monitoring regime has been imposed, designed to control the gathering and dissemination of information by domestic organisations in peripheral areas, even including scrutiny of the work of Western doctoral students in these regions.[56] Senior regime officials have also sought to directly influence how analyses written by Western actors are phrased and presented.[57] More generally the regime has long maintained a policy of aggressive engagement with policy makers and INGOs such as Human Rights Watch (both directly and through proxies such as the Whitaker Group) to ensure that such individuals and organisations remain 'informed' regarding particular details of the situation 'on the ground'.[58]

Conclusion

This article has explored the case of Uganda as a means of proposing a more agency-centred critique of the fragile states concept. In delineating how the country's Museveni regime has both embraced and contested donor perceptions of Ugandan state integrity, it has been argued that the regime has carved out a significant degree of agency for itself in an international system that otherwise relegates the country to a position of structural weakness and dependency. This 'agency' can be conceived of as transactional: Kampala has persuaded donors to view Uganda through perspectives that justify continued aid disbursements and limit criticism of domestic governance transgressions. In reshaping donor understandings of state integrity in Uganda, however, the regime has also secured agency at a deeper, more normative level. The Ugandan case therefore represents a challenge to the existing commentary on 'fragile states' that characterises the concept solely as a Western imposition on politically inert African states. It also highlights the importance of problematising and developing existing notions of agency and 'agencies' in the relationship between Western donors and the recipients of their aid.

Donors' acceptance of these two contradictory narratives on Ugandan state integrity also raises questions about how donors 'access' information on and in 'fragile states', as well as about the extent to which this process is affected or determined by their local experiences and interactions with local actors. The article has emphasised the importance of information asymmetry and centre–periphery dynamics in explaining how Uganda's donors have come to perceive the state as both strong and fragile, although there is clearly much work to be done on this subject at a broader level. Finally, the article has highlighted the conceptual weakness of the fragile states concept itself by showing how donor officials in one such state have been persuaded to view it as both strong and fragile. Like many other states Uganda is neither wholly strong nor wholly fragile, and international development interventions that proceed based on such stark and facile differentiations are far less likely to be effective than those taking a more nuanced approach – recognising and accounting for local and regional variations below the level of the monolithic 'state'.

Notes on Contributor

Jonathan Fisher is Lecturer in the International Development Department, University of Birmingham. His research focuses on the place of African states in the international system, donor–African relations and the political economy of development interventions. He has a particular interest in Eastern Africa and has published a number of scientific articles in journals that include *African Affairs*, *Journal of Modern African Studies* and *Conflict, Security and Development.*

Notes

1. For example, Stefan Kossoff, a Senior Governance Advisor at DFID, noted in an October 2011 presentation at the Overseas Development Institute (ODI), London, that '21 of DFID's 28 partner countries are now fragile or conflict-affected states.' DFID, *Why We Need to Work more Effectively*; ODI, *Donors and the 'Fragile States' Agenda*; and Zoellick, "Fragile States," 67–84.
2. Wainwright, "Responding to State Failure," 491.
3. OECD, *Fragile States 2013*, 2, lists '47 fragile states' including 24 (51%) from the African continent.
4. The Fund for Peace ranked Uganda as number 21 in the 2013 version of its influential 'Failed States Index'. http://ffp.statesindex.org/rankings-2013-sortable.
5. Fisher, "International Perceptions and African Agency," 250–293.
6. This generalisation is less applicable to the UK's DFID, which since 1997 has devolved most key decision making on aid disbursements to country offices. Interviews with DFID officials, London and Kampala, April 2009–November 2010.
7. Bøås and Jennings, "Insecurity and Development," 387.
8. Helman and Ratner, "Saving Failed States," 3–20; Jackson, *Quasi-states*; Rotberg, *When States Fail*; and Zartman, *Collapsed States*.
9. DFID, *Why We Need to Work more Effectively*; European Commission, "EU Response to Fragile Situations"; ODI, *Donors and the 'Fragile States' Agenda*; United Nations Development Programme, *Governance for Peace*; White House, "I: International Strategy"; and White House, *National Security Strategy*.
10. Bøås and Jennings, "Insecurity and Development," 385; Call, "The Fallacy of the 'Failed State'," 1496; Easterly and Freschi, "Top 5 Reasons"; Hagmann and Hoehne, "Failures of the State Failure Debate," 42; and Nuruzzaman, "Revisiting the Category of Fragile and Failed States," 288.
11. Bilgin and Morton, "Historicising Representations of 'Failed States'," 55–80; Gruffydd Jones, "The Global Political Economy of Social Crisis," 180–205; and Hill, "Beyond the Other?," 139–154.
12. Bøås and Jennings, "'Failed States'," 475–585; Chandler, *Empire in Denial*; Hehir, "The Myth of the Failed State," 307–322; and Kabutaulaka, "'Failed State' and the War on Terror," 1–8.
13. But see Bøås and Jennings, "Insecurity and Development," 389–393.
14. Brown and Harman, *African Agency in International Politics*; and Whitfield, *The Politics of Aid*.
15. Bayart, "Africa in the World," 219–226.
16. Whitfield and Fraser, "Negotiating Aid," 41; and Whitfield, "Aid and Power," 344.
17. Beswick, "Peacekeeping," 739–754; Beswick, "From Weak State to Savvy International Player?"; Fisher, "International Perceptions and African Agency," 404–423; and Fisher, "'Image Management'," 1–31.

18. Mwenda and Tangri, "Patronage Politics," 452–453.
19. There is insufficient space here to explore the background and activities of these groups; for more detailed analysis, see Prunier, "Rebel Movements and Proxy Warfare," 365–383; and van Acker, "Uganda and the Lord's Resistance Army."
20. Prunier, "Rebel Movements and Proxy Warfare," 373–374; and Tripp, *Museveni's Uganda*, 156–157.
21. Tripp, *Museveni's Uganda*, 153–154.
22. Ibid., 169-171; and author's interviews with a former senior UK official, London, 27 November 2008 and two former US diplomats, Washington, DC, 28 October, 17 November 2009.
23. Author's interview with a former senior US official, Washington, DC, 5 November 2009.
24. The Whitaker Group, supplemental statement submitted to the US Department of Justice (DOJ) on 28 August 2003, Washington, DC, 2003.
25. Tripp, *Museveni's Uganda*, 141.
26. Channel 4 Television, *The Bank, the President.*
27. Fisher, "'Some More Reliable than Others'," 16–19.
28. Tangri and Mwenda, "Military Corruption," 539–552.
29. Channel 4 Television, *The Bank, the President*; Dolan, *Social Torture*, 97; and Doom and Vlassenroot, "Kony's Message," 20.
30. Fisher, "'Some More Reliable than Others'," 16–19.
31. Fisher, "Managing Donor Perceptions," 413–416.
32. Author's interview with a former UK diplomat, London, 20 July 2009.
33. Author's interview with a senior Ugandan military official, Kampala, 25 April 2013.
34. Ibid.
35. Author's interview with a former UK diplomat.
36. Author's interview with a former US official based in Kampala, London, 1 May 2011.
37. Canada TV, "Interview with President"; Council on Foreign Relations, "Freedom from Fear"; and Woodrow Wilson Center, "Speech by His Excellency Yoweri Museveni."
38. Channel 4 Television, *The Bank, the President*; Council on Foreign Relations, "Freedom from Fear"; and Wilkerson, "An Interview with Sam Kutesa".
39. For example, a 1996 NRM election poster declared to voters, 'Don't forget the past...YOUR VOTE COULD BRING IT BACK' above a photo of skulls of the victims of Uganda's civil war. Human Rights Watch, *Hostile to Democracy*, 47. Likewise, in the lead-up to the 2011 elections, government billboards were erected around Kampala that displayed Museveni's face above the slogan 'Peace, Stability and Security: 28 rebel groups have been defeated since 1986...Vote NRM, Vote Yoweri K Museveni!' Author's personal observations on a visit to Kampala, November 2010.
40. Council on Foreign Relations, "A Conversation."
41. Towns, "Speech of Hon Edolphus Towns."
42. Landrieu, "Speech of Hon Mary Landrieu."
43. Council on Foreign Relations, "A Conversation"; Museveni, "Keynote Speech"; and Museveni, "Speech at General Debate."
44. Kuteesa et al., *Uganda's Economic Reforms.*
45. The Whitaker Group, supplemental statement submitted to DOJ on 12 October 2007, Washington, DC, 2007.
46. Museveni, "Keynote Speech."
47. Museveni, speech delivered at an event entitled 'Uganda through an Artist's Eyes' at the Royal Commonwealth Society, London, 10 March 2009 (attended by the author).
48. Harrison, "Post-conditionality Politics," 659–663, 672–673, 675–694; Hauser, "Ugandan Relations with Western Donors," 633–644; and Mwenda and Tangri, "Patronage Politics," 466–467.
49. Author's interviews with two DFID officials, London, 30 March, 25 September 2009; with two former senior US officials, Washington, DC, 4, 11 November 2009; and with a former UK diplomat, London, 5 May 2009.
50. Donor concerns over high-level corruption have increasingly eroded this community's confidence in Uganda's economic robustness, as evidenced by a variety of corruption-related aid cuts since 2010.
51. Author's interview with a UK diplomat, London, 22 May 2009 and with a European donor official, Kampala, 9 February 2010.
52. Author's interview with a former UK diplomat, London, 20 July 2009; and National Audit Office, *Department for International Development*, 27.
53. Duffield, "Risk-management and the Fortified Aid Compound," 470.
54. Author's interviews with a former senior UK official, London, 21 December 2009, and with an aide to a former senior US official, Washington, DC, 5 November 2009.
55. Duffield, "Risk-management and the Fortified Aid Compound," 455–457, 466.
56. Dicklitch and Lwanga, "The Politics of Being Non-political," 496-505; and Dolan, "Understanding War and its Continuation," 45–46.
57. Author's interview with a former US diplomat, Washington, DC, 13 November 2009.
58. Fisher, "International Perceptions and African Agency," 159–160.

Bibliography

Bayart, Jean-François. "Africa in the World: A History of Extraversion." *African Affairs* 99, no. 395 (2000): 217–267.

Beswick, Danielle. "Peacekeeping, Regime Security and 'African Solutions to African Problems': Exploring Rwandan Involvement in Darfur." *Third World Quarterly* 31, no. 5 (2010): 739–754.

Beswick, Danielle. "From Weak State to Savvy International Player? Rwanda's Multi-level Strategy for Maximising Agency." In *African Agency in International Politics*, edited by William Brown, and Sophie Harman, 158–174. London: Routledge, 2013.

Bilgin, Pirnar, and Adam David Morton. "Historicising Representations of 'Failed States': Beyond the Cold-War Annexation of the Social Sciences?" *Third World Quarterly* 23, no. 1 (2002): 55–80.

Bøås, Morten, and Kathleen M. Jennings. "Insecurity and Development: The Rhetoric of the 'Failed State'." *European Journal of Development Research* 17, no. 3 (2005): 385–395.

Bøås, Morten, and Kathleen M. Jennings. "'Failed States' and 'State Failure': Threats or Opportunities?" *Globalizations* 4, no. 4 (2007): 475–585.

Brown, William, and Sophie Harman, eds. *African Agency in International Politics*. London: Routledge, 2013.

Call, Charles. "The Fallacy of the 'Failed State'." *Third World Quarterly* 29, no. 8 (2008): 1491–1507.

Canada TV. "Interview with President Lt General Yoweri Kaguta Museveni." Murray Oliver, Canada Television Africa Bureau. Ottawa, 30 August 2002.

Chandler, David. *Empire in Denial: The Politics of State-building*. London: Pluto Press, 2006.

Channel 4 Television. *The Bank, the President and the Pearl of Africa*. Documentary directed by P. Chappell. Channel 4, UK, 1997.

Council on Foreign Relations. "Freedom from Fear: Forging US–Africa Partnerships against Terror." Speech delivered by Yoweri Museveni, President of the Republic of Uganda, 13 June 2003, Washington, DC.

Council on Foreign Relations. "A Conversation with Yoweri Kaguta Museveni, September 21, 2005." Washington, DC.

Department for International Development (DFID). *Why We Need to Work More Effectively in Fragile States*. London: DFID, 2005.

Dicklitch, Susan, and Doreen Lwanga. "The Politics of Being Non-political: Human Rights Organizations and the Creation of a Positive Human Rights Culture in Uganda." *Human Rights Quarterly* 25, no. 2 (2003): 482–509.

Dolan, Chris. "Understanding War and its Continuation: The Case of Northern Uganda." London School of Economics: PhD diss, 2006.

Dolan, Chris. *Social Torture: The Case of Northern Uganda 1986–2006*. London: Berghahn Books, 2009.

Doom, Ruddy, and Koen Vlassenroot. "Kony's Message: A New Koine? The Lord's Resistance Army in Northern Uganda." *African Affairs* 98, no. 390 (1999): 9–36.

Duffield, Mark. "Risk-management and the Fortified Aid Compound: Everyday Life in Post-interventionary Society." *Journal of Intervention and Statebuilding* 4, no. 4 (2010): 453–474.

Easterly, William, and Laura Freschi. "Top 5 Reasons Why 'Failed State' is a Failed Concept." Accessed October 26, 2012. http://aidwatchers.com/2010/01/top-5-reasons-why-%E2%80%9Cfailed-state%E2%80%9D-is-a-failed-concept.

European Commission. "EU Response to Fragile Situations." Accessed October 26, 2012. http://europa.eu/legislation_summaries/humanitarian_aid/r13019_en.htm.

Fisher, Jonathan. "International Perceptions and African Agency: Uganda and its Donors, 1986–2010." DPhil diss.: University of Oxford, 2011.

Fisher, Jonathan. "Managing Donor Perceptions: Contextualizing Uganda's 2007 Intervention in Somalia." *African Affairs* 111, no. 444 (2012): 404–423.

Fisher, Jonathan. "'Image Management' and African Agency: Ugandan Regional Diplomacy and Donor Relations under Museveni." In *African Agency in International Politics*, edited by William Brown, and Sophie Harman, 97–113. London: Routledge, 2013.

Fisher, Jonathan. "'Some More Reliable than Others': Image Management, Donor Perceptions and the Global War on Terror in East African Diplomacy." *Journal of Modern African Studies* 51, no. 1 (2013): 1–31.

Gruffydd Jones, Branwen. "The Global Political Economy of Social Crisis: Towards a Critique of the 'Failed State' Ideology." *Review of International Political Economy* 15, no. 2 (2008): 180–205.

Hagmann, Tobias, and Markus Hoehne. "Failures of the State Failure Debate: Evidence from the Somali Territories." *Journal of International Development* 21, no. 1 (2009): 42–57.

Harrison, Graham. "Post-conditionality Politics and Administrative Reform: Reflections on the Cases of Uganda and Tanzania." *Development and Change* 32, no. 4 (2001): 657–679.

Hauser, Ellen. "Ugandan Relations with Western Donors in the 1990s: What Impact on Democratisation?" *Journal of Modern African Studies* 37, no. 4 (1999): 621–641.

Hehir, Aidan. "The Myth of the Failed State and the War on Terror: A Challenge to Conventional Wisdom." *Journal of Intervention and Statebuilding* 1, no. 3 (2007): 307–322.

Helman, Gerald, and Steven R. Ratner. "Saving Failed States." *Foreign Policy* 89 (1992): 3–20.

Hill, Jonathan. "Beyond the Other? A Postcolonial Critique of the Failed States Thesis." *African Identities* 3, no. 2 (2007): 139–154.

Human Rights Watch. *Hostile to Democracy: The Movement System and Political Repression in Uganda*. New YorkNY: Human Rights Watch, 1999.
Jackson, Robert. *Quasi-states: Sovereignty, International Relations and the Third World*. Cambridge: Cambridge University Press, 1990.
Kabutaulaka, Tarcisius Tara. "'Failed State' and the War on Terror: Intervention in Solomon Islands." *Asia Pacific Issues* 72 (2004): 1–8.
Kuteesa, Florence, Emmanuel Tumusiime-Mutebile, Alan Whitworth, and Tim Williamson. *Uganda's Economic Reforms: Insider Accounts*. Oxford: Oxford University Press, 2010.
Landrieu, Mary. "Speech of Hon Mary Landrieu of Louisiana in the Senate. June 17, 2004. S6990." Congressional Record, 108th Congress (2003–2004). Washington, DC, 2004.
Museveni, Yoweri Kaguta. "Keynote Speech by HE President Museveni of Uganda." Given at Investing in Africa: Does It Really Mean Business? Oxford: University of Oxford, 1998.
Museveni, Yoweri Kaguta. "Speech at General Debate of the 64th Session of the UN General Assembly." New York, 2008.
Mwenda, Andrew, and Roger Tangri. "Patronage Politics, Donor Reforms and Regime Consolidation in Uganda." *African Affairs* 104, no. 416 (2005): 449–467.
National Audit Office (NAO). *Department for International Development: Tackling Rural Poverty in Developing Countries*. London: NAO, 2007.
Nuruzzaman, Mohammed. "Revisiting the Category of Fragile and Failed States in International Relations." *International Studies* 46, no. 3 (2009): 271–294.
Organisation for Economic Cooperation and Development (OECD). *Fragile States*: 2013 *Resource Flows and Trends in a Shifting World*. Paris: OECD, 2012.
Overseas Development Institute (ODI). *Donors and the 'Fragile States' Agenda: A Survey of Current Thinking and Practice*. London: ODI, 2006.
Prunier, Gérard. "Rebel Movements and Proxy Warfare: Uganda, Sudan and the Congo (1986–99)." *African Affairs* 103, no. 412 (2004): 359–383.
Rotberg, Robert. *When States Fail: Causes and Consequences*. Princeton, NJ: Princeton University Press, 2003.
Tangri, Roger, and Andrew M. Mwenda. "Military Corruption and Ugandan Politics since the late 1990s." *Review of African Political Economy* 30, no. 98 (2003): 539–552.
Towns, E. "Speech of Hon Edolphus Towns of New York in the House of Representatives. Wednesday, September 14 2005 – Extension of Remarks. E1842." Congressional Record, 109th Congress (2005–2006). Washington, DC, 2005.
Tripp, Aili Mary. *Museveni's Uganda: Paradoxes of Power. Boulder*, CO: Lynne Rienner, 2010.
United Nations Development Programme (UNDP). *Governance for Peace: Securing the Social Contract*. New York: UNDP, 2012.
van Acker, Frank. "Uganda and the Lord's Resistance Army: The New Order No One Ordered." *African Affairs* 103, no. 412 (2004): 335–357.
Wainwright, Elsina. "Responding to State Failure: The Case of Australia and Solomon Islands." *Australian Journal of International Affairs* 57, no. 3 (2003): 485–498.
White House. "I: Overview of America's International Strategy." Washington, DC, 2002.
White House. *National Security Strategy*. Washington, DC: White House, 2010.
Whitfield, Lindsay, ed. *The Politics of Aid: African Strategies for Dealing with Donors*. Oxford: Oxford University Press, 2009.
Whitfield, Lindsay. "Aid and Power: A Comparative Analysis of the Country Studies." In *The Politics of Aid*, edited by Lindsay Whitfield, 329–360. Oxford: Oxford University Press, 2009.
Whitfield, Lindsay, and Alastair Fraser. "Negotiating Aid." In *The Politics of Aid*, edited by Lindsay Whitfield, 27–44. Oxford: Oxford University Press, 2009.
Wilkerson, Michael. "An Interview with Sam Kutesa." *Foreign Policy*, August 10, 2009.
Woodrow Wilson Center. "Speech by His Excellency Yoweri Museveni, President of the Republic of Uganda, 14 May 2002." Washington, DC: Woodrow Wilson Center.
Zartman, William. *Collapsed States: The Disintegration and Restoration of Legitimate Authority*. Boulder, CO: Lynne Rienner, 1995.
Zoellick, Robert. "Fragile States: Securing Development." *Survival* 50, no. 6 (2008): 67–84.

State fragility and failure as wicked problems: beyond naming and taming

Derick W. Brinkerhoff

RTI International, Washington, DC, USA

Conceptualising state fragility and failure as a wicked problem set reveals the complex, ill-defined and interdependent nature of the reality behind these labels. This essay builds on the contributions to this special issue by examining why the fragile/failed state concept remains in good currency despite its analytic weaknesses. The discussion reveals that the parsing of state fragility into its component parts and the development of related indicators reflect efforts to tame the wickedness of the problem set; this has led to peace-building and state-building interventions whose plans and actions do not effectively take account of what is necessary to achieve their intended aims. A better problem-solving match would look beyond naming and taming, incorporating lessons from the implementation literature and international development practice. However, achieving this would depend upon the political will of both labellers and the labelled.

Introduction

Something wicked this way comes. (William Shakespeare, *Macbeth*, Act 4, Scene 1)

Like the witches' remark upon Macbeth's arrival at their doorstep, the international community's experience with fragile and failed states reflects the basic features of the class of problems referred to as 'wicked'. Wicked problems are defined as those whose definition is contested and whose contours are ill-formulated and inherently complex; no matter how they are defined, the problem at hand can be viewed as a nested symptom of another problem. Solutions are debated on the basis of conflicting objectives and values, may be unmeasurable or untestable and may entail high stakes with important consequences for peoples' lives.[1] State fragility and failure epitomise the essence of a wicked problem set. As the contributions to this special issue reveal, they are subject to vague, competing and sometimes contradictory conceptualisations. Their limited utility as an analytic categorisation is commonly acknowledged, yet the terminology remains in common usage. Problematising fragile and failed states underscores the importance of the international discourse on fragility, the relations between those countries labelled as fragile and the international community, and the political economy that allocates power and resources to tackle the fragility problem set.

This essay explores state fragility and failure as addressed by the authors in this special issue in terms of the characteristics of wicked problems, with two aims. First, I offer some insights into why the state fragility concept remains in good currency, despite its recognised analytic weaknesses. Second, I argue that effective responses to state fragility and failure must go beyond 'naming' (applying the fragility label to particular countries) and 'taming' (reducing the degree of wickedness in the fragile states problem set) to consider realistic implementation strategies for achieving sustainable change. The introduction to this issue notes the divide in the fragile states literature between 'critical scholars' and 'problem solvers', and the articles within it fall largely on the critical scholar side of this divide.[2] However, my main focus here is on problem solving and implications for practice. I make no claim to comprehensiveness. Given the vastness of the literature and the experience base, my aim is to add to the rich and diverse exchange among scholars, analysts and practitioners.

I first examine the characteristics of wicked problems and their manifestation in state fragility before briefly reviewing the articles in this issue. I then discuss the purposes that the state fragility label serves in relation to taming the wickedness of the fragility problem set. I next remark upon the gap between policy discourse and peace-building and state-building operations on the ground as a prelude to a discussion of the need to move beyond naming and taming. I offer some lessons from international development that might help to address the wickedness characteristics of interventions in fragile states. In conclusion, I note that making progress in confronting the challenges of state fragility will require cooperation between the labellers and the labelled.

Wickedness and state fragility

Drawing on Rittel and Webber, who first coined the term, the major features of wicked problems are the following:[3]

- Wicked problems cannot be clearly defined. The parameters of the problem vary depending on who is asked, leading to differing conceptions and debate among stakeholders regarding both the nature of the problem and potential solutions.
- Wicked problems are comprised of multiple interdependencies and causal connections. These features are hard to identify in advance and are often revealed only once a particular solution is attempted. Solutions tend to have internally conflicting goals, calling for trade-offs. Disagreements among stakeholders regarding causality and goals contribute to difficulties in defining the problem and developing solutions.
- Wicked problems have no clear solution. Responses to wicked problems cannot be assessed in terms of right or wrong; solutions are often a matter of 'good enough', driven by resource constraints or politically determined

timetables. Perceptions of success or failure vary according to stakeholders' positions and views.
- Each wicked problem is fundamentally unique. Because of the complex interplay of factors, connections among aspects of the problem, the specific social context and the limitations of *a priori* knowledge, wicked problems call for customised solutions and contextual adaptation. Rarely are all the unique aspects of the problem apparent before a solution is attempted, calling for learning and adaptation.
- Attempts at solutions to wicked problems produce unforeseen consequences. Because of the complexity, interconnectedness and multiple causal factors contributing to wicked problems, solutions often reveal new aspects of the problems as they are implemented. Pre-testing of solutions is not feasible. Some of these consequences may be negative, causing unanticipated harm and spurring further disagreement over the nature of the problems and what is needed to address them.

These features of wicked problems are readily observable in the fragile states arena and in the international community's responses to state fragility and failure, as the extensive academic literature – including the articles in this special issue – documents and the discussions of operational agencies confirm. Defining the fragility problem draws upon several research streams, each of which provides a different but often overlapping view. Carment et al. identify analytic streams from development economics, comparative politics, international relations and conflict studies.[4] On the operational side definitions emerge from humanitarians, peacekeepers and military planners. Definitional efforts have spawned a multitude of analytic tools, assessment methodologies and guidance.[5] A recent and comprehensive overview of fragility and conflict, which addresses definition and offers suggestions for interventions, is provided by the World Bank's 2011 *World Development Report*.[6]

A common aim of these assessment tools and methodologies is to tame the wickedness of the problem by parsing fragility into its component parts; this yields a set of sub-problems that are considered to be relatively less complex, more readily monitored by conflict early-warning systems and more amenable to solution. The interventions designed to address these sub-problems are covered in the various peace-building and state-building templates produced by both civilian and military actors.[7] Numerous analysts and observers have noted that policy and operational efforts to simplify the fragile states dilemma have led to coordination problems, inter-agency turf battles and perverse outcomes.[8] In sum, the consequences of dealing with the wicked problem of fragile states have included oversimplification, unclear and conflicting objectives, intervention policies and strategies, fragmentation of effort and limited results. Following this discussion of wickedness as a background, I next briefly overview the articles in this special issue.

State fragility: what's in a label?

The contributors use discourse analysis to explore the contours, contents and application of the state fragility concept from two perspectives: those of the labellers and the labelled.[9] Several of the papers examine the inputs to, and influences on, donors' definitions and operationalisations of the fragile state concept. Lemay-Hébert and Mathieu examine recent OECD documents and reports, supplemented by selected interviews with OECD officials, revealing the dual logics that the international donor community uses in analysing state building and legitimacy: neo-Weberian institutional–functional versus sociological–social cohesion. The authors argue that, while both logics are critical to a comprehensive understanding of the dynamics of state fragility and state building, the institutional approach that views legitimacy as emerging in response to the fulfilment of basic functions by the state has dominated OECD discourse, and has become the norm for 'best practices'. The primacy of this logic is driven to some extent by the emergence of an epistemic community consisting of OECD officials and the analysts who have been contracted to produce the reports and documents that reinforce that normative perspective.

Nay adds to the examination of knowledge production with respect to the fragile state concept in the OECD, including the World Bank in his analysis. He reviews the role of these two organisations in defining and disseminating the expert knowledge-driven concept of state fragility, as well as its gradual acceptance as the foundation for international donor doctrine, informing policy and interventions within the development–security nexus.[10] He argues that the resulting doctrine reinforces the hegemony of OECD and World Bank member states in their relations with countries labelled fragile. In her analysis of the European Union's official publications, strategy papers and communications, Grimm reveals the indecisiveness of the EU on questions of state fragility, drawing three conclusions. First, EU bodies have yet to define the problem in a way that supports strategy development. Second, as a result, the EU tends to react to proposals from others rather than advancing a coherent agenda of its own. Third, EU bodies refrain from using the fragility label with country partners to avoid causing offence, which impedes effective analysis.

Other papers address the reactions of countries labelled as fragile in terms of their treatment of the labellers. Siqueira analyses the evolution of the use of indicators of fragility in the World Bank to label and categorise countries. She recounts how the so-called g7+ countries accepted the fragile label but launched a process to develop ownership and consensus around their own set of fragility indicators, which are intended to emerge from country-level dialogue and deliberation rather than from expert-driven externally generated analytics. Gabrielsen-Jumbert, writing about Sudan, argues that the fragility discourse that led to international intervention in Darfur, justified under the responsibility to protect principle, undermined efforts by local actors to address the actual sources of the conflict. Furthermore, the labelling process, which led to indictments of Sudan's president in the International Criminal Court, stiffened the government's resolve to resist international efforts to mitigate the crisis.

Both Fisher and Heiduk present cases in which country governments have been able to manipulate the fragile state label and discourse, shaping donor responses to their own ends. Fisher recounts how Uganda's Museveni government has presented itself as both fragile and strong, resulting in continued external support, despite ongoing donor concerns over the regime's lack of commitment to democratic governance. Heiduk describes how the Indonesian military and the country's political elite, following the fall of the Suharto regime and the transition to democracy, were able to preserve much of their privileged position and power by highlighting Indonesia's risk of state disintegration in their dealings with the international community. This fragility message resonated with international actors' concerns over regional security and stability and led to continuing support for civilian and military assistance, despite human rights abuses, notably in East Timor, Aceh and Papua.

Taming wickedness

If the fragile states label and its associated indicator sets are so obviously problematic and detrimental to effective policy and action, why is this label still so widely invoked in international discourse and policy? The contributors here emphasise the extent to which the label serves the political interests of Western donor governments. A complementary answer is that its use represents an effort to tame the wickedness of the state fragility/failure problem set. The global governance literature provides insights that expand on that answer, suggesting a number of reasons for the label's continued use, some of which complement the views of the contributors to this issue. Davis et al. identify six benefits for international policy and decision making of relying upon indicators for complex concepts such as state fragility: efficiency, transparency, consistency, authority, norm- and standard setting and avoidance of contestation.[11]

Simplified conceptualisations of state fragility and reliance upon a set of indicators reduce the burden of information processing for decision makers in global governance organisations (such as the United Nations) and in multilateral and bilateral donor agencies. As indicator databases proliferate, their use becomes self-reinforcing. More production leads to increased reliability, improved aggregation and expanded acceptance of their use, thereby stimulating even more production. Simplification serves to reduce wickedness by subdividing fragility, which enables decision makers to address the individual components, thereby redefining the problem as a set of more manageable and measurable pieces.[12]

The second and third benefits flow directly from the first. Using indicators as a basis for decisions provides transparency, as this makes it easier to demonstrate to others the metrics and rationale behind one's choices. In addition to transparency, the use of indicators facilitates consistency, since decisions over time can be based upon demonstrable changes in the indicators employed to support choices, reinforcing the shared views of the epistemic community that Nay and Lemay-Hébert and Mathieu describe.

The claim that indicator-based conceptualisations of state fragility are empirical and scientific lends authority to the actors employing them to make decisions. This science-based authority reinforces the position-based authority of international actors who apply the fragile/failed label to countries and who participate in taking decisions regarding interventions in fragile/failed states within the security–development nexus. Siqueira illuminates this point in her discussion of the power dynamic involved in assertions of the objective scientific validity of fragility indicators. She notes how the country members of the g7+, with Timor-Leste in the lead, have sought to counter the donor power exerted through fragility measurement and categorisation by developing their own assessment tools and fragility classifications in hopes of expanding their leadership and margin for manoeuvre.

A by-product of authority is the ability to set norms and standards that determine the validity and acceptance of knowledge regarding state fragility, thereby reinforcing authority. Nay's analysis of the OECD and the World Bank explores this norm-setting capacity in detail. Such knowledge is often encapsulated in widely circulated indices – for example, Foreign Policy's Fragile States Index, or Transparency International's Corruption Perception Index. These norms and standards bolster common understandings and perceptions among policy- and decision makers with regard to the state fragility/failure problem set. The result is the creation of what Adler and Bernstein call an epistemic 'bubble', within which actors share interpretations of cause-and-effect relationships and solutions to the problem set.[13] In this way they contribute to reducing wickedness through problem simplification and minimising the fragmentation of perspectives on the problem.

Another benefit of relying upon indicator-based conceptualisations of state fragility is the avoidance of contestation. While actors may engage in debates regarding numerical values or the criteria used in constructing indicators, the indicators themselves are often treated as 'a fact that describes a country's situation'.[14] This feature also serves to reduce fragmentation, as the various actors come to accept the validity of the 'facts'. Over time, however, the producers of indicators and the analysts who rely upon them have been increasingly drawn into political debates and push-back. Thus, contestation is not completely avoidable, as the case studies by Fisher, Heiduk, Siqueira and Gabrielsen-Jumbert reveal. Some of this debate has been sparked by the shortcomings of international peace-building and state-building interventions and the gap between the policy rhetoric and the results achieved in the field, a topic I turn to next.

From rhetoric to reality

A focus on discourse and official policy rhetoric is important in explaining the conceptual frameworks for intervention and action and uncovering the political and power dimensions of donor–country relations with respect to questions of fragility. However, many analyses from the international relations disciplinary perspective underappreciate what happens 'on the ground'. A core finding of the policy implementation literature is the gap between policy statements and what actors responsible for implementation actually do. Lipsky, for example, explores the role of front-line service providers (whom he calls 'street-level bureaucrats') as the translators of policy into real programmatic interventions that may be more or less faithful to the intent of the policy makers.[15]

Similarly, within the peace-building and state-building literature, a number of analysts have examined the micro-dynamics of interactions between front-line humanitarian and development actors and those they seek to assist, in order to assess the success or failure of interventions in fragile/failed states. These studies document the gap between the rhetoric used in high-level discourse and the international community's policy documents on fragile states and outcomes in the field. For example, Barnett and Zürcher analyse how dynamics of capture, compromise and confrontation between peace builders and country elites played out in Tajikistan and Afghanistan to undercut the espoused normative objective of cooperative peace building.[16] Auteserre documents how top-down paternalistic interventions in the Congo undermined the potential for local-level solutions to conflict and violence, thereby contributing to ongoing fragility.[17] In a special issue of *International Peacekeeping*, Millar et al characterise the policy–outcomes gap in terms of 'friction' between external peace-building and state-building templates and indigenous sources of capacity to address fragility and conflict.[18] Patrick and Brown and Stepputat and Greenwood evaluate the pluses and minuses of whole-of-government approaches, which in principle seek to better match operational responses to the wicked-problem features of state fragility.[19] Both these assessments highlight various examples of gaps between intent and the impacts resulting from a lack of policy coherence, ambitious and conflicting objectives, insufficient resources, differing time horizons, stove-piped programming, bureaucratic politics among donor agencies, and weak engagement with country actors.

Beyond naming and taming

The contributions to this special issue clarify the political dynamics between labellers and the labelled and reveal how the wicked-problem characteristics of fragile and failed states have influenced donor–country interactions. As discussed above, the labels and associated indicators have sought to tame the wickedness of state fragility/failure by unpacking the problem set into manageable pieces, facilitating the development of intervention blueprints and universal solutions. The track record on the ground has been mixed at best, with a strong chorus of cautionary tales driven most conspicuously by negative assessments of the US-led state-building efforts in Iraq and Afghanistan, although the circumstances of these interventions were significantly different from those of most peace-building and state-building operations.[20] In reaction the international community is in search of new approaches that will encourage stronger policy realism and coherence, enable more effective operational responses and achieve better results. This search is informed by the various High Level Forums on Aid Effectiveness (particularly the 2011 Busan New Deal for engagement in fragile states), which have proposed new donor–country partnerships based on local ownership and shared accountability.

The wide range of diagnostic frameworks and indicator sets for fragility assessment remains useful to policy makers, analysts and practitioners for the reasons outlined above, particularly for conflict monitoring and early warning. Moving beyond simply naming, however, will require actors to exit the epistemic 'bubble' and recognise the limitations of these frameworks and indicators. Such tools are highly dependent on the quality of information and the availability of sources, and the categories they employ encourage selective 'seeing and listening', focusing on what peace-builders and state-builders are predisposed to consider relevant. Acknowledging local practices and institutions and hearing local voices are important prerequisites for an understanding of what is going on in post-conflict spaces.[21]

Outside the 'bubble' in which state-building solutions are premised on liberal democracy, informal institutions and governance are more readily accepted as potential sources of problem solving, capable of establishing positive relationships between citizens and their government. As Roberts cautions, 'Not everything local is necessarily good and helpful for building peace, but much that is good and local is missed'.[22] From this viewpoint moving beyond naming incorporates what has been called 'working with the grain' – encouraging externally supported peace-building efforts to recognise and (when possible) work in conjunction with local leaders and institutions.[23] This recognition serves as a reminder that the degrees of freedom accorded to outsiders to promote state-building reforms are constrained by the embedded nature of state–society relations.[24] Even when conflict-affected countries are highly dependent upon external resources, the ability of outsiders to exert influence is circumscribed in various ways that are not always apparent. For example, local actors are often proactively involved in 'gaming' donor relationships and peace-building operations to their advantage; Fisher makes this point in his study of Uganda, as does Heiduk in his Indonesia case study.[25]

Going beyond taming involves acknowledging the messiness and complexity of the fragile/failed states wicked-problem set and modifying the top-down, externally driven intervention templates associated with peace building and state building. The reductionism inherent in intervention models that break down peace building and state building into discrete sets of tasks ('lines of effort', in the parlance of military stabilisation planners) is ill-matched to wicked problems, as this strategy tends to ignore interdependencies and contributes to fragmentation. Responsibility for these task sets is often assigned to individual agencies and their partners; in the absence of effective coordination, this exacerbates fragmented action and can lead to perverse outcomes.[26]

International development practice offers some useful insights, drawn from accumulated experience with project and programme implementation. First, to better account for wickedness, linear approaches to problem-solving (gather data-analyse data-design solution-implement-evaluate) must be replaced with a continuous problem-solving process that cycles iteratively and relatively rapidly between problem specification and solution, with sufficient flexibility to make changes based on learning and adaptation.[27] Arguably experienced peace builders employ such rapid and adaptive problem solving at the micro level, but these processes do not tend to trickle up to influence bureaucratic practices within individual donor agencies or across joined-up partners.

Second, dealing with the inevitable fragmentation that arises from confronting wicked problems requires the establishment of shared understandings among key stakeholders with respect to the aims, benefits, costs and tasks associated with a given reform (in this case, peace building or state building), along with the creation of a collective commitment to success that will enable the requisite resources to be allocated and effort to be expended.[28] These key stakeholders are not just the international peace builders, but must include country actors at all levels (and not only elites).

A third insight is linked to the second: without a solid grasp of contextual factors (including history, politics, power dynamics and incentives) and the willingness to incorporate these as inputs to both intervention design and implementation, attempts to build constituencies and align with country actors will fall short. Recognition of the importance of context, of the constraining influence of path dependence and of the interplay between formal and informal governance institutions has become increasingly accepted as critical to successful international development programming and practice.[29] This is not to say that technology, tools and system-transfer approaches have disappeared or do not serve a useful purpose. However, their effective application in programmes intended to build capacity and achieve lasting results has shifted from 'best practice' to 'best fit', where reforms are designed and implemented on the basis of a more profound understanding of countries and actors.

There is some evidence suggesting that peace-building and state-building intervention approaches are evolving to better respond to the wickedness features of fragile states, and that they are moving, albeit in limited ways, beyond taming. Roberts et al note the emergence of hybrid peace-building operations that involve 'the mixing and melding of international and local structures and practices'.[30] McCandless recounts dialogue processes between donor countries and representatives of fragile states that lead to stronger mutual alignment and commitment to addressing fragility under the New Deal, as well as to recognition of the limitations of template approaches to intervention.[31] Some donors are placing more emphasis on iterative, smaller-scale efforts to address conflict and limit its spread, sending resources to local actors who are already engaged in conflict mitigation and peace building and enabling them to move ahead without predetermined blueprints; this approach is being pursued by the US Department of State's Bureau of Conflict and Stabilization Operations.[32] The UK's Conflict Pool seeks to improve the flexibility and nimbleness of multi-agency responses to conflict and fragility, and a recent evaluation notes some progress along these lines, despite ongoing operational problems.[33]

Conclusions

The contributions to this special issue offer confirmation of how the wicked-problem characteristics of fragile and failed states have affected both the international policy discourse and the design of peace-building and state-building interventions. They also illuminate the coping strategies of the actors on the receiving end of these diagnostics and interventions. Applying the rubrics I use in this essay, the authors examine naming, taming and, in some instances, gaming. With the exception of Siqueira, they stop short of considerations of bringing the labellers and labelled together to address the fragility problem set. International development practice offers some potentially helpful insights for going beyond naming and taming, as I have briefly described. Their application, however, must confront the forces at work that have created the self-reinforcing epistemic 'bubble' and that buttress Western governments' political dominance, as the authors explore here. Successfully confronting wicked problems will require mutual understanding and the identification of common ground for developing iterative solutions. A key challenge for the international community and those states labelled as fragile will be whether there is sufficient political will on both sides to bridge the divide between labeller and labelled.

Notes on Contributor

Derick W. Brinkerhoff is Distinguished Fellow in International Public Management at RTI International (Research Triangle Institute), and is an associate faculty member at George Washington University's Trachtenberg School of Public Policy and Public Administration. He has published extensively, including eight books, numerous articles and book chapters. His co-authored book, *Managing Policy Reform* (2002), has sold over 5000 copies and his most recent book is an edited volume, *Governance in Post-Conflict Societies: Rebuilding Fragile States* (2007). He is an editor of *Public Administration and Development*.

Notes

1. Churchman, "Wicked Problems"; Rittel and Webber, "Dilemmas."
2. Introduction to this issue. See also Lemay-Hébert, "Review Essay."
3. Rittel and Weber, "Dilemmas." See also Conklin, *Dialogue Mapping*.
4. Carment et al., *Security, Development, and the Fragile State*.
5. See, for example, Verstegen et al., "The Stability Assessment Framework"; and USAID, "Conducting a Conflict Assessment."
6. World Bank, *Conflict, Security, and Development*.
7. See US Army, *Stability Operations*; and US Institute of Peace and US Army Peacekeeping and Stability Operations Institute, *Guiding Principles*.
8. See, for example, Paris and Sisk, *Dilemmas of Statebuilding*.
9. Several of the authors supplement their literature reviews and document data with interviews.
10. Duffield, *Development, Security and Unending War*.
11. Davis et al., "Introduction."
12. See, for example, Carment et al., *Security, Development, and the Fragile State*, 84–105. The authors' fragility index subdivides fragility into six indicator clusters: governance, economics, security and crime, human development, demography, and environment. While the authors explicitly recognise the interaction effects among these fragility components, subdividing them enables cluster-specific analysis and intervention programming.
13. Adler and Bernstein, "Knowledge in Power," 296.
14. Davis et al., "Introduction," 20.
15. Lipsky, *Street-level Bureaucracy*.
16. Barnett and Zürcher, "The Peacebuilder's Contract."
17. Auteserre, *The Trouble with the Congo*.
18. Millar et al., "Peacebuilding Plans and Local Configurations."
19. Patrick and Brown, *Greater than the Sum of its Parts?*; and Stepputat and Greenwood, "Whole-of-Government Approaches."
20. Lake, "Iraq"; Marton and Hynek, "'Liberal' Statebuilding in Afghanistan."
21. See, for example, Jackson, "Chiefs, Money, and Politicians"; and Anderson et al., *Time to Listen*.
22. Roberts, "Hybrid Politics," 102–103.
23. See Booth, "Aid Effectiveness."
24. Migdal, *State in Society*.
25. In the fragile state policy and operational arenas 'naming' and 'taming' are actions that the labellers engage in, by virtue of their superior power, authority and resources. 'Gaming', which refers to manipulating or bending rules and procedures to achieve a desired outcome, applies to the actions taken by the relatively more disempowered labelled states.
26. Patrick and Brown, *Greater than the Sum of its Parts?*; and Stepputat and Greenwood, "Whole-of-Government Approaches."
27. See Brinkerhoff and Ingle, "Integrating Blueprint and Process"; and Andrews, *The Limits of Institutional Reform*. In addition, Conklin, *Dialogue Mapping*, provides a useful discussion on the process of addressing wicked problems.
28. An extensive literature addresses the importance of paying attention to process and participation for the success of reforms. See, for example, White, *Implementing Policy Reforms*; Brinkerhoff, "Process Perspectives on Policy Change"; and Odugbemi and Jacobson, *Governance Reform*.
29. Numerous sources focus on contextual factors. See, for example, Kelsall, "Going with the Grain"; Brinkerhoff and Goldsmith, "Good Governance"; and World Bank, "The World Bank's Approach to Public Sector Management."
30. Roberts, "Hybrid Politics"; and Millar et al., "Peacebuilding Plans and Local Reconfigurations," 138.
31. McCandless, "Wicked Problems in Peacebuilding."
32. See http://reliefweb.int/report/world/cso-one-year-progress-report.
33. See the discussion of the Conflict Pool in Stepputat and Greenwood, "Whole-of-Government Approaches," 23–24.

Bibliography

Adler, Emmanuel, and Steven Bernstein. "Knowledge in Power: The Epistemic Construction of Global Governance." In *Power in Global Governance*, edited by Michael Barnett, and Raymond Duvall, 294–319. Cambridge: Cambridge University Press, 2005.

Anderson, Mary B., Dayna Brown, and Isabella Jean. *Time to Listen: Hearing People on the Receiving End of International Aid*. Cambridge, MA: CDA Collaborative Learning Projects, 2012.

Andrews, Matt. *The Limits of Institutional Reform in Development: Changing Rules for Realistic Solutions*. Cambridge: Cambridge University Press, 2013.

Auteserre, Séverine. *The Trouble with the Congo: Local Violence and the Failure of International Peacebuilding*. Cambridge: Cambridge University Press, 2010.

Barnett, Michael, and Christoph Zürcher. "The Peacebuilder's Contract: How External Statebuilding Reinforces Weak Statehood." In *The Dilemmas of Statebuilding: Confronting the Contradictions of Postwar Peace Operations*, edited by Roland Paris, and Timothy D. Sisk, 23–53. London: Routledge, 2009.

Booth, David. *Aid Effectiveness: Bringing Ownership (and Politics) Back In*. Working Paper No. 336. London: Overseas Development Institute, 2011.

Brinkerhoff, Derick W. "Process Perspectives on Policy Change: Highlighting Implementation." *World Development* 24, no. 9 (1996): 1395–1403.

Brinkerhoff, Derick W., and Arthur Goldsmith. "Good Governance, Clientelism and Patrimonialism: New Perspectives on Old Problems." *International Public Management Journal* 7, no. 2 (2004): 163–185.

Brinkerhoff, Derick W., and Marcus Ingle. "Integrating Blueprint and Process: A Structured Flexibility Approach to Development Management." *Public Administration and Development* 9, no. 5 (1989): 487–503.

Carment, David, Stewart Prest, and Yiagadeesen Samy. *Security, Development, and the Fragile State: Bridging the Gap between Theory and Policy*. London: Routledge, 2010.

Conklin, Jeff. *Dialogue Mapping: Building Shared Understanding of Wicked Problems*. Chicester: John Wiley, 2006.

Churchman, C. Westman. "Wicked Problems." *Management Science* 14, no. 4 (1967): B141–B143.

Davis, Kevin, Benedict Kingsbury, and Sally Merry. "Introduction: Global Governance by Indicators." In *Governance by Indicators: Global Power through Classification and Rankings*, edited by Kevin Davis, Angelina Fisher, Benedict Kingsbury, and Sally Engle Merry, 3–29. Oxford: Oxford University Press, 2012.

Duffield, Mark. *Development, Security and Unending War: Governing the World of Peoples*. Cambridge: Polity Press, 2007.

Jackson, Paul. "Chiefs, Money and Politicians: Rebuilding Local Government in Post-war Sierra Leone." *Public Administration and Development* 25, no. 1 (2005): 49–59.

Kelsall, Tim. "Going with the Grain in African Development." *Development Policy Review* 26, no. 6 (2008): 627–655.

Lake, David A. "Iraq: US Approaches to Statebuilding in the Twenty-first Century." In *The Routledge Handbook of International Statebuilding*, edited by David Chandler, and Timothy D. Sisk, 293–304. London: Routledge, 2013.

Lemay-Hébert, Nicolas. "Review Essay: Critical Debates on Liberal Peacebuilding." *Civil Wars* 15, no. 2 (2013): 242–252.

Lipsky, Michael. *Street-level Bureaucracy: Dilemmas of the Individual in Public Services – 30th Anniversary Expanded Edition*. New York: Russell Sage Foundation, 2010.

Marton, Péter, and Nik Hynek. "'Liberal' Statebuilding in Afghanistan." In *The Routledge Handbook of International Statebuilding*, edited by David Chandler, and Timothy D. Sisk, 304–315. London: Routledge, 2013.

McCandless, Erin. "Wicked Problems in Peacebuilding and Statebuilding: Making Progress in Measuring Progress through the New Deal." *Global Governance* 19, no. 2 (2013): 227–248.

Migdal, Joel S. *State in Society: Studying How States and Societies Transform and Constitute Each Other*. New York: Cambridge University Press, 2001.

Millar, Gearoid, Jair van Millar, and Willemijn Verkoren. "Peacebuilding Plans and Local Reconfigurations: Frictions between Imported Processes and Indigenous Practices." *International Peacekeeping* 20, no. 2 (2013): 137–143.

Odugbemi, Sina, and Thomas Jacobson, eds. *Governance Reform under Real-world Conditions: Citizens, Stakeholders, and Voice*. Washington, DC: World Bank, 2008.

Paris, Roland, and Timothy D. Sisk, eds. *The Dilemmas of Statebuilding: Confronting the Contradictions of Postwar Peace Operations*. London: Routledge, 2009.

Patrick, Stewart, and Kaysie Brown. *Greater than the Sum of its Parts? Assessing 'Whole of Government' Approaches to Fragile States*. New York: International Peace Academy, 2007.

Rittel, Horst W. J., and Melvin W. Webber. "Dilemmas in a General Theory of Planning." *Policy Sciences* 4, no. 2 (1973): 155–169.

Roberts, David. "Hybrid Politics and Post-conflict Policy." In *The Routledge Handbook of International Statebuilding*, edited by David Chandler, and Timothy D. Sisk, 94–106. London: Routledge, 2013.

Stepputat, Finn, and Lauren Greenwood. *Whole-of-Government Approaches to Fragile States and Situations*. DIIS Report No. 2013: 25. Copenhagen: Danish Institute for International Studies, 2013.

US Agency for International Development (USAID). "Conducting a Conflict Assessment: A Framework for Strategy and Program Development." Office of Conflict Management and Mitigation, USAID, Washington, DC, April 2005.

US Army. *Stability Operations*. Field Manual No. 3-07. Washington, DC: Department of the Army, Headquarters, October 2008.

US Institute of Peace and US Army Peacekeeping and Stability Operations Institute. *Guiding Principles for Stabilization and Reconstruction*. Washington, DC: US Institute of Peace, 2009.

Verstegen, Suzanne, Luc van de Goor, and Jeroen de Zeeuw. *The Stability Assessment Framework: Designing Integrated Responses for Security, Governance and Development*. The Hague: Clingendael Institute, for the Netherlands Ministry of Foreign Affairs, 2005.

White, Louise G. *Implementing Policy Reforms in LDCS: A Strategy for Designing and Effecting Change*. Boulder, CO: Lynne Rienner, 1990.

World Bank. *Conflict, Security, and Development: World Development Report 2011*. Washington, DC: World Bank, 2011.

World Bank. "The World Bank's Approach to Public Sector Management 2011–2020: Better Results from Public Sector Institutions." World Bank, Washington, DC: Public Sector and Governance Board, 2012.

Index

For Product Safety Concerns and Information please contact our
EU representative GPSR@taylorandfrancis.com Taylor & Francis
Verlag GmbH, Kaufingerstraße 24, 80331 München, Germany